Levi Yitzhak of Berditchev

OTHER BOOKS BY THE AUTHOR

Prayer, Humility and Compassion
The Jewish Dietary Laws
The Zaddik
Three Paths of God and Man
The Jew in American Life
God, Man and Atomic War
The Sabbath
Between the Generations

Levi Yitzhak of Berditchev

Portrait of a Hasidic Master

by Samuel H. Dresner

HARTMORE HOUSE
New York • Bridgeport

©Copyright 1974, by
HARTMORE HOUSE, *publishers*
1363 Fairfield Avenue
Bridgeport, Connecticut 06605

All Rights Reserved

Manufactured in the United States of America

LIBRARY OF CONGRESS CATALOGING IN PUBLICATION DATA

Dresner, Samuel H.
    Levi Yitzhak of Berditchev: portrait of a Hasidic master.

  Bibliography: p.
  1. Levi Isaac ben Meir of Berditchev, 1740-1809.
I. Title.
BM755.L44D83   296.6'1'0924 [B]   73-91739
ISBN 0-87677-144-4

Contents

	Preface	7
	Map (Hasidic Centers of Eastern Europe)	11
	Prologue: The Hasidic World	13
1	The Life of a Tzaddik	18
2	Love of Israel	47
3	Prayer	91
4	Doing the Mitzvot	110
5	The Messiah	134
6	Day-to-Day	142
7	Humility	155
8	Between God and Man	166
9	Days of Awe	179
10	Death of the Rebbe	197
	Epilogue	203
	Chronology	207
	Notes	208
	Glossary	219
	Bibliography	223

Preface

IN THE CHAIN of *Hasidic* masters, which stretches more than seven generations through a hundred communities in Eastern Europe, there is no one—except the Baal Shem Tov himself—about whose life so many glorious tales have been told as that of Levi Yitzhak of Berditchev.

The mystics said that within the "holy one from Berditchev" was the soul of Rabbi Akiva. So sublime was his fervor in prayer, so glorious his performance of the *Mitzvot*, so warm his love for the people Israel, so radiant his holiness, that only through tales and anecdotes could his contemporaries portray him. There may have been men wiser than he; there may have been profounder writers and greater leaders; but there was no one among that remarkable group of *Tzaddikim* (nor, for that matter, in the history of the Jewish soul) whose heart was purer or who was more beloved by the people.

We do not know how many of the stories of Levi Yitzhak are accurate, how many are the product of pure fancy, and how many contain something of both. But when we piece these stories together, there emerges the image of a man in whom the divine fire burned so brightly that his prayers to God could awaken sleeping souls, his compassion for the needy could arouse the miser to charity, his observance of the *Mitzvot* could open to men a new path of service. His words of Torah struck fire in the hearts of his generation, his songs gave them hope, and his dancing brought them joy. His illimitable love of the people Israel at times led him to cry out in their defense—even against Heaven itself.

So seriously did he appear to have taken the word and presence of God that we might be tempted to question whether such a man really lived—and, if he did, to ask whether he might have been just another of God's fools. Yet, just because our age does not produce such a man, we must not judge the past too hastily.

There were times in Jewish history when the spirit was cultivated at least as seriously as the body, when refinement of the soul was at least as important as the search for power, when the object of books and their study was to sanctify thoughts and deeds rather than to gather knowledge for personal gain, and when God was a loving Father before Whom people prayed, sang, and lived.

In those days, simply to mention the word *Berditchev* was enough to evoke a burning sigh of remembrance for the saint who dwelt there and who brought a blessed balm of warmth and joy and hope to countless Jews—wise and simple, old and young, pious and skeptic—for whom he was a living witness to the presence of Heaven on earth.

"The Holy One, blessed be He, is the *Tzaddik* in Heaven," said Rabbi Shneur Zalman. "Rabbi Levi Yitzhak is the *Tzaddik* on earth."

In this book I have sketched the life and the spirit of Rabbi Levi Yitzhak of Berditchev. My principal sources have been the stories and legends which have been handed down for the more than a century and a half since his death, as well as his book *Kedushat Levi*.

From some of the stories we might suspect that Levi Yitzhak was a lovable simpleton who did not belong in our world. Yet, from historical sources we learn that he was not only a saintly soul but also a wise counselor in public affairs and an eminent Talmudist; and from his book *Kedushat Levi* we discover the added dimension of a profound and creative mind. Indeed, one cannot truly understand him without delving into his philosophy, and I must apologize for having done so only peripherally in this work. It is this paradox of innocent and sophisticate, storyteller and Talmudic master, humble servant and stormer of the heavens, communal leader and celebrated mystic, which we must keep in mind as we try to understand the man behind the legends.

Even in his lifetime there were those who were concerned that Rabbi Levi Yitzhak might be judged too quickly and too easily.

Rabbi Aaron of Zhitomir was a noted disciple of Levi Yitzhak. His book, *Toldot Aharon*, contains many of the master's teachings. According to *Hasidic* tradition, Levi Yitzhak and the young Aaron were once on a trip together. They stopped at Lizhensk where the famous Rabbi Elimelekh lived. He invited them to remain for a few days, after which Levi Yitzhak returned home. But Aaron decided to remain. Aaron went to Rabbi Elimelekh's *Bet ha-Midrash* to study, without telling Rabbi Elimelekh anything about it.

Surprised to see him there later, Rabbi Elimelekh asked, "Why did you not leave with your rabbi?"

"I know my rabbi," Aaron replied. "I stayed here because I want to learn to know you too."

Rabbi Elimelekh went close to him and took him by the coat. "You think you know your rabbi!" he exclaimed. "Why, you don't even know his coat!"

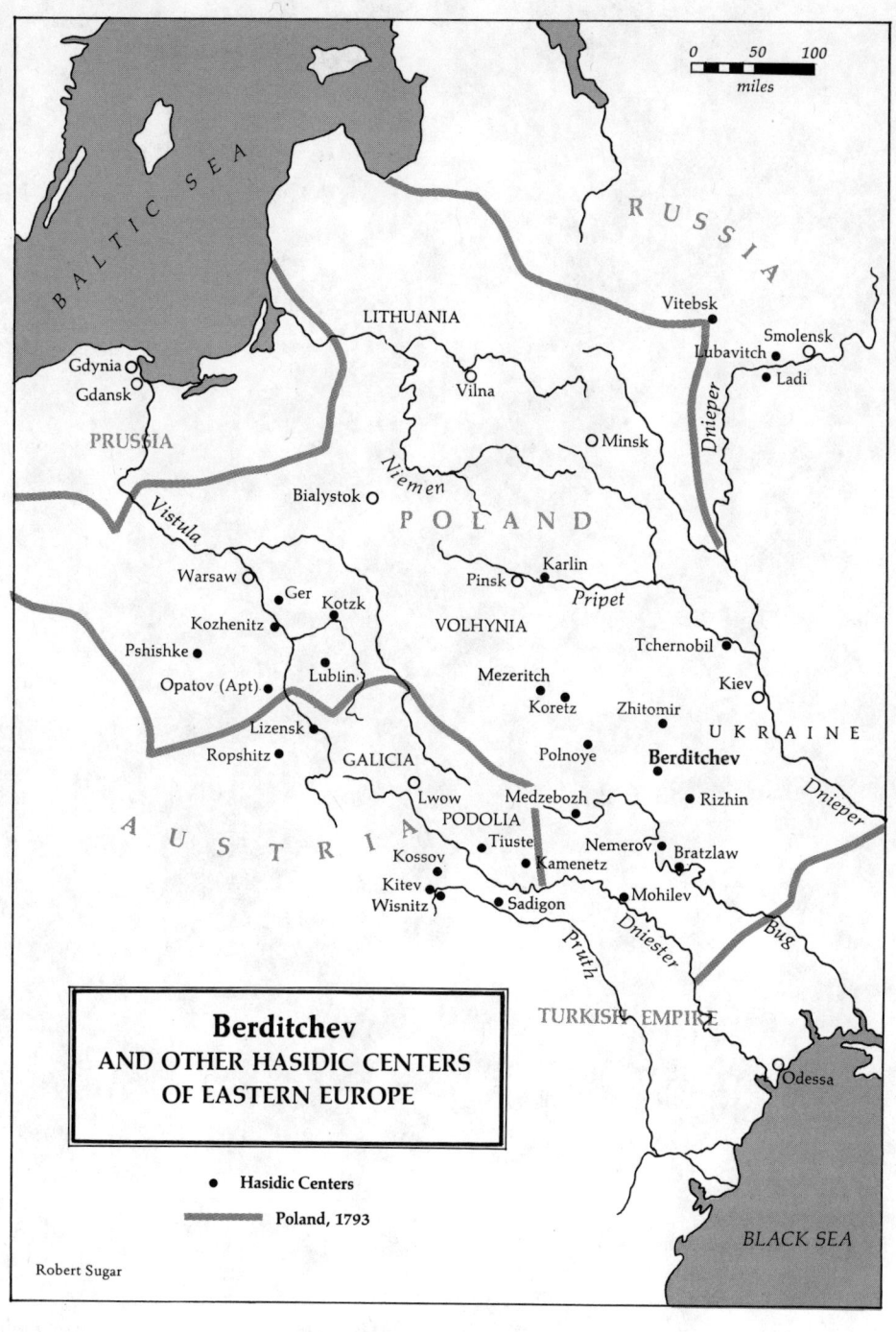

PROLOGUE

The Hasidic World

THE STORIES about Levi Yitzhak, his people and their problems, come from the world of *Hasidism* in Eastern Europe in the eighteenth and early nineteenth centuries. The last great flowering of the Jewish soul, Hasidism was founded by one of the most remarkable figures in Jewish history since the Middle Ages, the Baal Shem Tov (literally, "Master of the Good Name," also known as "Besht"). He appeared in a period when asceticism, scholarly pride, pedantry, and formalism were the hallmarks of the inner life, when worship of the "living God" was too often reduced to dull routine and mindless religious habits. One of the writers of the time summed up the whole purpose of Hasidism very simply. The Baal Shem, he wrote, came "to repair what had broken down."[1]

In opposition to asceticism, the Baal Shem taught that since God was in all things, He could be served through all things—even through the pleasures of life—and He should be served with joy.

In contrast to the scholars and rabbis who remained aloof from the unlettered masses and looked down upon them in contempt, he was the first rabbi of a new kind, called the *Tzaddik*. He was full of concern for all the people. He went to them in humility and love in an effort to raise them from their accustomed spiritual state to a higher one. [2]

He reacted against the danger of excessive formalism in religious practice wherein every detail of the law might be fulfilled in a man's actions while his thoughts were elsewhere. He urged, along with outward observance of the *Mitzvot* ("religious commandments"), the necessity of *Kavvanah* ("inner devotion") and *Simhah* ("holy joy"). He taught that the doing of the Mitzvah demands the mind and the heart as well as the body.

Around each Tzaddik there gathered his loyal followers, the Hasidim ("pious ones"), who comprised a brotherly commune in which they sought to share their material as well as spiritual goods. Every holy community was bound together by its loyalty to the master who was its center and its inspiration.

These Tzaddikim were an amazing group of men. According to Martin Buber, they "offer us a number of religious personalities of a vitality, a spiritual strength, a manifold originality such as have never, to my knowledge, appeared together in so short a time-span in the history of religion." [3]

It is not surprising then that within several decades—from 1750 to 1780—Hasidism began to sweep across Eastern Europe in such an irresistible tide that thousands of Jews—rich and poor, learned and ignorant—were embraced in its fold. In time, Hasidism succeeded in winning over to its ways the majority of the Jews of Eastern Europe. The Hasidic movement maintained its strength into the twentieth century—though not, perhaps, on the same exalted level as in early generations—until the Nazi hordes put an end to its life in Eastern Europe. Today only a scattered but vital remnant remains, principally in Israel, Brooklyn, Montreal, and Antwerp.

When the Baal Shem died in about 1760, he was succeeded by Rabbi Dov Ber, called the Great Maggid ("preacher") of Mezritch. More than any other leader, the Maggid was responsible for the organization, expansion, and consolidation of the Hasidic movement. Many of the great Hasidic masters of the second generation were disciples of the Maggid. Among these was Rabbi Levi Yitzhak. Others were Aaron of Karlin, Elimelekh of Lizhensk, Shmelke Horowitz of Nikolsburg, and Shneur Zalman of Ladi, author of *The Tanya* and founder of the still powerful Lubavitch dynasty, now transplanted to Brooklyn.

Hasidism did not conquer without opposition. The *Mitnagdim* ("opponents"), as those who resisted the new movement were called, engaged the Hasidim in fierce battle almost from the beginning. The old leaders took the enthusiasm of the Hasidim as a sign of frivolity. Moreover, the Tzaddikim's bold criticism of rabbinical pride was a danger to the status quo. (There were some early enthusiasts whose behavior did, indeed, give reason for legitimate concern.)

In Vilna at this time lived Rabbi Elijah, better known as the "Vilna Gaon." He was generally recognized as the outstanding representative of rabbinic learning of that era. Alarmed by reports about a new "sect," he issued a *Herem* ("ban") in 1772 against the Hasidim that created a lasting and devastating enmity between the two groups. Before, there had been bitter feelings, sharp words, and occasional "incidents"; now a decree from the highest possible source, the Gaon of Vilna, confirmed suspicions and set off a series of communal explosions that rocked Jewish life to its foundations. Stores where boycotted, rabbis driven from their positions, brother turned against brother. Marriages between adherents of the two groups were discouraged, and synagogues and communities were split into opposing factions. That same "causeless hatred" which, according to the sages of the Talmud, was responsible for the destruction of the Second Temple, was again rampant among the Children of Israel.

Because of this bitter strife, Rabbi Shneur Zalman went to Vilna to allay the fears of the Gaon by explaining to him the true nature of Hasidism. Rabbi Shneur Zalman was particularly suited to this mission, because, like Rabbi Elijah, he was a Lithuanian and famed for his Talmudic scholarship. Indeed, it was he whom the Maggid of Mezritch chose from all his students to compose a new code of Jewish law—a monumental task requiring a mastery of the entire legal literature. There was every reason to hope that the mission would be successful. But Rabbi Elijah of Vilna refused even to meet with Shneur Zalman! A second ban pronounced in 1796 by the Vilna Gaon further deepened the rift between the two groups, which was to continue for generations, leaving traces even today.

Much of the controversy with the Mitnagdim revolved around Hasidism's attempt to achieve a revival of the spirit of prayer in the life of the people. While Torah-study was exalted, prayer was neglected and had grown perfunctory. One of the great accomplishments of the Baal Shem Tov and his followers was to raise prayer to a station equal to that of the study of Torah. For, to the Besht, prayer was not just a commandment to be obeyed, nor even communion with God. Prayer *was* God: the divine within answering the call of the divine beyond.

Finding the synagogues spiritually stifling, the *Hazzanim* vain, and worship often reduced to mindless habit, the Hasidim established their own Houses of Worship, encouraged learned laymen or the *Rebbes* (Hasidic rabbis) themselves to lead the prayers. They adopted a new prayer book based upon the Sephardic rite according to the sixteenth-century mystic, the Ari, and sometimes delayed their prayers until after the prescribed time. A careful reading of the following parable, ascribed to Rabbi Levi Yitzhak, may help explain how some of these changes came about.

There once was a king who so loved music, that he directed his musicians to play before him at a certain hour each morning. Those who came at the appointed time and performed received a reward, and those who arrived early, even before sunrise, received a double reward. But whether they arrived at the appointed time or earlier, they came not for the sake of the reward but only out of love for the king. For many years all went well. The musicians delighted in playing each morning before the king, and the king delighted in hearing their music.

When, at last, the musicians died, their sons sought to take their places. But, alas, they had neither mastered the art of their fathers nor had they kept their instruments in proper condition. Worse still, the sons no longer loved the king as did their fathers but set their eyes only upon the reward, blindly following their fathers' custom of arriving early each morning at the palace to perform. But the harsh sounds that emerged were so offensive to the ear, that after a time the king no longer listened to their music. Intent upon the reward, however, greed closed the sons' eyes to this reality, and they continued to come each day to play as usual.

Still, there were among the sons of the old musicians, some who recognized that they were not worthy to play before the king. And they were determined to correct the situation. They set about the difficult task of relearning the forgotten art. Before coming to the king, they would now first try to tune their instruments, and in so doing would often arrive late. Upon entering the king's court and hearing the racket of the other musicians who were already present, they sought out an obscure corner for themselves where they could play undisturbed in accordance with their ability. It was there that they gathered each morning to perform, remaining long after the other musicians had departed so that they might improve their skill. And long before leaving their homes for the palace each morning they continued to struggle with their poor instruments. The king was aware of their efforts and it was good in his eyes. For even though they did not play with the same talent as their fathers, still they strove, within their limits, to once more bring joy to the king. Thus was their music received by the king with favor. [4]

1

The Life of a Tzaddik

RABBI ISRAEL BAAL SHEM TOV appeared one day before his disciples with drink and cakes, gave some to each, and told them to be seated and rejoice. They looked at one another in surprise. They asked the reason for the celebration.

Their teacher turned toward them and explained, "A holy soul will soon descend into the world, a soul who will stand fast for our brothers, the household of Israel."

The year was 1740. The man about whom he spoke was Rabbi Levi Yitzhak of Berditchev.

BEGINNINGS

Levi Yitzhak was born in 1740 in Husakov, Galicia. His father,

Meir, known as both a Talmudist and *Kabbalist*, was, according to tradition, the sixteenth generation of his family to serve in the rabbinate, being *Rav* ("rabbi") of the city. His mother traced her ancestry back to the sixteenth-century commentator on the Talmud, Rabbi Shmuel Edels. She was known for her wisdom and piety. The boy was raised in an atmosphere of learning and holiness. He was taught Talmud and the Codes by his father (whose teachings he quotes in his book, *Kedushat Levi*). At an early age, he was sent to the nearby town of Yaroslav to further his studies. Soon he became known as the *Illui* ("genius") of Yaroslav. [1]

Due to his reputation as a promising young scholar, in 1757, when he was seventeen, Levi Yitzhak became the son-in-law of the wealthy Israel Peretz of the city of Libertov in Poland. It had long been the custom among Jews that the chief qualities to recommend a young man for marriage were his learning and his character, and a father of means would search long and hard to find such a husband for his daughter.

Libertov was noted at that time as a center for Talmudic scholars. Rabbi Josef Tumim, author of the classic commentary to the Talmud, *P'ri M'gadim*, and one of the leading rabbinic authorities of his time, wrote:

> My lord and father ... was the head of the Yeshivah *in the city of Libertov, which was esteemed as an important community. Food and drink were generously provided for all of his students. Among the leaders of the community were four brothers, Israel, Moses, Jonah, and Tzvi Hirsh, who were men of both wealth and piety. These brothers put aside liberal sums of money to enable themselves to study with the best of the students.* [2]

"Israel" was Israel Peretz, Rabbi Levi Yitzhak's father-in-law, in whose home wealth and learning were joined. In Libertov, among such scholars as Rabbi Tumim, Levi Yitzhak pursued his study of the Talmud, its Commentaries and Codes, as well as the *Kabbalah*, rising higher on the rungs of learning, and delving ever deeper into the mystical writings.

Not far from Libertov was the city of Ritchvol, where the *Rav* and head of the Jewish court was Rabbi Shmelke Horowitz (later famous as the Rabbi of Nikolsburg), a disciple of the Maggid of Mezritch. When the young Levi Yitzhak heard of the new teachings of Rabbi Shmelke, a kindred spirit awoke in his heart, and he decided, against the objections of his father-in-law, to visit Ritchvol. He fasted to protest his father-in-law's edict. Israel Peretz relented and permitted him to go for a few days. This meeting was crucial; Levi Yitzhak decided to leave his home to learn the teachings and the ways of Hasidism.

On his return to Rabbi Shmelke to be admitted to the *Yeshivah*, he was brought before the rabbi, who asked him, "Do you know how to learn Torah?"

When he heard the word "Torah," Levi Yitzhak's face shone with a heavenly light, and he could only reply, "Torah—wonder of wonders!"

As a punishment for this reply, which the rabbi misconstrued as a lighthearted response, Rabbi Shmelke forbade Levi Yitzhak to enter the room of the *Yeshivah* for some time, and the student was forced to sit outside the door during the lectures, listening as best he could. It was not long, however, before he was permitted within. When Rabbi Shmelke recognized the rare talents of the young man, he knew that here among his students was one of the elect who possessed that happy joining of heart and mind which augured great things. He drew Levi Yitzhak close to him in love and called him "my son." He taught him not only the revealed writings—the Talmud, Codes and Responsa—but also the hidden writings—the mystical books; for while it was Rabbi Shmelke's custom to teach the former to his students publicly, he would study the latter in private in a small room of his own. In later years, whenever he wrote to him, Rabbi Shmelke referred to Rabbi Levi Yitzhak as "my student in *Nigleh* ['the revealed writings'] and my teacher in *Nistar* ['the hidden writings']."

THE GREAT MAGGID

Surely, Rabbi Shmelke thought, this one must be brought to the font of living waters, to the city of Mezritch and the Great Maggid, the successor of the Baal Shem and the acknowledged leader of the Hasidic movement. Mezritch at that time was at its zenith. It sheltered a brilliant group of young disciples and was visited by numerous rabbis, each already distinguished in his own right, who made the pilgrimage frequently to stay in touch with the Maggid.

Within the fellowship of this elite circle, and under the leadership of the Maggid, a new world of the spirit opened to Levi Yitzhak. The sparks which had been hidden were now kindled. Levi Yitzhak was overwhelmed by what he saw and heard: the fervor of prayers recited not by rote but with such an outpouring of spirit as to join the soul to the Source of all souls; the exposition of the mystic teachings in a new and startling way directed not so much toward heavenly matters as human ones, motivated not so much by the urge to hasten the coming of the Messiah as to purify the soul of the individual Jew; the study of Torah not only as an exercise of the mind but as an act of the spirit by which one communed with God's presence amidst the holy words, not in pride of achievement but with such selflessness and dedication that when the students read, for example, of the disputes between Rabbi Akiva and Rabbi Ishmael, the living images of the ancient sages arose before their eyes. *Kabbalah* had become ethos; study, another side of prayer; prayer, a bolt of lightning.

Levi Yitzhak became a devoted disciple of his new master and teacher, the Maggid, whose prayer, fulfillment of the Mitzvot, teachings of Torah, and even casual conversations—which Levi Yitzhak carefully wrote down for future study—were lessons so powerful that they transformed his life and confirmed his decision to walk in the way of the Baal Shem no matter what sacrifices this might entail.

Levi Yitzhak recounted the following incident with his master:

> *One year the first day of Rosh Hashanah fell on the Sabbath, when it is forbidden to blow the* Shofar, *while on the second day the Maggid was not well enough to blow it. The time for* Minhah, *["afternoon prayer"] came. My teacher arose to pray, and his words were a very flaming fire of God. It was always thus at* Minhah.

> *When I saw this, I left my place and stood near the window where my teacher always prayed, to pray there too. After he had completed the Amidah ["standing prayer"], it was his habit to pace back and forth for a few moments and over to the window. He turned slowly from the wall in front of which he had been praying, and I beheld upon his face such light and majesty as the glory of a heavenly rainbow. Fear and trembling fell upon me; I stumbled back; arms supported me lest I fall. But those who held me did not know the reason.*
>
> *My teacher noticed my trembling. He turned his face back to the wall and rested his head there for two or three minutes. When he moved away from the wall this time, there was no visible trace of his former appearance.*
>
> *Only at the time of my master's death did I see such splendor as this again. And it was from that light and splendor and majesty which shone from his face that I was able truly to understand his teachings.* [3]

When Levi Yitzhak returned from one of his early visits to Mezritch, his father-in-law said to him, "I am prepared to forgive this foolishness, but tell me what you learned at the Maggid's."

Levi Yitzhak replied that from his new teacher he had learned that there was a God in Heaven Who had created our world.

"Who does not know that?" scoffed his father-in-law and called for the maid.

"Do you know Who created the world?"

She replied, "God in Heaven!"

"Anyone can say this," explained Rabbi Levi Yitzhak, "but only he who has learned this from the mouth of the Great Maggid can know it."

THE TZADDIK

The world of eighteenth-century East European Jewry was suffering both physically and spiritually. Externally there was poverty and persecution; internally, decay, debasement, and despair. The study of Torah had turned to casuistry, communal corruption was rampant, rabbinic leadership was aloof and arrogant, and the hopes of thousands had been shattered and perverted by the false messiah, Sabbatai Zvi. The Baal Shem and the Maggid after him understood that the crisis of the times could not be met on every level. But if a new leader, who was humble and dedicated, could serve as a channel between God and Israel, all might be rebuilt around him, for is it not written in Holy Scripture that "the Tzaddik is the *foundation* of the world" (Proverbs 10:25)?

First from Rabbi Shmelke, and then from the Great Maggid, Levi Yitzhak learned of the new exalted leader, the Tzaddik, who cleaved to the Lord without separating himself from society, and whose concern for the people led him down to the unlettered masses with whom a bond was forged by which they could be drawn up to a higher spiritual level. The Tzaddik, according to Gershom Scholem, represented "the ancient paradox of solitude and communion. He who has attained the highest degree of spiritual solitude, who is capable of being alone with God, is the true center of the community.... To live among ordinary men and yet be alone with God, to speak profane language and yet draw strength to live from the source of existence—that is a paradox which only the mystical devotee is able to realize in his life and which makes him the center of the community of man." [4]

The mystery of this paradox was revealed to Levi Yitzhak. From it came the seeming strangeness of his ways, the apparent naïveté, the amusing simplicity, the fervor that seized him when he performed a Mitzvah and which surprised and enraptured those about him. Being alone with God did not set him apart from the community. He became its very heart.

Not all leaders, however, could achieve this.

> There are those who are able to cling to the Creator, blessed be He, at all times, even when conversing with their fellows. There are others who can cleave to the Creator, blessed be He, only when at prayer, studying Torah, or performing the

Mitzvot. **When they engage in worldly conversation, however, they are no longer able to cling to the Creator, blessed be He.*** [5]

For Levi Yitzhak, Noah and Abraham represented two types of leaders. Noah was among "those who themselves serve the Lord but do not bother to bring others to His service." "Noah was a righteous man in his generation" (Genesis 6:9). That is, he was righteous in that he took care to lead an unsullied life, carefully avoiding contact with—or concern for—sinners. " 'He walked with God' [*ibid.*]. That is, he walked only with God, but not at all with his fellowmen to draw them to God's service." This is the kind of self-satisfied leader who smugly looks on while the world moves to the brink of chaos.

Abraham, however, said Levi Yitzhak, was Noah's opposite, the prototype of a true leader. He walked "before" God (Genesis 17:1). That is, he went out into the world, leaving home and family, to bring others under the wings of the *Shekhinah* ("Divine Presence"). He pleaded with the Lord to spare the people of Sodom and Gomorrah without a thought for his own soul. Noah was concerned for his own piety; Abraham, for the soul of all mankind. Noah saved himself at the expense of others; Abraham attempted to save the world at the risk of his own life. [6]

Great is the reward for him who forsakes the security of the House of Prayer and Study to go out to the people; but great also is the danger. If the example of Abraham was to be a symbol for the new leader—the Tzaddik—then one had to be forewarned of the risk involved. At least a Noah, remaining secure, saves himself. Perhaps an Abraham, going among the people, will not only fail to win them over but will be drawn down into the pit himself.

This is what Levi Yitzhak meant when he said that the Tzaddik is like a broom. It sweeps clean, but in the process gets a little dirty.

---

*All passages in bold type are direct quotations from Levi Yitzhak's book *Kedushat Levi*.

And behold, My covenant is with thee, and thou shalt be as a father of a multitude of nations" [Genesis 17:4]. The purpose of the Tzaddik's serving God is to raise up the lower levels to the Creator, blessed be He. Beware, however, for in the Tzaddik's descent to the masses to bring them up, he himself may remain below; therefore must he first be bound up with the Lord. And this is the promise that God gives Abraham. "And behold, My covenant"—that is, My bond— that I shall be "with you" even when you will be a father of many nations. [7]

It was in Mezritch, under the Maggid's guidance, that the teachings of the Baal Shem were given new form and greater substance. The spiritual dialectic of binding oneself to God while at the same time going out and down to the common people, conversing with them on their level yet drawing them upward on the ladder of faith, was refined and perfected. A host of remarkable leaders, each a giant in his own right, emerged from Mezritch, spreading the message of Hasidism into Lithuania, Russia, Poland, and the Ukraine. These men were not of one cast; each possessed his own peculiar genius and labored in his own special way.

One of the Tzaddikim characterized the holy fellowship which was made up of the disciples of the Maggid as a single body: The Maggid himself was the head; the right hand, Rabbi Aaron of Titiyov; the left hand, Rabbi Barukh of Mezibosh (both grandsons of the Baal Shem); and the Rabbi of Berditchev—he was the heart. This one word, "heart," best describes Rabbi Levi Yitzhak. He was all heart, all compassion, all love, all feeling. And it was this which gave strength and direction to his prayers and to his deeds. [8]

ZHOLIKHOV

About 1761, Israel Peretz, the wealthy father-in-law of Levi Yitzhak, suffered financial reverses and fell into such debt that his son-in-law was forced to travel about the country to collect money for him. On one of these journeys, as night was falling, Levi Yitzhak came to a little town where he knew no one at all and could not find a lodging until, finally, a tanner invited him to his home. Levi Yitzhak wanted to say the evening prayer, but the smell of the hides was so terrible that he could not utter a word. So he left and went to the House of Study, which was quite empty, and there he prayed.

And then suddenly he understood how God must suffer for man, how the Divine Presence had descended to exile and now, with bowed head, stood in Tanner's Alley. He burst into tears and wept until he cried his heart out over the sorrow of the Divine Presence, and he fell in a faint. Then he saw the glory of God in all its splendor and heard the words: "Be strong, My son! Great suffering will come upon you, but have no fear, for I shall be with you...."

The time of undisturbed study, of mastering both the legal and mystical traditions, had come to an end for Levi Yitzhak. He accepted the call of the community of Ritchvol to succeed his former teacher, Rabbi Shmelke Horowitz, who had gone to another city. However, the bitter struggle against the innovations of the Hasidim had already broken out. The animosity of most of the rabbis and the leaders of the communities had reached the point of open hostility. Because he made his allegiance to the new movement, Rabbi Levi Yitzhak became an obvious target of persecution. Matters reached such a point that he feared for his life. On Hoshana Rabbah he fled, *Lulav* and *Etrog* in hand, to Koznitz, eleven miles away, where his friend, Rabbi Israel, lived. Not until he had walked half the distance on foot did a peasant take him in his wagon the rest of the way.

About 1771, Levi Yitzhak became *Rav* of Zholikhov in Poland. Here the struggle to establish Hasidism continued, for the ban of Elijah Gaon, issued in Vilna in 1772, created barriers of distrust and hatred even in Poland.

In the *Remembrance Book of the Zholikhov Jewish Community* [9] we are told how life was dominated by the learned and the rich Mitnagdim and how the poor, unlettered Jews were looked upon with disdain. Rabbi Levi Yitzhak threw himself into the task of renewal.

Within a short time he organized several study fellowships

("*Hevrahs*") for the simple Jews ("*Amkha Yidn*") who had neither the time nor the ability to delve into the Talmud—one for the tailors, another for the bakers, still another for those simple tradesmen who had until then been excluded from the study groups. Among those fellowships which he established was a *Hevrah Tehillim* ("fellowship for reading the Psalms"). Levi Yitzhak himself worked out the order of study for each *Hevrah*, determining what holy books the group should study and how much ground it should cover each day, and appointed a proper teacher. He insisted upon teaching the *Hevrah Tehillim* himself, and so, each morning, before or after the service, he would read and explain the Psalms to the *Amkha Yidn*. (In later years, when he had gained fame as the celebrated Rabbi of Berditchev, it was considered a special honor by the learned and wealthy—who had scorned his plan at first—to be accepted as a member of that *Hevrah*. It came to be known as the "Berditchever's *Hevrah Tehillim*" and continued to flourish until the community itself came to an end.)

The first large synagogue of Zholikhov was built through the efforts of Rabbi Levi Yitzhak. He revitalized the community and instituted a whole range of *Takkanot* ("reforms") in the ritual of Zholikhov and the surrounding area. Two such *Takkanot*, one a fact and the other probably a fable, are mentioned in the *Remembrance Book*. The *Tallit* ("prayer shawl") is worn only at the morning service and never at the evening service with one exception—at *Kol Nidre*, the eve of the Day of Atonement. But Levi Yitzhak decreed that on the eve of Rosh Hashanah also, for the *Minhah* and *Ma'ariv* services, the *Tallit* should be worn. Thus on the eve of Rosh Hashanah it is recorded that the Jews of Zholikhov would walk to synagogue with their prayer shawls pulled over their heads as on *Kol Nidre*, in silence, in fear, in devotion—a feeling of holy awe enveloping young and old alike.

The second *Takkanah* was to abolish *Dukhenen* (the recitation of the priestly benediction on festivals) whenever a festival fell on the Sabbath. For this change in the synagogue ritual, which was purely a *Halakhic* or legal decision, the people gave a more dramatic reason. It was, they said, a *Segulah*, that is, a miraculous protection against the total destruction of the town in the event—Heaven forbid—of fire. The *Takkanah* remained in force for many years, until it was changed by a later rabbi of Zholikhov, himself a priest ("*Kohen*"), who argued, "If when Levi Yitzhak was the rabbi he could issue a law according to his understanding, today I am rabbi and I decide according to my understanding." Thus on the next festival that fell on a Sabbath, in accordance with the new ruling, the priestly blessing was pronounced. That same year, according to legend, a fire broke out and destroyed half the city, including the synagogue and the House of Study. Strange things were told about this fire, the strangest of all being how the synagogue was consumed. This tall, strong, stately building, whose inside resembled the Temple of old, was devoured by hungry tongues of flame in what seemed only a few minutes. Immediately thereafter an army of white birds swooped down out of nowhere and picked up every bit of ashes so that no trace of the synagogue remained. After the fire, the *Takkanah* of Rabbi Levi Yitzhak was reinstated, and in that same year the rabbi who had changed the decree died. So did the people weave wonders about the life of the Tzaddik.

The records also contain a tale of Levi Yitzhak's departure from Zholikhov. He had not wanted to leave; too much of his heart and soul had been given to the community. But once again he could not withstand the power of those who hated him. Despondent, he took leave of his home and community, making his way on foot out of the city and beyond the surrounding villages. Suddenly a great weariness overcame him and, sick at heart, he sat down upon a large rock which—in contrast to the harsh, unyielding ways of the Mitnagdim of Zholikhov—felt like a downy pillow of comfort. Afterward, recalling his exodus, he made much of this resting place and named it the *weichstein* ("soft stone"). The tale of his departure became part of the legend, and for generations Jews traveling to and from Zholikhov would pause in wonder before the strange "soft stone," which, according to one version of the story, had been changed miraculously into a luxurious couch so that the beleaguered saint might find a moment of rest.

The *Remembrance Book* concludes by recounting that because

they abused their holy Tzaddik, the Jews of Zholikhov were punished in a manner befitting their folly. So long as Levi Yitzhak was their rabbi, each of his pronouncements of Torah was treasured by the townspeople and was engraved upon their memories; but when he was driven from the town, their minds became a blank.

Why this mild leader of men should have been chosen as one of the central targets of the Mitnagdim was a problem that troubled many.

The son of Rabbi Elimelekh of Lizhensk wrote to his father: "Why does the Hasid, Rabbi Levi Yitzhak, the head of the *Bet Din* ["court"] of Zholikhov, suffer so much from the attacks of the Mitnagdim?"

His father, Rabbi Elimelekh, replied: "Why does this surprise you? This sort of thing has always gone on in Israel. Alas for our souls! If it were not so, no nation in the world could subjugate us!"[10]

PINSK

In 1775, Levi Yitzhak was appointed Rav in the city of Pinsk, a key center of Lithuanian Jewry.[11] In Karlin, a neighboring suburb, Rabbi Aaron (d. 1772), one of the early Hasidic leaders and a foremost disciple of the Maggid, had served as Rav. He had succeeded in making serious inroads in this stronghold of the Mitnagdim. Though the appointment of Rabbi Levi Yitzhak to a community such as Pinsk was a tribute to his Talmudic scholarship, his election met with harsh opposition on the part of many of the communal authorities. They objected to the new rabbi's ecstatic manner of prayer and the bizarre fervor with which he fulfilled the Mitzvot—and the way he wasted his time associating with the simple and the sinner. All this was strange, even offensive, to the leaders of Lithuanian Pinsk.

Evidence of Levi Yitzhak's custom of befriending the outcast is found in the book *Toldot Aharon*, written by his disciple, Rabbi Aaron of Zhitomir. In explaining how Scripture could say, "And Isaac loved Esau" (Genesis 25:28), although Isaac surely knew that his other son, Jacob, was more deserving of his love than was this wild Esau, Rabbi Aaron writes:

> There are times when the Tzaddik must be more friendly with evildoers than with those who do good. For should the evildoer be permitted to go his own way, he might end his life in this same state of wickedness, Heaven forbid, and never repent. On the other hand, some who walk in an upright path take such pride in their goodness that at times it may be advisable to stay away from them. This was the way of the holy Rav of Berditchev: to befriend the stranger even more than his own students. He would say that his 'drawing away' was in reality a way of 'drawing near.' And there is in this much wisdom. Thus it is written: "And Yitzhak [that is, Levi Yitzhak] loved Esau"... because Esau did not walk in an upright path, and Yitzhak thought that by befriending him perhaps he would learn from his [Yitzhak's] ways.[12]

But what Aaron, the faithful disciple, understood as a wise principle of conduct whereby the lowly were raised and the lofty humbled, the Pinsk Litvaks looked upon as sheer foolishness and as time stolen from their rabbi's more proper task of studying the Talmud.[13] So it was that though the Hasidim rejoiced at the new rabbi's coming, the Mitnagdim threatened to drive him out. Matters reached such a point that even his relatives urged him to comply with the wishes of the majority. His wife alone remained loyal. But Levi Yitzhak stood fast in the maelstrom that swept around him. He ignored the accusations and insults as best he could and traveled to the Maggid as often as possible to gain guidance and strength.

Some idea of Levi Yitzhak's forbearance is given by a man who lived in Pinsk at this time:

> I was not fortunate enough to see with my own eyes that great fountain of holiness, the Maggid, and drink in his words, but a river came from the source and overflowed upon all those who drew near. This river was none other than the holy Gaon, Levi Yitzhak of Pinsk. Though I was not with

> *him many times, I can testify that he shone as a beacon in the darkness, withdrawing from all conflicts, devoted to the fulfillment of the Mitzvot in a manner most wonderful to behold. When he prayed, one could hear his voice even at some distance.*[14]

But his forbearance could be sorely tried, as it was in the case of Rabbi Avigdor. It is reported that in their youth Levi Yitzhak and Avigdor had studied together. But with the rise of the Hasidic movement, Avigdor was among its bitterest opponents. He was even a government informer in the celebrated case of Rabbi Shneur Zalman. Avigdor had set his sights on the rabbinical post in Pinsk, one of the most coveted in the land. He joined forces with those who plotted Levi Yitzhak's dismissal. Finally, he was named the rabbi, and later admitted paying a substantial sum for the appointment.[15]

While this agitation was at its height, Levi Yitzhak tried to make peace with Avigdor, but this stubborn, vengeful man ignored his every appeal. Indeed, whenever Rabbi Levi Yitzhak entered a building where Avigdor was, the latter immediately made his exit through another door.

It once happened that Rabbi Levi Yitzhak went into a house that had no other door, and when Rabbi Avigdor, who was also there, tried to leave, Levi Yitzhak blocked his way and said, "My dear Avigdor, why do you run from me? Stay and let us talk."

But Rabbi Avigdor pushed him aside and strode out.

Levi Yitzhak began to weep.

Hasidism met with astounding success in the south, in Galicia and the Ukraine. But it encountered stubborn resistance in the north, in Lithuania and northern Poland. The clash between the new way of Hasidism and the accustomed practices of many of the rabbis resounded in every quarter. It was highlighted by the publication of the first Hasidic book, *Toldot Ya'akov Yosef*, in 1780. This work combined a classic exposition of the teachings of the Baal Shem with a devastating critique of the contemporary rabbinic and lay leadership.

All of this combined to rouse the fury of the Lithuanian

Mitnagdim. In the summer of 1781 a new *Herem* against the Hasidim was proclaimed in the synagogues throughout Lithuania, and the persecution of the Pinsk Hasidim was intensified. Argument and counterargument, claim and counterclaim reached such a feverish pitch that Levi Yitzhak, man of peace though he was, could no longer remain aloof from the controversy. Once during a visit he told the Maggid of Koznitz that he intended to go to Vilna, the center of the opponents of Hasidic teachings, in order to debate with them.

"I should like to ask you a question," said the Maggid. "Why do you go contrary to the custom, in that you recite the *Shemoneh Esreh* prayer with open eyes?"

"Dear heart," said the Rabbi of Berditchev, "do you think—when I do this—I see anything at all?"

"I know very well," the Maggid replied, "that you see nothing whatsoever. But what will you say to those others when they ask you this question?"

Shortly before 1781 Levi Yitzhak was chosen to represent the leaders of the Hasidic movement in a public debate in Warsaw with the noted Rav of Brisk, Rabbi Abraham Katzenellenbogen, who referred to him as "chief among the arrogant ones."[16] No official record remains of what transpired there. But a later popular account runs as follows:

"Why do you shout so much during your prayers," asked the *Brisker Rav*, "as if, Heaven forbid, God does not hear even the slightest whisper?"

"We do not shout because of God, Who surely hears every whisper," replied Rabbi Levi Yitzhak, "but because of your Mitnagdim, that you might hear our prayers in Brisk and Vilna and not spread gossip that we Hasidim do not pray."

"Why do you jump and leap from place to place when you pray, as if the fear of Heaven were not upon you? Such conduct is not proper before even a human king."

"Do not bring proofs from a human king," replied Rabbi Levi Yitzhak. "He fills only the place where he sits, and thus we must stand opposite him, face to face. Not so with the King of kings, the Holy One, blessed be He, Whose glory fills the world, for there is no place where He is not, and wherever we turn there He is. Therefore, it is proper to leap and jump after the Master of the World, always searching for Him. And through each of our movements toward Him we cry out to all the world—the Lord is everywhere!"

"Why do you say your prayers after the proper time?"

"Rabbi of Brisk," replied Levi Yitzhak, "we have not heard that there is a clock in Heaven at which the angels look in order to determine whether or not to pray. I, Levi Yitzhak, believe that each moment of the day a Jew should rise and proclaim that we have but One God. He should worship the Lord at all times and not only when the clock tells him to!"[17]

According to Hasidic tradition, Levi Yitzhak and his family were physically evicted from their home and community. The cause of this may very well have been a letter from the illustrious Elijah Gaon and other leaders of the Jewish community of Vilna to "the leaders of the congregation of the holy community of Pinsk." This letter is one of the most important historical documents that deal with Levi Yitzhak's early struggles with the Mitnagdim. It contains valuable information about the situation in Pinsk. In it the leaders of the Pinsk community were once again urged to dismiss their rabbi. Although the name of the rabbi is not mentioned, the date of the letter is clear evidence that it was Levi Yitzhak. The epistle begins by calling attention to

> that one who has been appointed in your community as Rav and Gaon. He encourages the evildoers who have cast off the yoke of Torah and Mitzvot and innovates customs of which our holy forefathers knew nothing. They are the Hashudim ["suspected"] sect, who call themselves Hasidim. Already the lay and spiritual heads of the leading communities have joined to root out the thorns and thistles from the vineyard of Israel, by scattering these clusters of evildoers, driving them from us and annulling their strange customs which have no basis in our holy Torah. The desire of the Lord has been victorious: We have stood firmly against them, subduing and humbling them as the dust of the earth. . . .

> *Alas, however, Satan is yet among us . . . in that some of the leaders of [your] community are of that sect and strengthen the evildoers. . . . We have warned you in previous letters and have made known to you the restrictions and bans which communal leaders together with their rabbis have promulgated against the sect. . . . But your community—though there are God-fearing men among you—has ignored these warnings because of the powerful influence of those who belong to or support the sect. . . .*
>
> *Even though it would have been better to remove the scepter and crown of authority from the Rav and Gaon [of Pinsk] earlier, when you decided not to depose him, we accepted your decision—thinking that perhaps he would of himself turn from his erring way and cease leading the people along the crooked road! But if he refuses to bend his neck to the yoke . . . , then, as we have urged you in our former letters . . . , withdraw all authority from the above-mentioned Rav and head of the court of your community. Let him neither teach Torah nor render legal decisions. . . . Drive him out and be done with him! . . .*[18]

So the murmurings against Levi Yitzhak swelled to a deafening roar and the movement to oust him gained decisive momentum. One day while Levi Yitzhak was visiting the Maggid, perhaps taking counsel on how to deal with the recently proclaimed *Herem*, his home was broken into, his belongings seized, his wife and family evicted, his salary revoked; and a new rabbi—the infamous Avigdor—was hired to fill his post.[19]

Hardship, persecution and disappointment had followed Levi Yitzhak without respite, from Ritchvol to Zholikhov to Pinsk. Caught up in the holocaust that was then raging in the Jewish communities of Eastern Europe, his extraordinary powers of mind and soul seemed to be spent in vain.

His Hasidim lamented over this early period of their master's life, recounting this story:

The Baal Shem told his disciples that when the time came for the soul of Levi Yitzhak to descend into the world, great consternation arose in the Heavenly Court.

Satan was visibly shaken. He came before the Lord with a complaint. "I have heard about a new soul called Levi Yitzhak. He will be kind to strangers. He will defend the people. He will be a great scholar of Torah. Furthermore, his prayer will be like none since that of Rabbi Akiva, who would never complete his worship in the same corner that he began. Master of the World, this soul that now descends to the earth will cleanse the hearts of all our generation, and all my labors will be in vain."

The Holy One, blessed be He, answered Satan, "Do not fret, Satan. That soul of which you speak—the soul of Levi Yitzhak of Berditchev—will not have time to cleanse hearts. He will be a rabbi in Israel!"[20]

BERDITCHEV

In 1785, Rabbi Levi Yitzhak, weary from the incessant—and often violent—agitation that had followed him for almost fifteen years, at last found respite and glory. In that year, at the age of forty-five (and on the forty-fifth day of the counting of the Omer),[21] he was received with dignity and honor as the Rav of Berditchev. There he discovered the peaceful and the fertile soil for spiritual work that he had longed for. Perhaps he referred to this when he wrote that "The fullness of joy is found only where anguish once prevailed."[22]

The reverence in which he was held is reflected in the following.

> *The first day of the week,* parashat Noah, 1794
>
> *We praise God all the day long, for this is the day upon which we have waited. We have found and we have seen him whom our soul loves, who has been elevated as the head of the court of our community, the congregation of Yeshurun, the holy community of Berditchev, the honored master, the splendor of Israel, the father of mercies, the glory of the holy ones, the true Gaon, the distinguished Hasid, the divine teacher, Rabbi Levi Yitzhak—may his light continue to shine—who was previously the head of the court in Zholikhov and in the holy community of Pinsk and its environs. It is impossible to*

describe his learning or his holy service to God. He bears upon his shoulders the burden of all Israel, the people of God, to be for them a shield and a fortress, and to teach the people the way of wisdom, to chart a course through the sea of the Talmud and a path through mighty waters, to give the children of Judah a weapon with which to fight the battle of the Lord with devotion and yearning and love. To the Jews there is light, which is Torah, as if emanating from Heaven itself. He is our shepherd who watches the flock of Israel, to guide us to green pastures with heavenly words and with earthly advice, that we not stumble, God forbid, into the pits of danger and to bring down to us the bread of God from on high, rich with blessings. Our own ears can testify that all his words are the words of the living God and all his days he struggles for the welfare of his people, the house of Israel.[23]

If Vilna was the "Jerusalem of Lithuania" (the stronghold of the Mitnagdim), Berditchev was the "Jerusalem of Volhynia" (the stronghold of the Hasidim). It contained so many Jews that it was virtually a Jewish city. Its commercial growth was so great that the Polish government decided to move the great annual fair to Berditchev in 1765 and to hold it there regularly. So each year thousands of visitors came to the city. Among them were large numbers of Jews. The economic influence of Berditchev as the most important center for the merchants and farmers of the area, was equaled by its potential for spiritual influence. The Maggid, whose disciples were spreading the teachings of Hasidism throughout Eastern Europe, had long looked to Berditchev as a city that might, under proper conditions, become the focal point for the new movement in the Ukraine. By 1785 the Maggid had died and his disciples were scattered, but his hope was to be fulfilled.

In Berditchev many obstacles had to be overcome at first, though the opposition lessened as time went on. There was a group who was unfalteringly faithful to the memory of the great Rabbi Liber who had lived and taught in Berditchev. (He had died fifteen years before.) They were understandably cool to the newcomer. Once Rabbi Levi Yitzhak invited them to come to him and told them that he intended to immerse himself in Rabbi Liber's bath. Now what was called Rabbi Liber's bath was nothing but a pit full of water covered by a roof on four posts. In winter Rabbi Liber had had to break the ice with an ax before he could perform his holy ablutions. After his death the bath was neglected; the roof had caved in and mud filled in the pit. And so the Tzaddik was told that it was impossible to bathe in it. But he was firm in his purpose. He hired four workmen who dug in the pit for a whole day without striking water. They continued to dig for a week. Still no water was found. His enemies laughed at this curious new Rav. It was obvious, they said, that Rabbi Liber did not wish his bath to be used.

Finally Rabbi Levi Yitzhak asked all those who had known Rabbi Liber well to assemble early the following morning. He went to the bath with them, and once more the workmen began to dig.

After two hours one of them cried out, "I see water!"

Soon the bottom of the pit was thinly covered with water. "There is no need to dig any further," said the rabbi. He took off his clothes and, keeping only the cap on his head, went down into the pit. When he stepped into the water, everyone there saw that it barely lapped around his ankles. But in a moment it had risen to his mouth.

Then he asked, "Is there anybody here who remembers Rabbi Liber in his youth?"

Someone answered that in the new part of the city there lived a beadle, 116 years old, who had served Rabbi Liber in his youth. The Tzaddik sent for the old man while he waited in the water. At first the beadle refused to come, but when he was told what had happened, he changed his mind.

"Do you still remember the *Shammash*," the rabbi asked him, "who hanged himself from the chandelier in the House of Prayer?"

"I remember him," the old man answered in surprise. "But how are you concerned with him? All that was a good seventy years ago, long before you were born!"

"Tell us about it," said the rabbi.

The old man said, "He was a simple man. but he was very devout. And he had his own way of doing things. On Wednesday of every week he began to polish the great chandelier hanging from the ceiling to have it ready for the Sabbath. And while he did this, he always said, 'I do this for the sake of God.' But one Friday afternoon, when people came to the House of Prayer, they found him hanging from the chandelier in a noose knotted in his belt."

Rabbi Levi Yitzhak said, "That time—on the day before Sabbath—when everything had been cleaned and polished, and there was nothing more to be done, the simple beadle asked himself, 'What more can I do in honor of God? What more can I do in His honor?' His poor, weak mind grew confused, and because of all the great things in the world to him the chandelier had always been the greatest, he hanged himself from it in honor of God. And now that seventy years have passed since that day, Rabbi Liber appeared to me in a dream and told me to do whatever could be done to release the soul of that simple man. Therefore, I had the holy bath restored and immersed myself. Now tell me, is the hour come for the release of that poor soul?"

"Yes, yes, yes!" all called as if with a single voice.

"Then I, too, say, 'Yes, yes, yes!'" said the rabbi. "Go in peace."

With that he came out of the water, and the water sank so that it would barely have lapped at his ankles.

Rabbi Levi Yitzhak had a bathhouse built in that place and had the old bath restored. He had another dug next to it for himself. Only when he was about to prepare for some difficult work did he use the bath of Rabbi Liber. As long as the house with the two baths stood in the old part of the city, the people called the one bath that of Rabbi Liber, and the other that of Rabbi Levi Yitzhak.

The tailors and bakers in Berditchev, who were also among the opponents of Rabbi Levi Yitzhak, brought to the city a rabbi of their own.

It once happened that Rabbi Levi Yitzhak attended a *B'rit*

Milah where the majority of people were tailors and bakers, and with them was their rabbi, a Mitnaged. The other rabbi mockingly pointed to Rabbi Levi Yitzhak. "Here is that leader of the Hasidim from whom blessings pour forth so freely," he said. "Perhaps he will also bless those who are gathered here today with a blessing fitting the occasion and the assemblage."

"This," said Rabbi Levi Yitzhak, "is my blessing: that we should be worthy of receiving the Messiah in our own lifetime."

"And what does that blessing have to do with this gathering?"

"Our sages have taught us in the Talmud," replied Levi Yitzhak, "that 'in the days of the Messiah the earth will bring forth cakes and garments of fine wool.' So, since clothing and bread will be readily available in that time, there will be no need either for tailors or for bakers—or for their rabbi!"

Such sharp replies of Levi Yitzhak to his tormentors were rare. His customary manner is revealed in the following incident.

At the head of the many Mitnagdim in the city who opposed Levi Yitzhak and refused to accept his authority was Barukh Hamozag. He was a leader in the community and a man of wealth who had great influence in the court of the neighboring prince.

Once on the eve of a Sabbath when Rabbi Levi Yitzhak was not in the city, Barukh Hamozag took the rabbi's wife and children, put them on a cart filled with dung, and drove them out of the city.

Saturday night, immediately after *Havdalah* (marking the close of the Sabbath), a group of Berditchev Hasidim traveled to Rabbi Zev Velvel (the author of *Or Hameir*) in Zhitomir. They arrived at dawn the next day. Without delay, they angrily made their way to Rabbi Zev Velvel and poured out the entire story to him. Rabbi Zev Velvel told them to return after the morning prayer.

"Surely while he prays," they said, "he will curse that proud and evil man." And their rage diminished.

After Rabbi Zev Velvel had finished his prayers, the committee returned.

"What can I do?" said the rabbi. "Before I even lifted up the prayerbook to demand punishment for Barukh, already Rabbi Levi Yitzhak was standing there to beg mercy!"

> There are those who serve the Lord from fear, in order to receive a reward, and there are those who serve the Lord from love, and in great joy, in the knowledge that even the angels stand trembling before Him. The Tzaddik who serves the Creator from love is of so tender a disposition as to be unable to take vengeance upon those who despise him. But the Tzaddik who serves the Creator from fear is of so stern a nature as to delight in repaying his antagonists.[24]

Love for Israel burned deep in Levi Yitzhak's heart, for he was full of compassion toward every Jew. Indeed, mercy was the touchstone of his soul. When the decree was issued by the government ordering that a surname be added to the given name of every Jew, Rabbi Levi Yitzhak wrote down as the name of his family *Derbarmdiger* ("merciful"). His students and friends asked him about his choice of a name. He answered, "Are we not told by the Talmudic sages to follow after the ways of the Holy One, blessed be He? 'As He is merciful, so you be merciful.' Therefore let my name be called Derbarmdiger."

And so it was.

At that time, the winds of skepticism were blowing fiercely from Berlin, where Moses Mendelssohn and his circle had begun to urge the study of Western literature and thought in order to "modernize" the ancient faith of Israel. These winds reached even as far as Berditchev, which soon harbored a group of free thinkers. And these, too, added to the ranks of those opposed to the new rabbi.

Among them was a very learned man who had heard of the Rabbi of Berditchev and looked him up in order to debate with him, as he was in the habit of doing with others. He planned to refute the rabbi's old-fashioned proofs for the truth of his faith. When he entered the Tzaddik's room, he saw the rabbi walking up and down, a book in his hand, immersed in thought. Levi Yitzhak, who knew of the man, took no notice of him.

After a time, however, he paused, gave his visitor a brief glance, and said, "But perhaps it is true after all!"

The skeptic tried in vain to rally his self-confidence. His knees shook, for the Tzaddik was terrible to behold and his simple words were terrible to hear. Then Rabbi Levi Yitzhak turned to him and calmly addressed him.

"My son, the great Torah scholars with whom you debated wasted their words on you. When you left them, you only laughed at what they had said. They could not set God and His Kingdom on the table before you, and I cannot do this either. But, my son, only think! Perhaps it is true. Perhaps it is true after all!"

The doubter made an effort to reply, but the terrible "perhaps" beat on his ears again and again and broke down his resistance.

It was at this time, too, that the Gaon of Vilna, whose *Herem* against the Hasidim had turned all Israel into two warring camps, died. The Gaon had been influenced by hearsay reports to denounce the new movement. He had never met even one of its leaders. When the noted Rabbi Shneur Zalman came to Vilna to explain to the Gaon why his fears concerning Hasidism were unfounded, Rabbi Elijah fled the city to avoid a confrontation.

After the death of the Vilna Gaon, the following tale was told in Rabbi Levi Yitzhak's name:

See how stubborn the Mitnaged of Vilna was. When his soul ascended on high for judgment, the Heavenly Court could not find a single blemish. But when judging the great ones, the court is troubled by even a hair's breadth of guilt. Thus, accusation was made against Rabbi Elijah that he had sinned in persecuting the Hasidim. The court considered the matter and at last reached a decision. It found him guilty as accused and decreed that his atonement would be to listen to some of the teachings of Hasidism from the mouth of Rabbi Nahum of Tchernobil, whose custom it was to expound the Hasidic teachings before the heavenly family. If the Vilna Gaon refused to obey the decision, he would be permitted to enter Paradise only by way of *Gehinnom*.

To this judgment the Mitnaged from Vilna replied, characteristically, that it would be better for him to enter Paradise by way of *Gehinnom* than to listen to the teachings of Hasidism.

And do you think that the final decision of the Gaon was carried out? Immediately the tens of thousands of pages of all the holy books that he had studied and learned almost by heart during this lifetime—the Talmud, *Sifra, Sifre, Tosefta, Midrashim* and *Kabbalah*—swept into the room and arranged themselves into a massive wall across the doorway to *Gehinnom*. This created an impassable barrier between the Gaon and the lower regions.

A stubborn Mitnaged was he in this world, and a stubborn Mitnaged he remained even in the world to come. The Heavenly Court had no choice in the matter. It brought him into Paradise without his even hearing one word of the gentle and holy teachings of Hasidism.

After eight years in Berditchev, Levi Yitzhak suffered a nervous collapse. He could no longer bear the burden he had taken upon himself to forge a community of the faithful by shaping their minds and igniting their spirits. So complete was his effort, so wearing the task, so exalted the goal, and so constant the enmity that the bright flame of his spirit began to flicker.

Rabbi Yitzhak of Kamarna wrote:

> *See what they have done to the prince of our generation, our master and teacher, Rabbi Levi Yitzhak, may his memory live on to eternity! For my father-in-law, Rabbi Avraham of Pintchov, told me that Levi Yitzhak's enemies drove him to the very brink of despair. In 1793 he fell from his rung into a state of depression and would pray quickly from a small Siddur. My father-in-law said that Levi Yitzhak's disciple, the holy Maggid of Koznitz, sought to help his master. But, the Maggid reported, while the Heavenly powers ordinarily would not have permitted Levi Yitzhak to fall from his rung—God forbid!—they stood aside and did not prevent his "fall," because in that year he had so provoked them by defending the Children of Israel against divine punishment for their sins. My father-in-law visited Berditchev in 1794 and found Rabbi Levi Yitzhak returned to the vigor of his full powers. He remained there for a year to study Torah with him and to learn from him the fear and love of God.*"[25]

Levi Yitzhak's illness left him as suddenly as it had come, and he continued his work in double measure for the last fifteen years of his life.

The work of Levi Yitzhak reached its towering height. His fame began to spread far and wide. Berditchev, formerly known for its commerce, now became the destination for multitudes of Jews who traveled there to see and learn from the rabbi.

As Rav, head of the *Bet Din* and *Yeshivah*, Levi Yitzhak's authority was supreme in all matters relating to the law. Thus equipped, he proceeded to treat long-standing communal ailments. He prescribed new medicines—some quite strong—to insure a manifest well-being. Large numbers of students came to his *Yeshivah*. There he taught the Talmud and Codes. His son Meir wrote: "It is well known to all that my father and master has raised up many thousands of students whom he has instructed in the Oral Law."[26]

It is important to stress this rabbinic aspect of his life. He served the communities in which he lived not only as the Hasidic leader, or Tzaddik, but also—unlike most other Tzaddikim—as the traditional Rav. Because of this he was referred to not as *Rebbe*, as the Tzaddikim were commonly called, but as *Rav, Av Bet Din*, and *Reish Metivta*, titles given the communal rabbi who was a legal authority and functioned primarily as a teacher and judge. Also, he was not succeeded by his son in dynastic fashion as was the custom with most other Hasidic leaders. The majority of the stories about him stress the ecstatic or mystic aspect of his life—which was remarkable enough to deserve such fame—but beneath the popular image which tradition has fashioned for him is the immense rabbinic learning which, in good measure, must explain his being elected Rav of Lithuanian Pinsk at the time of the Vilna Gaon, or his being chosen to debate the Rav of Brisk. Talmud and *Kabbalah*, *Halakhah* and *Aggadah*, prose and poetry, were interwoven in his life.[27]

Each Sabbath afternoon, at the *Shalosh S'udot*—those soulful gatherings that took place toward the close of the Sabbath, as the shadows of evening lengthened—Rabbi Levi Yitzhak spoke to his followers on the great teachings of Hasidism. This spiritual meal, which the early Hasidic leaders had established as the central hour of the week, was marked by the singing of holy songs. Some of them, called *Niggunim*, overflowed with such yearning or joy that no words could contain the mood; the melody alone carried the meaning. The rabbi, full of fire, compassion, and holy joy, discoursed in a manner so unforgettable that records of his words have been handed down with love and care from generation to generation.

The writings of Rabbi Levi Yitzhak have survived in the form of his book, *Kedushat Levi*, the first part of which was published in his lifetime, in 1798.[28] Most of the early Hasidic literature was written by disciples from notes they had taken and, consequently, only reflect their masters' genius. But Levi Yitzhak wrote his book himself. This work secures its author a place among the great Jewish mystics. It was widely read and soon became one of the classics of Hasidic literature. For the written words of the author of *Kedushat Levi*, even as his spoken words, possessed the strange power to bring the heart of the reader to the love and fear of God. "Each time I open the book, *Kedushat Levi*, and begin to read it," wrote one scholar, "there rises before my mind's eye the image of a holy sage, adorned in *Tallit* and *Tefillin*, his face aglow from the glory of the *Shekhinah* Who hovers above, sitting and writing, trembling in ecstasy and writing—not with ink but with holy fire."[29] Indeed, there was for a time a widespread belief among the plain people that simply having this book in one's house gave protection against all evil.

It was the custom of a certain eminent scholar each week at the close of the Sabbath, after *Havdalah*, to spend an hour or more studying *Kedushat Levi*, reading each word slowly and with great care. Once, one of his disciples, who had observed this custom of his master, asked the following question: "Why is it that when my master reads the *Akedah*, which is a profound and difficult book, he goes through it quickly; but when he studies *Kedushat Levi*, which is written in so lucid a style that one who runs can read it, he proceeds so slowly?"

His master replied, "You are mistaken. The *Akedah* was written

THE LIFE OF A TZADDIK   45

in a manner that reflects the thoughts of its author. But this is not so of *Kedushat Levi*. For in this book there are hidden meanings and concealed allusions such as in the books of the Ari [the famous sixteenth-century Kabbalist, Rabbi Isaac Luria]."

Almost all we know of Rabbi Levi Yitzhak comes from the glowing reports and tales of his adoring disciples and the mass of his followers. Is what they say to be believed? How did those who stood against the new movement view him? One such testimony is found in the memoirs of a *Maskil*, an "enlightened" writer, who delighted in holding the Hasidim up to biting ridicule. About the Rabbi of Berditchev, however, he spoke differently. He described Levi Yitzhak as "a scholar of the highest rank, just and pious, who influenced countless lives for good." The *Maskil* goes on to say:

> *The ecstasy and compassion which marked the prayers of Rabbi Levi Yitzhak were known far and wide. Even as he entered the synagogue, the thunder of his voice would shake its walls. On the eve of Rosh Hashanah he did not walk upright to the synagogue in the ordinary fashion of others, but would go bent over almost to the ground, holding two* Shofars *in his hands. On those days his prayers were like the piercing sound of the* Shofar *itself, striking such terror into the hearts of the people that often they would burst into tears. When he stood before the Ark to lead the service, he could not remain in one place but would run hither and yon, dancing with all his might, crying out in an awesome voice. Suddenly he would seize a man by his coat and shout at him, "Whom do you serve?" Trembling, the Hasid would reply, "I serve the Lord of Heaven and Earth." With that Levi Yitzhak would turn to God in joy, saying, "See, O Master of the World, how Your children serve You! You alone they glorify and sanctify. Where is there a people like unto Your people?"*[30]

His utter simplicity, his ardent prayers, his love of Torah, his fervor in performing the Mitzvot, his deeds of kindness and compassion, his defense of his people, swept like a strong, cool breeze through the countryside, reviving, restoring, and renewing. An ancient faith that had been in danger of growing dry and hard found new life. Rabbi Levi Yitzhak became a legend in his own lifetime, and the city of Berditchev was transformed into a radiant goal for countless Jews from distant towns. As pilgrims going up to Jerusalem, they would travel through snow and sun alike, with all sorrow banished and with only joy in their hearts, to visit the holy man who lived there and whose holiness was felt by all Israel.

Rabbi Nahman of Bratzlav, the grandson of the Baal Shem, commanded his Hasidim that whenever the Rabbi of Berditchev was traveling in their neighborhood they should examine their *Tefillin*. Later he explained what he meant. "The *Tefillin* are referred to by the ancient sages as the 'glory of Israel.' So is the Rabbi of Berditchev."

2

Love of Israel

ACCORDING TO THE LEGEND mentioned earlier, the Baal Shem prepared a celebration for his students at the birth of Rabbi Levi Yitzhak, because he knew that a soul had come into the world to be a defender of all Israel. The prophecy of the Besht came true. The flaming spirit of the rabbi was more deeply marked by love for Israel than were those of all the Tzaddikim who preceded him and all who followed him.

Ahavat Yisrael, "love for Israel," is a golden thread that runs through the tapestry of Jewish faith. Scripture portrays the role of Israel, chosen to be "a kingdom of priests and a holy nation," the recipient of God's revelation for all mankind.

*Thus saith God the Lord,
He that created the heavens,
And stretched them forth,
He that spread forth the earth
And that which cometh out of it,
He that giveth breath unto the people upon it,
And spirit to them that walk therein:
"I, the Lord, have called thee in righteousness,
And have taken hold of thy hand,
And kept thee,
And set thee for a covenant of the people,
For a light to the nations;
To open the blind eyes,
To bring out the prisoners from the dungeon,
And those that sit in darkness
Out of the prison house.
I am the Lord, that is My name;
And My glory will I not give to another. . . .*

*For a small moment have I forsaken thee;
But with great compassion will I gather thee.
In a little wrath I hid My face for a moment;
But with everlasting kindness
Will I have compassion on thee. . . .*

*For the mountains may depart,
And the hills be removed;
But My kindness shall not depart from thee,
Neither shall My covenant be removed,
Saith the Lord that hath compassion on thee."*

(Isaiah 42:5-8, 54:7-8, 10)

But there was the shame of Israel as well as the glory, the curse as well as the blessing. The Bible recounts the story of a people confronted by God and of this people's repeated cycle of rebellion, judgment and return.

Hear, O heavens, and give ear, O earth,
For the Lord hath spoken:
"Children I have reared, and brought up,
And they have rebelled against Me.
The ox knoweth his owner,
And the ass his master's crib,
But Israel doth not know,
My people doth not consider.
Ah, sinful nation,
A people laden with iniquity,
A seed of evildoers,
Children that deal corruptly;
They have forsaken the Lord.
They have contemned the Holy One of Israel. . . .

They sell the righteous for silver,
And the needy for a pair of shoes;
And turn aside the way of the humble."

(Isaiah 1:2-4; Amos 2:6-7)

To Levi Yitzhak, however, there was no darkness, no curse, no shame. He saw—at least he claimed he saw—only light and blessing and glory. It was not that he knew nothing of the people's sins, but rather that he preferred to see their goodness, even if it meant occasionally closing one eye. His love was for all men, the evildoer as well as the righteous, the untutored as well as the learned, the humble as well as the mighty. He believed that no man, be he ever so deep in iniquity, was beyond turning back. It was not always easy to be charitable to his fellow man. It required a constant struggle with the baser side of his nature. "Until I remove the thread of hatred from my heart," he wrote, "I am, in my own eyes, as if I did not exist."

Levi Yitzhak saw two possible ways of dealing with the people: He could drive them from sin with harsh words, or draw them to God through kind words. The second, with rare exceptions, was the way of the Rabbi of Berditchev. He could not abide condemnation of the people, even by devoted leaders, even though what they said might be the truth. Thus, preachers saddened him when they dwelled only on the failings of the congregation, threatening fire and brimstone for all transgressors. About this practice, he wrote:

> Rashi and Nahmanides disagree on the nature of the sin that prevented Moses from entering the Promised Land. One said it was because Moses cried out against the people: "O ye, rebellious ones"; while the other said it was because he struck at the rock, in violation of God's command. But it would appear to me that a single reason—anger—was the cause of both.
>
> For there are two ways to urge Israel to do the will of the Lord. One way is to speak to them in a gentle manner, with kind words, reminding each Jew of the nobility of his heritage, of the fact that his spirit comes from the Creator, and of the great joy that pervades the world when even a single Mitzvah is performed. In such a fashion, one is able to touch the heart and turn it to do the will of the Creator and accept the yoke of the Kingdom of Heaven.
>
> The second way is to rebuke Israel with harsh words and shame them until they are forced to do the will of the Lord.
>
> The difference between them is this: He who speaks gently to the people raises their soul higher and higher, for he dwells always upon the holiness of Israel, of the good they have done and can yet do. He is worthy of being a leader of Israel. But he who bitterly reproves the people is not worthy. [1]

This was counsel that Rabbi Levi Yitzhak tried to follow in his own life. True, sin and evil existed. But why dwell upon it? Were there not enough gossips and sycophants who did so? How much rarer is the gentle word; how much more difficult to judge one's neighbor charitably. There was so much goodness in this people, so much willingness to sacrifice for the Mitzvot of the Lord. And even if from time to time the people turned from the path of righteousness, consider what suffering they had to endure. What of the insults and cruelties, the shame and the endless hardships that were inflicted daily upon them? What of the pogroms that burst from nowhere upon their heads, leaving behind terror, desolation and ruin? What of the web of wretched poverty from which there was no escape? What of their pitiable helplessness before the greedy count, the zealous priest, the ignorant peasant? All this, and more, they must endure.

The way of love, the way of understanding, forgiveness and compassion was Levi Yitzhak's choice.

> Since the Creator chose only the people of Israel as His own, how can one speak ill of them? ... Indeed, our tongues have been set in our mouths for two purposes alone: to study Torah and to praise Israel. And if you ask: What of those who seem only set on worldly gain, as they rush along the byways and through the marketplace? I say, they do all this only for the sake of Heaven: to earn enough so that they can give generously to charity, have their children taught Torah, and so they can provide well for Sabbaths and holy days. For the Holy One, blessed be He, is glorified by His people Israel in all their ways. [2]

Why did Levi Yitzhak choose the way of love? Because of the terrible suffering which the bitterness of exile had inflicted upon the people. Because men prefer to condemn and criticize, to pounce upon error and seek out transgression, while good is often bypassed. Because the way of love can be a wondrous way of winning people to Torah and God, for mercy is victorious when anger fails, and understanding opens gates barred to condemnation. Because Rabbi Levi Yitzhak lived his life a hand's breadth above the ordinary man. In the shadows of human existence he glimpsed those sparks which, under his gaze, joined to form such a wave of sunlight that all darkness vanished. Israel was the holy flock of the divine Shepherd—how could they go astray?

IN DEFENSE OF ISRAEL

Levi Yitzhak could not bear to hear evil spoken against his holy people. When it *was* spoken, whether it concerned all the people or only one Jew, it was his custom—even if he himself had witnessed what had transpired and had to blind himself for the moment to what was before him—to speak in defense of Israel.

It is said that if Rabbi Levi Yitzhak heard one Jew speaking ill of another of the Children of Israel, he would turn, seize him by the arm, and say, "My brother, how can you repeat such gossip, Heaven forbid, about the *Tefillin* of the Holy One, blessed be He, in which our sages tell us, is written: 'Who is like unto the people, Israel?' "

(The *Tefillin* of a man are his "glory." According to Rabbinic legend, God too wears *Tefillin*. Since, in God's *Tefillin* praise of Israel is inscribed, the Jews are symbolically described as "His *Tefillin*.")

Once a man of some standing came to visit Levi Yitzhak.

"Where have you come from?"

"From the land of *Gehinnom*," he answered mockingly.

"Throw this fellow out," Levi Yitzhak replied. "Israel knows nothing of *Gehinnom*."

One day when Levi Yitzhak entered the *Bet ha-Midrash*, he heard a preacher on the pulpit pouring fire and brimstone upon the congregation, omitting hardly a sin, minor or major, intentional or unintentional, whether between man and his fellow or between man and God. When at last the sermon was finished, Levi Yitzhak lifted his eyes heavenward and said, "Master of the World, give no heed to the faultfinding of this preacher. He speaks bitterness against Your people, but it is a bitterness which his own troubles have brewed. Poor fellow, he has a daughter at home who is of age but he lacks the means to bring about a marriage for her. Let him find money for a dowry and wedding, so that he will cease condemning Israel, Thy holy people."

And Moses said, "Let the Lord, the God of the spirits of all flesh, appoint a man over the congregation" [Numbers 27:16]. This verse instructs us to speak well of the people Israel. For if they are unable to do the will of the Creator at all times, as angels do, it is only because of the hardship in providing for their families. And so it was with Abraham our Father, a compassionate man, who would ever find merit in Israel. Therefore did he give food to the angels who came to visit him, though he knew angels do not eat, in order to teach them human needs, that they might appreciate our situation and not be harsh with Israel. And this is why Moses said, "The Lord, the God of the spirits of all *flesh*." Because man is flesh and blood he must labor for his livelihood, and, alas there are times when the weariness of the body may hamper his service of God. Therefore, Moses was careful to use the expression: "The Lord, the God of the spirits of all *flesh*." That is to say: Just as You are a Judge and Guide Who will always be merciful with Israel, because You understand the needs and frailties of the flesh, so may You appoint a man over the congregation who will understand, defend, and guide them as a shepherd his flock. [3]

"These are the words that Moses spoke to all Israel" (Deuteronomy 1:1). The phrase, "these are the words," is understood by the sages to mean "words of reproof." But how could Moses, the lover and defender of his people, speak "words of reproof"?

Rabbi Levi Yitzhak explained it quite simply:

Moses only said these words when he directed them "to all Israel." But when he spoke to the Holy One, blessed be He, he would never mention, Heaven forbid, the sins of Israel. On the contrary, he would dwell upon their praise, pointing out all their good qualities and indicating what they had achieved in spite of privation and temptation, thus acting as the defender of the people Israel.

TEXT:
"He does not behold iniquity in Jacob,
Neither does He see wickedness in Israel;
[For] The Lord is their God."

[Numbers 23:21]

EXPLANATION:
When the sins of Israel rise to heaven—God forbid—the Holy One, blessed be He, turns away in order not to look upon them . . . nor does He remember them afterward. But the good which Israel does, in that they crown "the Lord" as "their God," that is ever engraved before Him.[4]

Though one may fulfill the Mitzvah of *B'rit Milah* ("circumcision") at any time during the day, it was the custom of Levi Yitzhak to rise at dawn to attend to this commandment even before the morning prayer. Only once did he delay, and then until four o'clock in the afternoon. This is how it happened.

A son was born to Levi Yitzhak's daughter. Many friends and relatives from the city and beyond were invited to the *B'rit Milah* and the feast of celebration which followed. From far and near they came—scholars and unlettered men, rich and poor—to join in this rejoicing of the rabbi's household.

On the eighth day after the birth of the child—the day of the *B'rit Milah*—they awakened while it was still dark because of the holy rabbi's eagerness to fulfill the Mitzvah of bringing a child into the covenant of Abraham at the earliest possible hour. At the break of dawn, the rabbi's House of Study was already full. When the time for the morning prayer arrived and the rabbi remained in his room, the men sat down to wait. An hour passed, another hour, and still another. The older Hasidim rose, wrapped themselves in their *Talleitim*, put on their *Tefillin*, and completed the silent prayer, but the rabbi still did not appear. In astonishment they sat down again and waited. Finally Yosef Bunam, the son-in-law of the rabbi and father of the child, could restrain himself no longer and knocked on Levi Yitzhak's door. No answer, no sound, not even the slightest movement was heard.

Time for the afternoon prayer had arrived and still the holy rabbi did not leave his room. Beginning to grow afraid but without courage to penetrate the inner sanctum, several of the Hasidim at last drew near and looked through the keyhole. They saw the rabbi sitting in a chair, deep in thought, with a strange light playing upon his face. This frightened them so much that they did not return to the door. Not until four o'clock in the afternoon was the sound of steps heard inside the room. Then the door opened, and the rabbi appeared on the threshold. The men rose. The holy rabbi entered, looked about, and asked for the child. He performed the circumcision and made the blessing over the wine, and when he came to the prayer, "Blessed art Thou, O Lord, Who makest the convenant," he dipped his finger in the wine and touched the mouth of the child, saying, "Our God and God of our fathers, establish this child for his father and his mother, and let his name in Israel be called Moshe Yehudah Leib, the son of Yosef Bunam."

When the father of the child heard the name, he was bewildered. He did not know why the rabbi had chosen it. The *Minyan* prayed the afternoon prayer, washed their hands, said the blessing and sat down to the Feast of the Circumcision.

After the meal, the holy rabbi turned to his son-in-law, who sat next to him, and said, "My child, I see that you wish to ask a question."

"Yes, my master and teacher. Two things puzzle me. Why did you delay coming to the *B'rit Milah*? Is it not the custom always to perform a Mitzvah as early as possible, especially the Mitzvah of *Milah*? And why did you call the child—may he live many years—Moshe Yehudah Leib, a name unknown in our family?"

Levi Yitzhak said: "Listen my child and I will explain all to you."

A hush fell upon all those seated around the tables. So heavy was the silence in the House of Study that one could almost feel it. Rabbi Levi Yitzhak began to talk and spoke something like this:

"Today I arose very early to prepare myself to bring my dear grandchild into the covenant of Abraham our Father, may he rest with peace and blessing. At the first break of dawn I opened the window and, behold, I saw a deepening darkness in the heavens above and on the earth beneath. I turned here and there to discover why this was so, and it was made known to me that today a prince of Israel, the holy Tzaddik, Rabbi Moshe Yehudah Leib of Sassov, would die. I wept for that master of Israel who would go to his eternal rest and for us whom he would leave in mourning.

"While I was still sitting in sorrow, I heard a voice cry out: 'Make way for Rabbi Moshe Yehudah Leib, the son of Rabbi Ya'akov!'

"At this proclamation, the holy and pure souls of Heaven went out to honor the Tzaddik of the generation and lead him into their dwelling. As he had entered the upper region, the Tzaddikim and Hasidim formed a great circle around him. Suddenly he heard a voice reaching from one end of the world to the other and, fascinated, he began to follow after it until he had left the holy gathering far behind and reached the very gate of *Gehinnom*.

"He entered the nether region without permission. The guards of *Gehinnom* waited patiently, but he did not leave. They saw him walking back and forth, as if looking for someone, and thought that most likely he had come there by mistake, having lost his way. They went over to him and politely told him he was not in the right location, and requested him to ascend to the place that had been prepared for him in *Gan Eden*. Rabbi Moshe said nothing. The guards repeated their request, but he was silent. He refused to move. They did not know whether to drive him out or permit him to remain. The guards took counsel and decided to ask the Heavenly Court what could be done. But even those recondite creatures were puzzled, for never since the beginning of the world had there been such a case of a Tzaddik descending into the fires of *Gehinnom* of his own desire and wishing to remain there. The members of the court decided to bring this matter before the Throne of Glory. They recited the whole story of how the holy Tzaddik, Rabbi Moshe Yehudah Leib, the son of Rabbi Ya'akov, had died and after having been taken to the Upper Realm, as was fitting for such a saint, he had freely chosen to enter *Gehinnom*—without permission—and now refused to leave.

" 'Let him come himself before the Throne of Glory and explain this strange decision,' was the answer.

"A messenger of the court descended to *Gehinnom* and told Rabbi Moshe that his appearance was requested before the Throne of Glory and that he must obey at once.

" 'All my days in the World of Vanity,' he answered the messenger, 'I have tried to fulfill one Mitzvah with all my heart and all my might, no matter what the sacrifice. Now that I have come to the World of Truth, should I do less? I shall not move from this place until I have done that Mitzvah. If the Heavenly Court wishes to hear my complaint, then I am prepared to tell them, but only here, in this place.'

"The messenger brought his words before the Throne of Glory and it was decided to grant him his request.

"He began, 'Master of the World, You know how great is the Mitzvah of *Pidyon Shevuyim*—redeeming those who have been taken captive. Because of its primacy, You Yourself have fulfilled it, and not by means of an angel or by any messenger. For when the Children of Israel were captive in Egypt and Pharaoh hardened his heart and would not send them out from the house of slavery, You Yourself, in all Your glory, went down to redeem them. And I have sought to hold fast to Your qualities, as our rabbis, of blessed memory, have taught in explaining the verse: "This is my God and I shall glorify Him" [Exodus 15:12]. "How shall man glorify God?" they asked. "By following His ways: As He is merciful, so we should be merciful; as He redeemed captives, so we should do likewise" [Shabbat 133b]. I have labored hard in this Mitzvah all my days. I have never distinguished between the wicked captives and the righteous ones, between those who obeyed the Lord's commandments and those who did not. All of them were equally beloved to me, and whenever I learned where they were and who held them captive, I tried to redeem them, for there was no peace in my heart until I had succeeded in freeing them. Such is our lot in the World of Vanity. But lo! When I entered the World of Truth, here, too, I found many captives. Therefore I wish to fulfill this Mitzvah, which depends upon neither place nor time.'

"'And if You say the Mitzvot are given to us only in the World of Vanity so that we might purify our lives and the lives of those around us, but that in the World of Truth those who are righteous return to the original state of man's perfection and we are therefore no longer required to fulfill the Mitzvot, then by my life I say NO! I will not stir from this place until I shall fulfill this Mitzvah here, for, behold, it is well known to you that never was I like the servants who served their master only to receive a reward. To the contrary, so dear are Your commandments to me that I have done them no matter what the place or time or penalty might be. If it is possible for me to bring these miserable captives out into freedom, good; if not, it were better to remain with them in the fires of *Gehinnom* and suffer with them than to sit with the Tzaddikim and bask in the light of the *Shekhinah*!'

"So there he stood, straight and strong, and pleaded his case, his face shining with a holy light, his words flying before the Throne of Glory. The Holy One, blessed be He, Himself (if one may speak thus) uttered the decision.

"'Great are the Tzaddikim who are ready to hand over their souls for the sake of others, and great is the Mitzvah that encompasses both worlds. And because the merit of this Mitzvah is so great, let there be determined, therefore, how many persons Rabbi Moshe Yehudah Leib has redeemed from captivity during his lifetime, both they and their children who will come after them until the end of time. That number is he permitted to redeem also here.'

"At once the Book of Records was brought, opened, and read. The names of all those who had been redeemed by Rabbi Moshe were counted and their children and their children's children, and the final figure arrived at was sixty thousand. So it was that Rabbi Moshe Yehudah Leib was given permission to select sixty thousand souls among all those in *Gehinnom* to be taken to *Gan Eden*.

"Because the choice was his, the rabbi began to walk through the nether world from fire to fire, looking into the countless pits and caves. There he found desolate creatures who had suffered for hundreds of years and who had long ago lost all hope of redemption. They were not easy to find, because souls like these were scattered throughout all the rooms of *Gehinnom* and had to be ferreted out one by one from their hiding places. Exhausted from his effort, he gathered those whom he had selected and found their number to be sixty thousand. Column after column emerged from *Gehinnom*, marching with him at their head, until they arrived at *Gan Eden*.

"As the Tzaddik Rabbi Moshe Leib led this strange procession, I watched in marvel, unable to stir from my place. Have the sages not said, 'Greater are the Tzaddikim in their death than in their life?' For I had beheld the purity of heart of this Tzaddik from the moment he descended alone into *Gehinnom* until the gates of *Gan Eden* were opened before him and he returned with the sixty thousand he had redeemed. After all of them had entered, the gates were closed and I came back to this world.

"Only then did I recall the *B'rit Milah*. I opened the door of my room and found all of the holy congregation in the House of Study waiting impatiently. I hastened to bring your dear child—may he live for many years and may blessing and peace be upon him—into the covenant of our father Abraham. I called the infant Moshe Yehudah Leib, after the name of that holy and pure one who died today and went to his eternal rest, may his name be for a blessing.

"Happy are the Tzaddikim who bear blessings and work kindness in this world and in the World to Come, who turn Heaven's decree of justice to mercy, and who redeem not only themselves but others, too, not only in their lifetime but even in their death. My their merits be a protecting shield for us and for all Israel. Amen."

Here is a favorite tale told by Levi Yitzhak about the defense of Israel:

Two thieves were brought to justice before the Heavenly Court. Both were special cases. The one called Nahum'l the thief was the younger. All year he hid himself deep in the woods, plying his trade of robbing traveling merchants and stealing from the homes of the wealthy. Only once a year, on the day before Yom Kippur, did he leave his lair for the city where he would do a strange thing. First he would divide all his loot among the poor. Then he would enter the synagogue and remain there till the fast was over, standing the entire time and praying with such fervor and sweetness that the very stones beneath his feet almost melted with joy. After the fast day he would disappear for another year, during which he was again busy earning his "livelihood."

The other thief was Ya'akov Yoel, a Jew with a fine face and a long white beard. He had once been a shopkeeper, but in his old age had turned over his business to his sons so he could remain in the House of Study both day and night. Only once a year did he leave his study and prayers. During the annual season of the fair, when business was brisk and his sons were exceptionally busy with customers, they would ask their father to help them by tending the cash box. I need hardly add that no one could question the honesty of such a Jew, whose beard was so long and white and whose piety so unblemished. And what son would suspect that his own father would steal from him? Nonetheless, it was a shocking fact that from time to time the pious, white-bearded Ya'akov Yoel carefully looked about and then stealthily slipped money from the cash box into his pocket! With this money he would buy the liquor and sweets that he would enjoy with the other Hasidim each day after morning prayers.

"After all," Ya'akov Yoel explained, "it is from my own children that I took what I took, and from my own store. And, furthermore..."

Leaping forward, Satan interrupted him with a poisonous leer. "And what about the red handkerchief?"

At this Ya'akov Yoel was filled with shame and hung his head in silence. It was true. Almost every Rosh Hodesh and every market day after morning prayers he would go among the people in the synagogue with a red handkerchief, asking for a contribution for a "pressing need." All the while Ya'akov Yoel would smile into the corner of his beard thinking that after all, wasn't drinking with the other Hasidim a "pressing need"? And since no one suspected that Ya'akov Yoel, whose beard was so long and white, would misuse these monies, his handkerchief jingled gaily with copper, and sometimes even with a silver coin.

Nahum'l the thief, in his turn, began to speak slowly and simply. "What can I say, O Master of the World? All my deeds are known to You. All year I rob and steal and not one word of holiness comes to my lips. On the day before Yom Kippur I give my money to the poor, and during all of Yom Kippur I give my heart and tongue to the Lord. More than this I cannot say. Do with me as You will."

Satan began the indictment: "These are no simple thieves! Take this Ya'akov Yoel. His pious pretentiousness and all his learning are nothing but crooked paths to people's pockets! Hypocrite! Scoundrel! That's what he is. And Nahum'l—once a year he scrupulously keeps Yom Kippur. Why? For love of God? Not at all. To return to his thieving ways, forgiven for his past year's crimes. Nor is plain robbery enough for these two. Their thievery is a special kind; it hides behind false piety and charity which deceive the innocent."

The Good Angel who acted as the defense counsel listened to all this but did not lose hope. Quite the contrary. He said, "I should like to raise several questions which may reveal facts that have been overlooked. Have we considered what these two Jews did with the stolen money? Did anyone see Ya'akov Yoel eat a sumptuous meal even once? And did he in his old age ever lie down upon a soft bed instead of the hard bench of the House of Study? And the bit of drink that he bought with the few coins that he stole, did he enjoy it alone or in the company of Hasidim, that the hearts of fellow Jews might be warmed to praise the Holy Name? Would not his sons and the men in the House of Study have rejoiced to learn to what holy purpose their few coins were put, had they been told the truth?

"And what did Nahum'l do with his money? Although a young man, he did not spend much money on pleasures for himself. He divided his wealth each day before Yom Kippur among the poor, and all his heart he gave to prayer. If those who were robbed knew what was done with their money, I wonder whether they would complain very loudly.

"See how Nahum'l and Ya'akov Yoel have turned robbery into benevolence, drawing holiness out of evil and light out of darkness. How many Tzaddikim can accomplish this?"

Before passing judgment, the Court, having heard both sides, ordered Nahum'l and Ya'akov Yoel to weigh out their good and bad deeds on the Heavenly balance. And this is where a terrible thing happened.

Nahum'l rose, placed on the black side of the scale, year by year, all the years of his life. He shut his eyes tight for there was no year that was not full of robberies and no robbery that was not as heavy as iron. To offset this were only the days of Yom Kippur. These he began to put on the white side of the scale. Though they were few, their weight was great, for each day was saturated with tears, and each tear weighed more than iron. So he began to breathe easier. But, alas, when Nahum'l had set the last day of Yom Kippur on the scale, he saw that the indicator lacked only a hair's breadth to weigh out on the white side. For a hair's breadth his soul was lost!

Now Ya'akov Yoel rose and put all the red handkerchiefs and fairs on the black side. Each handerchief and each fair was full of coins, with each coin as heavy as iron. But when he began to weigh on the white side all his study and prayer and other good deeds, he was encouraged, especially at the weight of his songs and dances that had inspired each holy day and happy occasion. But, alas, the very same thing that had happened to Nahum'l happened to Ya'akov Yoel—the pointer lacked only a hair's breadth! For a moment Ya'akov Yoel thought he saw the indicator tremble, about to move. Both he and Nahum'l watched it desperately. But in vain!

They looked at each other knowingly. Nahum'l winked at Ya'akov Yoel, who nodded. Slowly they stretched out their hands to lighten the load on the black side of the scale, unaware that no one can steal from the scale of Heaven undetected. No sooner did their hands touch the scale, than an alarm began to ring so loudly that the firmament shook. Confusion reigned. It was Heaven's first robbery!

Like a black raven, Satan swept forward. "Now Your eyes have seen, O Lord, what comes of all this mercy You extend to Your creatures. They dare to rob Heaven itself!"

Nahum'l and Ya'akov Yoel, terrified at the consequences of

their deed, began to weep hopelessly. Tumult surrounded the Court as angels descended to it from *Gan Eden* and from all the other upper regions. Even the Good Angel who was counsel for the defense seemed to despair as he addressed the Heavenly Court.

"All seven heavens are in an uproar. Is there no one to plead for these two Jews? Let Rabbi Levi Yitzhak be brought here, for he alone may be able to defend them."

Now all of this took place on the holy day of Yom Kippur, at that very moment, in fact, when Rabbi Levi Yitzhak was leading his congregation in the *Musaf* prayer in the House of Study of Berditchev. Even before *Musaf* he had been aware of a disturbance in Heaven, for black clouds of judgment had covered the earth. As he prayed the words, "Man, his origin is dust . . ." he was summoned to the Heavenly Court, and when he saw the two hopeless Jews there, he extended his arms and said with a broken heart, "O Holy One! O Merciful One!"

At once a wave of love and compassion quieted the Heavenly assembly; only the weeping of the two lost Jews was heard. The Berditchever raised his head and began to pray in his holy way with song and sweetness.

" 'Man, his origin is dust'—son of man, frail creature who comes from the dust of the earth. 'And he returns to the dust'—his end is to be dust once again. 'By the peril of his life he obtains his bread'— sometimes he must even transgress to feed his body. But 'he is like a fragile potsherd'—when man sins, he is smashed like a broken bowl.

"Merciful One, Holy One. First You hide from us Your Paradise and Your Presence in the next world. Then You set the evil urge in us to inflame our hearts in this world. Is it any wonder then that we are burned by the fire which You Yourself have put in us? Let the heavens tremble, for what are they compared to the tears that flow from broken hearts?"

Again the Rabbi of Berditchev stretched forth his arms and raised his voice to plead with love and a broken heart, "Merciful One! Holy One! Merciful One! Holy One!"

All the gates of mercy now swung open, and Nahum'l and Ya'akov Yoel were elevated upon the mercies of the Lord. The

Rav, knowing that this was a rare moment of divine grace, begged mercy now not only for these two but also for all men.

"How long, O Lord, can we bear our pain? Let an end come! Let the Holy One show mercy and send the Messiah to redeem the world from suffering and sin!"

But Satan cried out, "Is it not enough that the Rav of Berditchev wants to bring thieving scoundrels into Paradise? Must he at the same time seek to hasten the Messiah?"

Before the Rav could open his mouth to reply, the proceedings of the Heavenly Court were interrupted by the noise of a disturbance that rose from the House of Study in Berditchev on earth. There, an aged Jew, weak from fasting on Yom Kippur, had fallen into a faint. In vain they tried to revive him. Immediately Rabbi Levi Yitzhak went over to the old man and embraced and caressed him and whispered in his ear until he regained his strength and opened his eyes.

Meanwhile, the moment of grace had passed.

Who knows, if that incident had not occurred in the House of Study, whether the Rabbi of Berditchev might not have brought the Messiah!

Rabbi Levi Yitzhak often appeared blind to the faults of his people. Once, he was walking down the street on Tishah b'Av, the ninth day of the Hebrew month Av, when the destruction of the Temple and the Exile is commemorated by a twenty-four hour fast. Coming upon a Jew eating and drinking in public, he turned to him and said, "My son, surely you have forgotten that today is Tishah b'Av."

"No, Rabbi," said the other. "I know that today is Tishah b'Av."

"If that is so," continued Levi Yitzhak, "then you must be unaware that on Tishah b'Av it is forbidden to eat and drink."

"No, Rabbi," replied the other sharply. "I know that today is a fast day."

"Then," added Levi Yitzhak, "it must be that you are sick and the fast would endanger your health."

"No, Rabbi," the other smiled. "I am quite healthy, thank you. May there be many in Israel as well as I am."

"Master of the World," cried the Tzaddik, lifting his eyes heavenward, "look down from Heaven and see who is like Your people Israel, a holy nation. A Jew would rather declare himself a sinner than permit a false word to escape his lips!"

Another time, the Rabbi of Berditchev saw the driver of a wagon arrayed for the morning service in *Tallit* and *Tefillin*. He was greasing the wheels of his wagon.

"Lord of the World!" Levi Yitzhak exclaimed with delight. "Behold this man! Behold the devoutness of Your people. Even when they grease the wheels of a wagon, they still are mindful of Your name!"

A disciple of the Rabbi of Berditchev experienced an "ascension of soul." When he awoke, he related this vision.

He said that he had entered into the upper realms and had wandered to and fro until he came upon the great Chamber of Justice. There he beheld a frightful sight: The people of Israel were being brought before the Heavenly Bar of Judgment! Satan and his faithful attendants were busy carrying in heavy cartons filled with Israel's sins, forming a pile that was growing larger every moment. Dismay seized him as he thought of the fate of his people. Then he looked further and, behold, he saw the holy Tzaddik, Rabbi Levi Yitzhak, acting as the Defender of all Israel. But alas, he was not able to stand against the Accuser and his helpers, who pointed with smug satisfaction to the many boxes of transgressions they had already gathered.

The rabbi, continued the storyteller, noticed on his right a door opening into Paradise, the dwelling place of the Patriarchs and the Tzaddikim, and on his left a door opening into *Gehinnom*, the place of burning fire and the furnace of pitch. He knew that this was no time to stand idly by while the Accuser continued to carry in more boxes of transgressions. When no one was looking, he quickly seized the boxes that had been heaped there and one by one cast them into the door which led down to *Gehinnom*, watching them fall into the terrible fire.

When Satan returned with his attendants and saw that all his work had gone up in smoke, he let out a piercing cry and fixed his blazing eyes upon the Rabbi of Berditchev, knowing that only he could have done this deed. Then he seized him by his coat, dragged him to the Heavenly Bar of Judgment, and demanded that the rabbi be punished as a thief, according to the law of the Torah. The Court returned judgment and decreed that the law of the Torah should be fulfilled: Rabbi Levi Yitzhak had stolen and must pay for the loss. If he could not do so, he would be sold into servitude.

So it came about that the Rabbi of Berditchev, unable to pay so large a fine, was to be sold at public auction. A great hue and cry arose in the Upper World; the holy Patriarchs and the Tzaddikim of long ago left their places in Paradise and came before the Heavenly Court to redeem him.

But Satan and his followers, who had long waited for just such an opportunity, were not to be put off so easily. They, too, wanted to buy him and so rid themselves at last of their most formidable opponent. So each time the Patriarchs offered a sum, Satan offered more.

Finally, when all seemed lost, a great roll of thunder pealed forth and the Holy One Himself, in all His glory, stepped forward and said: "The earth is Mine and the fullness thereof. I purchase him for Myself. From now on the Rabbi of Berditchev will be My servant."

Rabbi Levi Yitzhak defended not only his own generation but past generations as well. For example, a *Midrash* relates that at the time of the giving of the Torah, Moses had to awaken the Children of Israel because they had fallen asleep. The Maggid of Koznitz writes that his teacher, the Rabbi of Berditchev, explained this Midrash thus: "Heaven forbid that we suspect the people Israel of indifference, of choosing that holy moment before Sinai to nap. The reverse was the case. With such trepidation did they approach the hour of revelation that they wished first to rest so that, refreshed, they might accept the Torah with a clear mind."

And what of Satan, the foremost of all Israel's accusers? Rabbi Levi Yitzhak explained the passage from the evening prayers, "Remove Satan from before us and behind us," by saying, "At the time when each Jewish family sits around the Purim table partaking of all the good food and drink upon it and begins to jest with one another in a merry mood, then Satan points an accusing finger at them, saying, 'See how frivolously these Jews carry on!'

"But we are able to answer him, 'Consider yesterday, the day *behind us* which was a day of fasting, the Fast of Esther, when all Israel sat in sorrow and poured out their hearts to their Father in Heaven.'

"Likewise, on the day before Yom Kippur at the final meal, Satan comes and complains, 'See, the Final Judgment is soon to come and these Jews can think of nothing but to fill themselves with food and drink.'

"Again we answer him, 'Consider tomorrow, the day *before us*, which will be a day of fasting and tribulation and prayer.'

"Therefore we utter these words of prayer to the Almighty, since there is no cause or case, 'Remove Satan from *before* us and *behind* us!' "

WARSAW

The popular image of Levi Yitzhak which emerges from the many tales of wonder and love that were woven about him is that of a beloved saint. His personality deepens when, as mentioned earlier, we add the dimensions of Talmudic master and profound thinker, which his role as communal Rav and his authorship of the celebrated work *Kedushat Levi* attest to. His full stature, however, emerges when we recognize that he was an advocate of the people Israel not simply in the mystic or personal sense through divine or human dialogue, but in practical deliberations which helped determine the fate of much of Polish Jewry.

In 1791 the Ukraine, in which Berditchev served as an economic center, was still a part of Greater Poland. The partition of Poland was yet to come. A new constitution was being drawn up by the Sem (the Polish Parliament), a portion of which would deal with the conditions of the Jews. A moment of crisis had arrived. It was of the highest importance that the most influential and wisest leaders of Polish Jewry should convene at once and deliberate how they could best protect the religious, social, and economic rights of the Jews which were soon to be formulated. The historian, Israel Halperin, has recently proven that among that memorable gathering of Jewish notables who met in Warsaw in 1791 was Rabbi Levi Yitzhak.[5]

One writer recalled later how the Rabbi of Berditchev had prepared for this meeting.

> *In those days Rabbi Levi Yitzhak, who had formerly been Rav of Zholikhov in Poland, occupied the rabbinical seat in Berditchev. He was pure, righteous, and God-fearing and was widely renowned for his marvelous manner of serving God. ... Now the city of Berditchev was a metropolis in which many Jews resided and many more visited from neighboring communities in order to do business, so that whatever transpired in Berditchev was soon known elsewhere. When it was learned that dark days were destined for the people Israel, the elder, Rabbi Levi Yitzhak, sent out a call to the Tzaddikim of the time to come to Berditchev, that counsel might be taken with them to assure the welfare of the people Israel.*[6]

Another observer, who was in Warsaw at the time and writing in French for the Gentile reader, also noted Rabbi Levi Yitzhak's presence. "Among the Jewish representatives was one of the great rabbis of the Hasidim who had recently left his community [Pinsk] because of dissension and had traveled [to Warsaw] from deep in the Ukraine."[7]

The Hasidim of Warsaw treasured the memory of Rabbi Levi Yitzhak's visit to defend the rights of his people. They held sacred that place in the Bet ha-Midrash in the "Courtyard of the Iron Gate" near Bagno Street where he came to worship during his visit, and, until the time of the Holocaust, one could see displayed there a board from the pulpit before which Levi Yitzhak used to pray. When he departed Warsaw from that visit, they said, he left three blessings behind: the first blessing was that in the adjoining room, where they studied and which had no oven or double windows, the students would never feel the bitter cold; the second blessing was that the young men who studied there would be delivered from the hands of the Goyim (i.e., not be conscripted into the army); the third blessing was that no fire would destroy the courtyard in which the synagogue stood.[8]

IN PRAISE OF ISRAEL

Rabbi Levi Yitzhak delighted in seeing his people fulfilling the Mitzvot. It was then that he loved to speak in praise of Israel.

It was late at night on the eve of the Gentile New Year, and the Hasidim of Rabbi Levi Yitzhak were still sitting and studying in the *Bet ha-Midrash*.

Suddenly the door to the rabbi's private room opened and Levi Yitzhak emerged. *"L'shanah Tovah Tikatevu V'tehatemu,"* he cried. "May you all be inscribed and sealed for a good new year!"

With that he returned to his room and closed the door. The Hasidim were astonished. Surely their rabbi knew that this was not Rosh Hashanah, but the Gentile New Year? Why then should he greet them so?

Later the door opened again and the rabbi repeated the same greeting. A short time afterward it happened for a third time.

Puzzled by the rabbi's behavior, the disciples asked one of the older Hasidim to go to their master's room and inquire into the meaning of his action.

This is what the Hasid reported Rabbi Levi Yitzhak told him:

Last Rosh Hashanah, the Day of Judgment for all Israel, the Jews prayed with fervor in their synagogues. Their prayers and the sound of the *Shofar* ascended to heaven. Moved by the waves of supplication, the Holy One, blessed be He, left His Throne of Justice to ascend the Throne of Mercy. There He wrote a decree which stated that the coming year would be a year of health and happiness for the Jewish people.

When Yom Kippur came and He saw how all Israel fasted and wept and poured out their hearts in prayer, He lifted the pen to sign the good decree for the Jewish people.

At that moment Satan approached to protest.

"Yes, O Lord," he argued, "on Yom Kippur they fast and have remorse, dressed in white as the angels in Heaven. But what of all the rest of the year when they are filled with sin and wickedness?"

The decree was not signed.

When the Jews began to put up their *Sukkot*, Israel's Defending Angel appealed, "O Lord, do You not see these *Sukkot* which even the poorest of Your Jews are building with so much joy, according to Your command? It is for You that they are building them. Sign the decree now."

And so it would have been, had not Satan objected. "Yes, for You, O Lord, they are building *Sukkot*—shaky huts of branches and boards which are here today and gone tomorrow. But for themselves—for their homes, their businesses, their entertainment—they erect strong buildings of brick and stone and glass that last forever!"

Then came Simhat Torah. The Jews embraced the Torah and danced with it in their synagogues in wild abandon. Again the Defending Angel argued that the Holy One, blessed be He, should sign the decree. "See, O God, how Your children are happy with Your Torah!"

Satan, however, intervened. "Yes, for one night they dance merrily with Your Torah, their heads turned and their spirits lifted by a drop of schnapps. But in a more sober mood when their minds are clear, do they fulfill the Mitzvot which are written in the Torah?"

The decree was not signed.

And so it is that the judgment written in Israel's favor on Rosh Hashanah has remained unsigned all these weeks. Until tonight. For when the Gentile New Year began and with it commenced all the drunkenness and the shouting and the brawls that usually occur on that night, the Defending Angel approached God and said, "O Lord, see how they begin their New Year tonight. Listen to the screams of pain and the sounds of dissipation. Look at the debauchery and the corruption—and remember how Your children began the New Year on Rosh Hashanah, with prayer, with repentance, and with holiness."

To this Satan could add not a word.

And so it was that, after some four months of delay, the Holy One, blessed be He, at last signed the good decree for the Jewish people.

"Therefore," concluded Rabbi Levi Yitzhak, "did I greet you tonight with *L'shanah Tovah Tikatevu V'tehatemu!* May you be inscribed and sealed for a good year."

Moses said to the Children of Israel, "What does the Lord your God require of you, but to fear the Lord your God?" (Deuteronomy 10:12).

"And is the fear of Heaven then such a small thing?" asked the rabbis of the Talmud, commenting on this verse. "Yes," they answered themselves, "in regard to Moses, it was a small thing."

Rabbi Levi Yitzhak puzzled over these words of the Talmudic sages. What did they mean by saying that the fear of Heaven which is a nigh impossible rung, was a "small thing" for Moses? And what does all this mean for us today? This was the explanation he gave:

"In regard to Moses, it was a small thing. That is to say, in regard to the generation of Moses. For to the generation of Moses, who witnessed the ten plagues, the splitting of the Sea of Reeds, and all the miracles of the Exodus from Egypt, certainly the fear of Heaven was "a small thing"—a mere trifle, hardly worth mentioning.

"But in these dark generations, when the glory of Your Presence is hidden, is there anything greater, O Master of the World, than a Jew who is a Jew?"

> "And Joseph my son is still alive" [Genesis 45:28]. That is, even in Egypt, a land steeped in filth, did Joseph remain righteous and reject the evil about him. And now, too, dwelling amidst defilement, does Joseph, which is all Israel, live in holiness. . . .

Thus shall I explain, with the help of Heaven, why it is written: "Six hundred thousand of the people in whose midst I am" [Numbers 11:21]. The first and second commandments—*I* am the Lord thy God," and "Thou shalt not have any other Gods *except Me*"—were heard by the people themselves, while the rest of the commandments were told to them by Moses. Therefore the divine "I" was engraved upon and sealed into the midst of every Jew, to the end that they might ever cling to His great name. And this is the meaning of "six hundred thousand of the people in whose midst *I* am." That is, an imprint of the divine "*I*" remains in their midst forever. *I* will go down with you into Egypt and *I* will surely bring you up" [Genesis 46:4].⁹

On the day before Passover, Rabbi Levi Yitzhak, while walking through the marketplace, met several Gentiles who were known to be smuggling goods across the border.

"Do you have any smuggled silk?" he asked them.

"We do," they answered.

"How many yards do you have?" he continued.

"Don't worry, Rabbi," said the smuggler. "We have as much as you need."

He left them and soon met a Jew.

"Do you have any *Hametz* ['leavened bread']?" he asked.

"*Hametz*?" asked the astonished Jew. "Heaven forbid that a Jew should have *Hametz* after the sixth hour on Erev Pesah."

Soon he met a second Jew and again asked, "Do you have any *Hametz*?"

"What did you ask, Rabbi?" answered the distraught man. "*Hametz* at this time? Am I not still a Jew?"

Rabbi Levi Yitzhak lifted his eyes toward Heaven and said, "Master of the World, look down from Heaven and see how Your people Israel tremble at Your word and hasten to fulfill Your commandments. The Russian Czar is a mighty and fearsome ruler who has many generals and guards and prisons to enforce his decrees. And he commands thousands of soldiers to protect the border to see that no merchandise is brought across it unlawfully. Nevertheless, daily they smuggle in all manner of merchandise and fear not to sell it openly in the market. But You, O Lord, Who have no generals or guards or prisons, have simply written in Your Torah, 'There shall no leavened bread be seen with thee.' And on Erev Pesah, long before the evening comes, there is not a trace of *Hametz* to be found among all the people of Israel."

> Other nations are driven by the promise of reward to follow the ways of their faith. Not so Israel ... of whom it is written, "Chosen shall you be from among all the nations." It is for this reason that Israel did not receive the Torah directly after escaping Egypt or after crossing the Sea of Reeds. For had this been so, one might have suspected that they took it only in gratitude for the miracles that befell them. Thus it was that the Holy One, blessed be He, delayed until they had quite forgotten the miracles and had begun to complain. As we learn in the Scriptures: "There was no water for the people to drink, so they quarreled with Moses" [Exodus 17:2]. Only then did they receive the Torah, crying out, "We will observe it and we will hearken to it," proving that they accepted it only out of love.[10]

Then there was the day in the *Bet ha-Midrash* when one of his disciples came to Rabbi Levi Yitzhak with a question.

"The sages in the Talmud have written, 'During his lifetime Rabbi Zera never walked more than four cubits without wearing *Tefillin*.' How are we to understand this message? For we know that on the Sabbath and on festivals we are not permitted to wear *Tefillin*, nor may they be worn even on ordinary days in unclean places. How, then, could they have said that Rabbi Zera never walked more than four cubits without wearing *Tefillin*?"

To this question Rabbi Levi Yitzhak had an answer: "Israel wears *Tefillin*. And in Israel's *Tefillin* are written the words, 'Hear, O Israel, the Lord is our God, the Lord is One.' But the Lord, too, we are told, wears *Tefillin*. And what is written in His *Tefillin*? In the Lord's *Tefillin* there is written, 'Who is like Thy people, Israel?' Thus we see that in the *Tefillin* of the Holy One, blessed be He, there is written praise for Israel, while in the *Tefillin* of Israel there is written praise for the Lord. And it was with this in mind that our sages wrote that Rabbi Zera never walked more than four cubits without wearing *Tefillin*; that is to say, even when he no longer wore his *Tefillin*, he busied himself either with the praise of the Holy One, blessed be He (as is written in the *Tefillin* of the Children of Israel), or with the praise of the people of Israel (as is written in the *Tefillin* of the Lord)."

Levi Yitzhak referred his disciples to this passage from Scripture:

> *He does not behold iniquity in Jacob,*
> *Neither does He see wickedness in Israel;*
> *The Lord his God is with him.*
>
> [Numbers 23:21]

Then he explained it. A man who is loyal to God and to His holy ones does not seek out Israel's sins but, on the contrary, looks for reason to praise the people and each member of the people. If "He does not see iniquity in Jacob," this is a sign that "the Lord his God is with him" and the fear of God is in his heart.

Can praise of Israel lead one to place it higher than Torah? At first the question, "Which is greater, Torah or Israel?" appears absurd. Each is in need of the other, without which it is useless, meaningless. Israel without Torah is merely one nation among many, an inconsequential, Middle-Eastern people who would have disappeared from the face of the earth twenty-five hundred years ago. Why should they have lived on in exile, with no land, no king, no power, at the mercy of every petty tyrant, if not for the eternal task given them in the Torah?

And, conversely, the Torah without Israel is a book without a reader, a call without an ear to listen, a vision without an eye to see. Of what use the glory, the thunder and the pathos, without a human heart to give it life? The Torah, it has been recounted, was offered to many peoples before Israel accepted it, but those others rejected it, fearing both the grandeur and the misery of becoming its agent. Thus, if there had been no Israel, there would have been no Torah, no one to record for eternity the Divine encounter.

Torah and Israel—both are necessary.

And yet there have been thinkers in Israel's history who have given greater weight to the one or to the other. The philosopher Saadiah, for example, proclaimed that "Israel exists only by virtue of the Torah." To him Torah was primary; Israel—its witness, its servant—was secondary.

And among those who claimed the reverse—as you might well have surmised—was the Rabbi of Berditchev:

TEXT:
"As the Lord commanded Moses, so did he number them in the wilderness of Sinai" [Numbers 1:19].

EXPLANATION:
The Lord gave the Torah to Israel. The six hundred thousand Israelites are the six hundred thousand letters of the Torah; that is, the souls of Israel are the body of the Torah, for each one of Israel is a letter of the Torah. Thus, when Moses numbered the people, it was as if he were studying the Torah.[11]

A favorite hymn in the Passover Haggadah is *"Dayyenu."* In it the miraculous events of God's deliverance of Israel from Egypt are recounted. After each event follows the refrain, *Dayyenu*—"It would have been enough."

One passage from that hymn has always been particularly puzzling:

Had God brought us to Mount Sinai
And not given us the Torah,
It would have been enough.

Strange! What good would Israel's reaching Mount Sinai have been, if they had left without the Torah?

But let us recall, observes the Rabbi of Berditchev, that, according to the sages, our father Abraham, who lived long before Moses, was so wise and saintly that he fulfilled all the commandments of the Torah of Moses even before they had been given. What was true at the beginning, for the single man Abraham, was later true of the entire people of Israel when they stood at Mount Sinai. They reached such heights of purity and holiness at that moment that, even if the Torah had not been given to them, they could have grasped by themselves all the mysteries of the revelation![12]

It is well known that there are two Torahs—the Written Torah and the Oral Torah—the Written Torah, which was revealed on Mount Sinai, and the Oral Torah, which is called the people's Torah. (For Rashi explains the verse: "And in His [God's] Torah shall you meditate day and night," to mean that after one meditates in it, it is called "his" [man's] Torah.) And the reason why the Oral Torah is called "the people's Torah" is because it testifies to the power of the Jewish people. That is to say, the great sages of the Talmud and afterward explained and commented upon the Written Torah according to their understanding, *even though, according to Heaven, it may not have been the correct meaning.* This is the intent of the story from the Talmud which records Rabbi Eliezer's dispute with the other sages:

On that day Rabbi Eliezer brought all the proofs in the world [in support of his opinion], but the sages did not accept them.

He said, "If the law agrees with me, let this locust tree prove it!"

The locust tree moved a hundred cubits; others say four hundred cubits.

The sages said to him, "No proof can be brought from the locust tree."

Then he spoke to them again, "If the law agrees with me, let this stream of water prove it."

The stream began to flow backward.

They said to him, "No proof can be brought from a stream."

Then he spoke to them again, "If the law agrees with me, let Heaven itself prove it!"

A voice came forth from Heaven saying, "Why do you

dispute with Rabbi Eliezer? The law agrees with him in every case!"

Thereupon Rabbi Joshua arose and said, "It is not in Heaven" [Deuteronomy 30:12].

What did he mean by "not in Heaven"? Rabbi Jeremiah says, "The Torah was given once and for all from Mount Sinai; we do not listen to voices from Heaven. For it was written in the Torah on Mount Sinai: 'After the majority must one incline' " [Exodus 23:2; Talmud Bava Metzia 59a].

Just as in days of old, so too do the Tzaddikim in our time possess this power: to explain the Torah according to their understanding, even though in Heaven it is not so. They have the power, if one may dare to utter the thought, to bend the will of Heaven to their will![13]

The power of man is great. Even greater the power of the people Israel. Greater still the power of the Tzaddik. According to Rabbi Moshe of Tchortkov, Levi Yitzhak explained the first words of the Ten Commandments which the Creator spoke to Moses at Mount Sinai—"I am the Lord your God" (Exodus 20:2)—in this way:

> *Now the Torah is eternal, and God spoke not only at Sinai but to every generation.*
>
> *In our generation the Holy One, blessed be He, says to the Tzaddik, who now stands in the place of Moses: "I, the Lord, am your God! You may"—dare one utter the words?—"do with Me as you wish!" For what the Lord decrees the Tzaddik may annul; but what the Tzaddik decrees, the Lord will confirm.*
>
> *And the words of the wise are filled with grace!*[14]

IN PROTEST AGAINST GOD

A strange episode is related in the Bible. It is about Abraham, the chief of the Patriarchs, whom we speak of as "our father" and whom Scripture calls the "man of faith"; who, tradition tells us, smashed the idols of his family and was the first to know the One

God. This same Abraham stood before the Lord on hearing of the impending destruction of the city of Sodom and pleaded—no, demanded—"Shall not the Judge of all the earth do justly?" (Genesis 18:25).

These are bold words, words that have over the centuries acquired a history of their own through comment and super-comment. Job spoke such words. The rabbis of the Talmud and later spoke similar words. Contemporary writers frequently use them. While for some it may be only a literary foil, for others it describes the narrow ridge between faith and despair upon which they stood in fear and trembling. But for Abraham and for Levi Yitzhak, the matter was something different: not the questioning of faith but the rebellion that arises out of the profoundest confirmation of that faith.

In all Jewish history there is no figure better known for his complaints against God because of the sufferings of the Children of Israel than Rabbi Levi Yitzhak of Berditchev. The problem of evil—that is, the suffering of the innocent and the flourishing of the wicked—has troubled every thinking man. Philosophers pose the apparent contradiction between divine perfection and human misery: If God is all good, where does evil come from? If God is all powerful and just, why does He permit the innocent to suffer and the wicked to dwell at ease? After inquiry exhausts the mind, there comes a point when reason halts before the enigma—and then the soul cries out.

It was such an outcry of the soul that the Rabbi of Berditchev uttered. With a zeal born of unutterable love for a people chosen, yet despised and profaned, he came before the Lord with a wail of woe. Often while he was leading the congregation in prayer before the Holy Ark—especially during the Days of Awe—Levi Yitzhak would pause, leave the written text, and express in the simple language of the people the feelings that overflowed his heart. He would speak to God as an aggrieved son would talk to his father, often by way of commenting on a passage in the prayer book, in words that were meant only for the privacy of Heaven at that very moment, but which impressed themselves indelibly upon the hearts of those who heard them in such fear and wonder that they were destined to become the priceless treasure of his people for all generations. These words were not written down in a book. They were not uttered in discussion with his disciples about the justice of God—though such complaints were expressed then, too. But—and this is the unique element—these words were spoken to God in the very midst of congregational prayer. They happened!

Upon reading the examples which follow you may ask yourself: Are they true? Did Rabbi Levi Yitzhak really stand in the congregation before the Holy Ark and speak the words that generations of Hasidim have ascribed to Him? It is doubtful that he is responsible for all of them, certainly in the precise form that have come down to us. In all probability, Hasidic legend added to and embellished them as it did much of the other material in this book. But there can be no question that many of these episodes are genuine. Little wonder that Jews traveled hundreds of miles to pray with the Tzaddik of Berditchev, then told what they had seen and heard to all who would listen. These tales became the cherished record of the outpouring of one whose love for God and for God's people was so strong, that he did not fear to call the Master Himself to account for the misery of the children. Rabbi Barukh, the grandson of the Baal Shem, said, "According to Rabbi Levi Yitzhak of Berditchev, the Holy One, blessed be He, has not done justice to even one Jew."

"God of Abraham, Isaac and Jacob," said the Rabbi of Berditchev, interrupting his prayers, "You ask us—and rightly so—to follow after Your ways. And indeed, we try to do so. Why then do You not, at times, follow after our ways? Why, for example, do you not treat us in at least the same manner that any simple Jew would? If a simple Jew were to drop his *Tefillin* or notice that they had fallen to the ground, he would at once lift them up, wipe them clean, and kiss them. For the *Tefillin* are 'the glory of Israel,' and in them are written the words: 'Hear, O Israel, the Lord is our God, the Lord is One.'

"Your people, Israel, are the *Tefillin* of Your head, for the *Tefillin* glorify their wearer, and it is though Israel that You are glorified. For what verse is enclosed in Your *Tefillin*? It is a verse of David's, of Your anointed: 'Who is like Your people, Israel, a unique nation on earth!'

"Lord, Your *Tefillin* have fallen to the ground and have lain in the dust of exile and suffering lo! these two thousand years. Why do You not raise them up once again?"

Then he added: "If You will forsake Your way and adopt our way and forgive our sins and redeem us, all will be well. If not, I shall be compelled to reveal publicly that Your *Tefillin* are false."

Another time Levi Yitzhak exclaimed:

"Master of the World, the sages and prophets of old speak of the covenant at Mount Sinai as a marriage between God and Israel. But what kind of marriage is it? Israel brought great *Yihus* ['nobility'] to the marriage, for are we not the children of the Patriarchs, Abraham, Isaac and Jacob? But what *Yihus* did You bring, Lord? Who were Your ancestors? You brought wealth to the marriage—that was Your part of the bargain, as it is written of You, 'Mine is the silver and Mine is the gold.' Therefore, Master of the World, open up Your vast treasure house for us, ease our dreadful needs, and act like the One to Whom all the world belongs!"

"Lord of the Universe," prayed Levi Yitzhak before the sounding of the *Shofar* on Rosh Hashanah, "You have commanded us, 'A day of sounding the *Shofar* shall there be for you.' And because of this commandment in Your Torah, we, Your children, sound a hundred *Shofar* blasts each Rosh Hashanah, and thousands upon thousands of Jews have sounded these hundred blasts for many centuries.

"Now these thousands upon thousands of Jews, Your loyal children, cry out and pray and beseech You, and have beseeched You for these many centuries, to sound but *one* blast for our freedom on the Great *Shofar*.

"Still You have not blown it!"

When all seemed dark and hopeless, the Rabbi of Berditchev pleaded:

"Master of the World, what claim do You have against Your people? By my life, had I not seen with my own eyes the way in which the Children of Israel hasten to perform Mitzvot—giving charity, keeping the Sabbath, and studying Torah—I would not have believed it was in the power of flesh and blood to do such things while confined to this bitter exile!"

Once, in the *Musaf* service of Rosh Hashanah, when he reached the words "And Your throne will be established in mercy and You shall sit upon it in truth," Levi Yitzhak stopped praying to explain the meaning of these words to the Almighty.

"O Lord, if You want the throne of Your glory to be established so that You may sit upon it in that glory which alone is fitting for the King of kings, then deal mercifully with Your children and issue decrees for their salvation and consolation. But if You deal with us harshly and issue harsh decrees, Heaven forbid, then Your throne will not be established and You will not sit upon it in truth. For the Tzaddikim of the generation will not permit You to sit upon Your throne. You may decree, but they will annul. Therefore I entreat You, O Eternal King: If 'Your throne be established in mercy,' then 'You will sit upon it in truth.' "

"Master of the World, David Your servant said, 'They stand this day for Thy judgments, for all things are Thy servants' [Psalms 119:91], and I, Levi Yitzhak, will explain these words:

" 'They stand this day for Thy judgment,' that is, the Children of Israel, the people You have chosen, the people who fulfill Your law, they stand this day—if one may utter it—to judge You!

" 'For all things are Thy servants,' that is, they judge You for everything we bear—wicked and cruel decrees, pogroms and persecutions, poverty and sorrow—all these things are come upon us only because 'we are Thy servants.' Just as King David said elsewhere: 'For Thy sake are we slain all the day long, and are we taken as sheep for the slaughter' [Psalms 44:23]. O Master of the World, since it is 'for Thy sake' that we die before our time, the judgment is that You must redeem us, and without delay."

Whenever Rabbi Levi Yitzhak would come to the verse in the Book of Exodus, "Thou shalt not afflict the orphan" [22:21], he would cry out: "Master of the World, warning after warning and prohibition after prohibition have You given in Your holy Torah that one should not afflict an orphan. And we have hearkened to Your word all these years, caring for the fatherless with tender mercy and at great sacrifice. But, Lord, are not we too orphans? Is not Israel an orphan today? Is it not written in Scripture, 'We are become orphans with no father' [Lamentations 5:3]? Where, then, is Your mercy? Why do You permit us to remain in the misery of exile after all these years?"

It was during one Yom Kippur service, when the people had confessed their sins and were asking for forgiveness, that suddenly everyone grew silent as they noticed their rabbi turn from the prayer book before him and say: "Eternal Lord, there was a time when You went around with that Torah of Yours and were willing to sell it at a bargain, like apples that have gone bad. Yet no one would buy it from You; no one would even look at You! And then we took it! Because of this I want to offer You a proposition. We have many sins and misdeeds, and You an abundance of forgiveness and atonement. Let us exchange! But perhaps You will say: 'Oh, like for like!' My answer is, 'Had we no sins, what would You do with Your forgiveness?' So You must balance the proposition by giving us life, and children, and food besides!"

On another Yom Kippur he spoke in a more demanding tone, quoting chapter and verse: "Master of the World, I have several complaints—four in number—to register against the legal decisions of Your Court, for I am a Rav in Israel and am acquainted with Your laws.

"First, it is written in the Talmud, tractate Ketuvot, 'You may acquit the accused in his absence, but you may not convict him in his absence.' How then is the Heavenly Court able to find us guilty when we do not appear before them?

"Second, our sages have written in *Pirke Avot*: 'Do not judge your fellowman until you have been in his place.' How then can those who abide in Heaven judge those who abide on earth, since they have never experienced earthly life?

"Third, our sages decreed in the Talmud, tractate Sanhedrin, that 'no man may be appointed as a member of the *Sanhedrin* ["religious court"] who is childless, for children teach a father to have compassion.' How then can angels, who have no children, qualify as judge?

"Fourth, there is a principle in our laws of jurisprudence that 'the accuser must come to the accused.' Since they above are the accusers and we below are the accused, let the Heavenly Judges come down to us and render judgment in our courts of justice according to the law!"

One Yom Kippur evening Rabbi Levi Yitzhak stood before the Ark to chant the *Kol Nidre*. For almost an hour he stood there silent.

The congregation waited in fear and trembling before the holiness of the day. The sun had already sunk among the trees. The time for *Kol Nidre* was almost past; and still he stood there and did not chant the prayer.

Then he stirred himself, turned to the people, and asked the *Shammash*, "Is Berel the tailor here?"

"No, master," replied the *Shammash*.

"Go out," commanded Levi Yitzhak, "and find him."

The *Shammash* went out, found Berel the tailor, and brought him to the synagogue.

"Berel," asked Rabbi Levi Yitzhak, "why do you delay the prayers of Israel?"

"What should I do, my lord," answered Berel. "There is no one before whom I can summon Him to judgment. Would our rabbi act as judge in this case?"

"Commence," said Rabbi Levi Yitzhak, "and state your claim."

So Berel began to plead.

"The week before *Selihot* the count called me to his estate to make a new fur coat for the winter season, which was not too far off. I took my tools and some bread in a basket (for I would not eat the bread made by Gentiles) and went to the manor of the *poritz*. He gave me a number of beautiful skins, soft and rich, out of which I should make the coat.

"I thought to myself, I am a poor man. All my earnings have gone to raise my sons. Now my daughter is reaching the age of marriage and I have not known where I would find the means to provide her with a dowry and wedding. Here is a way to fulfill my duty to my daughter. I shall leave out ten pelts, that they may serve as part of a dowry for my daughter. No one will be the wiser, and the count has caused us enough misery so that I have no qualms about his contributing unwittingly to this good deed.

"And so I did just as I planned. I sewed the coat for the count with all the skill for which I am known, and still had left over ten pelts for myself. But how would I find a way to take the furs out of the house of the count? Then a thought occurred to me. When the time for my departure came, I took my loaf of bread, removed the insides, stuffed the pelts within the crust, put the bread in my sack, which I threw over my back, and was on my way.

"I had not gone two miles when I heard behind me a rider on horseback chasing after me. Woe and alas! A terrible fear seized me, for I was certain that the theft had been discovered and I was to be apprehended and sent to prison for at least ten years.

"Quickly I hid my sack under a tree, sat down on the grass, and waited for the rider, my heart throbbing as if to burst all the while.

" 'Berkah [Berel], return to the manor,' commanded the rider. 'The count wants you.'

"I returned to the count, and believe me, when I entered the room where he sat, the fear of death was upon me. Who knows, I thought, what my punishment will be?

" 'Berkah,' the count said to me, 'look at this. Is this what you call finishing your work? You forgot to sew a strap on the inside fur by which to hang up my coat.'

"I heaved a sigh of relief and gave thanks to the Almighty. I sewed on the strap and went briskly on my way once again, hastening to the tree where I had hidden the sack that contained the key to my daughter's happiness.

"But when I came to the tree—lo and behold! My sack was nowhere to be found! No sack, no bread, no pelts. I searched until my arms and legs ached, but I found nothing. Then I sat down and began to turn the matter over in my mind, considering it from every angle. At last the truth dawned upon me. This was no other than His work"—here he pointed up toward Heaven—"He does not want a Jew, one of His chosen flock, to steal pelts, even to provide a daughter's dowry and marriage, even from an evil Polish count who has hounded and robbed us all these years and would never even miss the loss.

" 'If that's the way it is,' I said to myself, 'I am quits with Him. I don't want to be one of His "Chosen People" any longer!'

"I made my way home, entered the house, and found the evening meal on the table.

"My wife greeted me, 'Berel, wash your hands and come to the table.'

"Angrily, I refused to wash my hands. I sat down, took a piece of bread, and did not say the blessing. I ate well, and did not say grace. Afterward I did not pray the evening service. I went to bed, and did not say the *Shema*. The next morning I continued my rebellion. No prayers, no blessings. So the days passed.

"When the time for *Selihot* came, I did not heed the call of the *Shammash* in the early dawn to go to the synagogue, nor did I go to the synagogue on Rosh Hashanah—not even to hear the *Shofar*. I could not forgive Him for what He had done to me.

"But when at last the holy day arrived, the Day of Atonement, I began to think: Perhaps today I should forgive Him, for does He not forgive us too on Yom Kippur? But only on one condition: that He forgive everything, even the sins of mine which Yom Kippur does not atone for, for it is written that Yom Kippur atones for the sins man commits against God, but not those he commits against his fellowman. If He will forgive everything, then I am willing to forgive Him too. But if not, I too shall not forgive.

"Tell me, rabbi, which of us is right?"

"You are, Berel, you are," answered Levi Yitzhak with great joy. "You are right, and the judgment is hereby rendered in your favor. Let Him forgive everything."

With that, Rabbi Levi Yitzhak began the *Kol Nidre*.

The document which testifies best to Levi Yitzhak's love of Israel is not a story or a saying but a song, an event that became a poem.

While leading the congregation in prayer one Rosh Hashanah, the Rabbi of Berditchev, grieving over Israel who, despite its sufferings, persisted in sanctifying God's Name, broke from the fixed words of the Hebrew liturgy to cry out in the folk tongue that not only the people, but the Lord as well, understood.

THE KADDISH OF RABBI LEVI YITZHAK

Good morning to You, Lord, Master of the Universe.
I, Levi Yitzhak, son of Sarah of Berditchev,
I come to You with a Din Torah from Your people Israel.

What do You want of Your people Israel?
What have You demanded of Your people Israel?
For everywhere I look it says, "Say to the Children of
   Israel,"
And every other verse says, "Speak to the Children of Israel,"
And over and over, "Command the Children of Israel."

Father, sweet Father in Heaven,
How many nations are there in the world?
   Persians, Babylonians, Edomites.

The Russians, what do they say?
   That their Czar is the only ruler.
The Prussians, what do they say?
   That their Kaiser is supreme.
And the English, what do they say?
   That George the Third is the sovereign.

And I, Levi Yitzhak, son of Sarah of Berditchev, say,
"Yisgadal v'yiskadash shmei raboh—
Magnified and sanctified is Thy Name."

And I, Levi Yitzhak, son of Sarah of Berditchev, say,
"From my stand I will not waver,
And from my place I shall not move
Until there be an end to all this.
Yisgadal v'yiskadash shmei raboh—
Magnified and sanctified is only Thy Name."

Gut morg'n Dir, Ribbono shel olom!
Ich, Levi Yitzhok ben Soroh mi-Berditchev,
Bin tzu Dir gekoomen mit a Din Torah
Far Dein folk Yisroel.

Un vos host Tu tzu Dein folk Yisroel?
Un vos host Tu Zich ongezetzt
Oif Dein folk Yisroel?
Az vos nor a zach iz, "Tzav es bnei Yisroel,"
Un vos nor a zach iz, "Emor livnei Yisroel!"
Un vos nor a zach iz, "Dabeir livnei Yisroel!"

Tatenyu! Kamo umos ba'olom?
  Bavloyim, Parsoyim, Edomin!
Die Deitschlender vos zogn zei?
  "Unzer Koenig iz a Koenig!"
Die Englender vos zogn zei?
  "Unzer Malchus iz a Malchus!"

Un ich, Levi Yitzhok ben Soroh mi-Berditchev, zog:
"Yisgadal v'yiskadash shmei raboh!"

Un ich, Levi Yitzhok ben Soroh mi-Berditchev, zog:
"Lo ozuz mimkomee; ich vel zich fun ort nit riren!
Un a sof zol dos zein, un an ek zol dos nemen!
Yisgadal v'yiskadash shmei raboh!"

The soaring strains of this song of divine dissent sounded far beyond the narrow confines of Berditchev, echoing in the hearts of Jews scattered throughout poverty-stricken, persecution-ridden communities in Eastern Europe and, in time, even in far-off America and Israel. It gave voice at one and the same time to the misery and the grandeur, the tragedy and glory, which inhabited the soul of this people. It was as if the song took on a life of its own, moving from its point of origin in time and space as a millennial outcry from the pit of anguish—irrevocable, unfaltering, eternal. Incredible was the song the Jews continued to sing: Despite all the claims of kings of flesh and blood, there is but one King and one Kingdom—the doxology of Israel.

Nor was the mysterious power of this song understood only by the Jews. There were countless others who were drawn to it because they heard in it the deathless hope of the human soul. Paul Robeson, for example, the noted Negro singer, sang it following World War II at the great rallies for European Jewry and for the State of Israel during the early years of the young state's struggle for independence and subsistence.

He sang it in 1958 in Moscow at a special concert. The hall was filled to overflowing with military and government officials, persons of influence and culture. Among those present were also a large number of Jews. It was well known that Robeson's repertoire contained many Negro folk songs, African freedom songs, and several Jewish songs. Robeson's procedure was to explain the meaning of each song before he sang it. Conscious of the suffering of the Russian Jews, he had decided to sing the Berditchever's *Kaddish* and listed it on his program. Suddenly he received a note from a member of the sponsoring committee, which read: "No one in the audience understands Yiddish. It would, therefore, be out of place to sing any Jewish songs this evening."

Robeson was perplexed. Yiddish had been listed in the last Russian census as the mother tongue of thirty-five percent of the Jews, who were well represented in the audience. Granting the assumed ignorance of Yiddish, would the African songs that he would sing in the languages of Ghana and the Congo be better understood?

He began his program in his usual manner, explaining each song before it was sung. First he introduced a series of songs from the Congo and Ghana, indicating their anti-colonial character, which reflected the new spirit of the rising nationalism there.

Then he boldly announced, "And now I shall sing an anti-imperialist song for you which you may not have heard in some time. It was written more than one hundred and fifty years ago by a Russian as a protest against the Czar. The name of the author is Levi Yitzhak, and he lived in the city of Berditchev."

So it was that he began to sing Rabbi Levi Yitzhak's *Kaddish*. When he came to the words:

> What do You want of Your people Israel?
> What have You demanded of Your people Israel?
> For everywhere I look it says, "Say to the Children of Israel,"
> And every other verse says, "Speak to the Children of Israel,"
> And over and over, "Command the Children of Israel."
>
> Father, sweet Father in Heaven,
> How many nations are there in the world?

a tremor passed through the auditorium, scattered sighs and muffled sobs were heard. And when he began to thunder:

> And I, Levi Yitzhak, son of Sarah of Berditchev, say,
> "From my stand I will not waver,
> And from my place I shall not move
> Until there be an end to all this...."

weeping could be heard from parts of the auditorium. Tears flowed freely from dozens of faces. The applause, sporadic at first, reached a crescendo which threatened to shake the walls. The song became a rallying cry among the frightened Jews of Moscow for weeks to come.

Do you wonder how a single song can possess such power? Then read the words again. Read them in Yiddish if you can, or in

English if you must. But read them with your heart as well as your mind.

The voice of Rabbi Levi Yitzhak still speaks.[15]

"The very utterance of the name 'Rabbi Levi Yitzhak of Berditchev,'" said the Rabbi of Rizhin, "lessens the harsh powers of judgment on high and brings a sigh of joy to those who dwell here below."

Then his son, Rabbi Avraham Ya'akov, added, "Even if one does not mention the holy Rabbi Levi Yitzhak by name, but only utters the name of the city, 'Berditchev,' it is sufficient. . . . "

In later years, when the rabbis recounted these tales of love, they spoke with wonder of the time during which Levi Yitzhak lived, and lamented the narrowing of spirit that had been brought about subsequently.

"My grandfather, Rabbi Menahem Mendel of Kotzk," said Rabbi Shmuel of Sokotchov to his Hasidim, "was once asked a question by one of his disciples.

" 'Why is it, O our teacher, that the great love which used to exist between the Hasidim of the first generation has so diminished in our generation?'

" 'In Heaven,' Rabbi Menahem Mendel replied, 'there is a palace whose name is love. It was Rabbi Levi Yitzhak of Berditchev who opened the door to that palace and brought forth from it boundless love for one's fellowman. But the evil ones of that generation used this great power for hateful purposes. Therefore, the Tzaddikim sealed up the door to the palace once again, and thus, because of our many sins, love has ceased.' "

3

Prayer

> Pray not to gain a reward
> Neither in this world nor in the world to come;
> Pray only out of love for the Almighty. [1]

SOME MEN live by the plenitude of their power; others by the nimbleness of their wits. But there are those rare souls who find the meaning of their lives in that which dwells beyond both matter and mind, in the recondite realms of the spirit. They pierce the veils which confound our world, perceiving the truth which lies at the heart of the human undertaking—that the life of man is part of the life of God, that we live not only in the dimensions of physical reality which science describes and philosophy charts, but in another dimension, a holy dimension, which can be neither weighed nor measured.

The Rabbi of Berditchev was one of those souls. He was a man of prayer who taught his generation as much by worship as by words. The psalmists, seers, and saints of old lived again in him. The spark of the divine within him communed with the divine beyond. And the fire of the spirit which was kindled in his soul was to shed new light on the destiny of all Israel.

> There is the ordinary Tzaddik who, when he prays before the Lord, finds it necessary to bind himself to the letters of the prayers, that the holy letters may lead him on.
>
> But there is also the grand Tzaddik who dwells upon a higher rung; he is able to lead the letters on.... [2]

HIS WAY OF WORSHIP

Prayer is a venture of the soul upon uncharted seas. To embark on such a voyage one needs to prepare.

> "And I entreated the Lord in that time, saying" [Deuteronomy 3:23]. In this verse, the word "saying" appears superfluous. But the explanation is thus: first he "entreated" the Lord, in order that, afterward, he should be able to pray. For "saying" means what he wanted to say but was first unable to say, because he felt unworthy before the Lord. Thus it was necessary for him to pray in order that he should be able to pray. [3]

"How is it possible for a Jew to simply enter a synagogue, open the prayer book and pray, without a moment of forethought?" asked Rabbi Aaron of Zhitomir.

> *For all things require preparation. And surely if we are to appear before a king, we must consider beforehand what we*

would say, how we would say it and by what means. Indeed one needs more time to prepare for prayer than to recite the prayers themselves. But how many of us can achieve this? Therefore, we are counseled to rely upon the Tzaddikim of the generation who pass half the night making themselves ready for prayer, as for example, our master, the holy Rav [Levi Yitzhak], may his merit be a shield for us, so that when we come to the synagogue all preparations are already made for us; we open the prayer book and begin at once to pray.[4]

Such lengthy preparations often caused Levi Yitzhak to begin his prayers later than the prescribed time, so that he would conclude after the others. One reason given in his name is that, "like the camp of Dan 'which was the rearward of all the camps' [Numbers 10:25], so the Tzaddik waits until all Israel has completed their prayers that he might raise them to Heaven." [5]

It is reported that when Levi Yitzhak was about to pour forth his prayer before the Lord, he would tremble violently and his heart would nearly melt within him for love and awe of the glory of the Lord. If he was praying in one corner of the room at the beginning of the service, he might very well be in another an hour later because of his violent and wonderful movements.

"When Rabbi Levi Yitzhak led the service and uttered the call to prayer, 'Borkhu' "—his disciple Shmuel Kaminker reported—"he stood on the same rung of fervor as did the Maharsha when he composed one of his celebrated responsa.[6]

It was his habit to put on two sets of *Tefillin*. And the sound of his voice, it was said, could be heard at a distance. During his worship—particularly when he recited the words of the *Kaddish*—"*Yisgadal v'yiskadash shmei raboh*"—his soul was kindled and burned with ecstasy as a quivering flame. During those moments when he cleaved to the Source of all life, it seemed to some as if he had departed this world. [7]

Once Rabbi Barukh of Mezibosh observed him in the trembling fervor of his prayer, and when he had finished, remarked to him,

"Levi Yitzhak, my friend, if Aaron the priest had performed his service in your manner when he kindled the lights of the *Menorah*, surely he would have poured the oil in the wrong place and broken the *Menorah* itself!"

Another time Rabbi Levi Yitzhak was passing through the city of Zholkeva, which was the home of the Tzaddik Rabbi Abraham Avush. Levi Yitzhak stood at the side of his host during the morning worship. And in the midst of his prayer he was seized with ecstasy, as often happened to him.

When Rabbi Abraham Avush had finished his prayer, he said to his neighbor, "If I would measure myself by the prayer of this one, then I must admit that I have never really prayed from childhood until this day."

Others said that when they were in his *Bet ha-Midrash* while Levi Yitzhak prayed, the hair on their necks stood on end, and they were seized with a holy awe. Even evil men were moved. Their hearts would melt within them when they heard the words and song of his prayer, which burned with holiness and purity. Such men would often leave their evil ways and turn to the Lord. Indeed, Rabbi Avraham Ya'akov of Sadigorah said that, "the great fervor with which the Rabbi of Berditchev prayed exhausted his body as well as his soul. However, it was he who chose this way of service not alone for his own sake but likewise in order to draw the hearts of men near to the Holy One, blessed be He."

> It is right that a man should be modest in his service of God, as it is written in the morning prayers, "Let a man fear the Lord in private...." But in order to lift up the holy sparks that are hidden in others, it may be necessary to reveal his own fear of God, for by this means he may turn them also to the fear of the Lord. And this was the purpose of Israel's wandering through the wilderness. [8]

The owner of a tavern in Berditchev was not in favor of the Hasidic way of life, but liked to listen when Hasidim told each other of the deeds of their leaders. On one such occasion he heard them speak of the wondrous prayers of Rabbi Levi Yitzhak. They said that when he came to the portion of the service called *Keter*, where the words, "Holy, holy, holy," are said, and in the chanting of which those who dwell in Heaven unite with men, the angels themselves would come to listen to him.

"Do you really think that this is so?" asked the innkeeper.

"Yes, it is so."

"And where do the angels go after that?" he inquired mockingly. "Do they remain floating in the air?"

"No," the Hasidim answered him. "They fly down and stand around the rabbi."

"Well, I shall see this matter for myself. He won't get me to budge from the spot!"

"We shall show you."

The opportunity came on Rosh Hodesh, when Rabbi Levi Yitzhak was leading the prayers in his *Bet ha-Midrash*. When he reached the *Keter* prayer in the *Musaf* service and was removing his *Tefillin*, ecstasy began to seize him. So consumed with the fire of holiness was he that he could not properly guide his hands, and mistakenly put his *Tefillin* into the *Tefillin* bag of another. Soon the entire congregation was kindled with the flame of his fervor and his holy way.

Immediately they called for the Mitnaged innkeeper.

The Mitnaged came, and saw with his own eyes and heard with his own ears; and his heart began to tremble and understand. As the service continued, the fire of Rabbi Levi Yitzhak's fervor mounted higher and higher, until at last it began to reach the Mitnaged himself.

Gathering all his strength, he fled from the house of worship. But from that time forth he, too, began to believe in the Tzaddikim. [9]

When the boy Kalman was five years old, he hid under the *Tallit* of the Rabbi of Berditchev, as children liked to do, and looked up into his veiled face. A burning strength entered his heart, suffused it, and took possession of him.

After many years, Rabbi Elimelekh took some of his noblest disciples to the Rabbi of Berditchev. Among them was young Kalman. Levi Yitzhak recognized him. "That one is mine!" he said.

In later years, Rabbi Kalman used to say that because he once hid under the *Tallit* of Rabbi Levi Yitzhak, a pure fire of holiness entered his heart and continued to burn all the days of his life.

"When I was a child," Rabbi Kalman wrote in his book *Ma'or V'shemesh*, "I happened to be in the *Bet ha-Midrash* with Rabbi Levi Yitzhak of Berditchev—may the memory of that righteous one be for a blessing—when he was standing in prayer. Suddenly a group of soldiers entered the room, for war was raging at the time. Everyone fled, but I hid under a bench. Only the Rav from Berditchev, lost in worship, remained. He did not stir from his place. The soldiers called to him but he did not answer. They even struck him several hard blows. When they observed that still he did not move and that he acted as if he felt no pain, they shouted, 'This fellow isn't human!' and left.

"After he had concluded his prayers, Levi Yitzhak went home. His household noticed a bruise on him, removed his clothes, and found his body covered with blood."

Rabbi Barukh of Mezibosh, the grandson of the Baal Shem, was the only one of the Tzaddikim of his generation who would, at times, speak slightingly of the Rabbi of Berditchev. Once when Rabbi Moshe Zhverel, the son of Rabbi Mikhal of Zlotchov, was spending the Sabbath with Rabbi Barukh, one of the latter's Hasidim began to describe the strange motions and movements which the Rabbi of Berditchev was known to make during his prayers. Rabbi Barukh laughed and made fun of this. Angered at such frivolity, Rabbi Moshe decided to return home immediately after the Sabbath. When later he came to receive the blessing of departure from his master, he was asked why he was leaving so soon. Unable to restrain himself, Rabbi Moshe confessed with a pained heart that he could not remain and listen to the holy service of the Rabbi of Berditchev being taken so lightly.

"Let me explain the matter to you," said Rabbi Barukh. "You know that for these many years the angels on high have looked with jealousy upon the holy manner in which the Rabbi of Berditchev serves the Lord, for it is like a constant devouring flame. Indeed, Satan himself has claimed that, because of the prayers of Rabbi Levi Yitzhak, there is no longer any need for the Temple service of the High Priest or even the coming of the Messiah. In order to silence these complaints and dispel this heavenly jealousy, from time to time I laugh, belittle the ways of Rabbi Levi Yitzhak, and appear to slight him.

"But in truth I know and recognize his great holiness."[10]

Rabbi Levi Yitzhak was a master of prayer. Prayer was a discipline by which he ordered his hours, a mystery to which he surrendered his soul, and a meaning with which he struggled all his life to comprehend. Some of the noblest passages in his writings deal with prayer.

He taught, for example, that melancholy contracts the spirit, weakens the soul, and dims the divine light that burns within; it is the fruit of selfishness and denotes an absence of gratitude to God for the marvels of the simplest facts of life and for the wonder of life itself. Melancholy is tantamount to denial of the goodness of God and stands as a wall between Heaven and earth, defeating the purposes of prayer. The opposite of melancholy is joy. God must be served with joy, Rabbi Levi Yitzhak said, and this was a characteristic of his own service. Indeed, his grandson, the Rabbi of Neshkhiz, remarked that it was in part due to the quality of joy in which Levi Yitzhak immersed himself that the great power of his prayers was manifest.

> In truth the Holy One, blessed be He, desires to pour out His love upon the Children of Israel at every moment and at every hour, but the Evil One prevents this. When Israel is aroused in joy, however, then the power of this joy dispels the power of the Evil One, and a mighty flood of divine love flows forth unimpeded.[11]

Elsewhere, Levi Yitzhak tells us that prayer can serve as man's loadstone, his marker, the standard by which all his thoughts are judged. For prayer is the bond of holiness that joins God and man; it touches and illumines the divine within man.

> There is a way a man may determine whether the thought he thinks is pure: If when he prays to God, the thought does not obstruct or distract his prayer but, on the contrary, strengthens it, then the thought is pure. But should it in any way disturb or weaken his prayer, then he is obliged to cleanse his mind, as one would refine a precious metal by removing the dross—even though, at first, he believed this to be a holy thought.[12]

In this way the soul can guide the mind.

> How is it possible that this clod of clay which is man is able to rise up to praise the Master of all, Whom no angel or seraph can extol according to the majesty of His Holiness? But the question itself contains the answer. For if in truth there were even a single creature in all the worlds who was able to glorify God as He deserves to be glorified, then it would be fitting that only he should do so. Since, however, there is no one, whether in heaven above or earth below, who can praise Him properly, therefore anyone is permitted to praise Him, even the humblest of the humble—even man.[13]

Moreover, said Levi Yitzhak, the words a man utters to God have the power to lift up to Heaven the words he later speaks to his fellowman. The nobility of spirit to which a man ascends during the hour of his worship exalts him even afterward when he goes out among his neighbors to attend to his daily affairs. Thus, upon concluding the *Amidah* prayer, when we take leave of the King of kings, moving three steps backward and bowing, we say, "O God, guard my tongue from evil and my lips from speaking guile...." For prayer to God with words that are pure and true and come from the depths of the soul will keep a man from frivolous speech afterward, since he will then say to himself, "Only a moment ago I uttered words before the great and awesome King. In a few hours I will again pray to Him Whose glory fills the world. How, then, dare this very same mouth speak wasteful, meaningless words now?"

> If a man keeps his ears pure by guarding them from all gossip and slander, then is he worthy to hear what is proclaimed each day from above: "Repent, O My children, repent!" And when he hears these words, his heart fills with shame that he has sinned before the Lord, before Whom all worlds tremble.[14]

KAVANNAH

But above all else, Rabbi Levi Yitzhak taught that the success or failure of prayer depends upon the intention of the heart: the inward feeling that fills the soul, the state of preparedness with which one enters the moment of prayer (the Tzaddikim often delayed their prayers beyond the proper time in order to study and pray in preparation for prayer), the openness of the soul to hear the word of God, to feel His presence, to permit the Lord to enter his life—in a word, *Kavannah*. It is not, as another Hasidic sage observed, how much of the prayer book a man goes through, but how much of the prayer book goes through him.

The following stories illustrate this point:

One Rosh Hashanah, the Rabbi of Berditchev was preparing to blow the *Shofar*. He went and immersed himself in the *Mikveh*, dressed in his *Kittel*, put on his *Tallit*, recited the Psalms *Lamnatzeiah* and *Min ha-Meitzar* with the congregation, verse by verse, and read passages from the Zohar. Then he took the *Shofar* in his hand and paused for a moment. The congregation stood trembling with anxiety, ready for the blessings and the blowing. But there were no blessings and no blowing. Rabbi Levi Yitzhak put the *Shofar* down, lifted it up again, and once again put it down. Minutes passed, half an hour; still no sound from the *Shofar*.

"My friends," Rabbi Levi Yitzhak finally said, "back there near the door sits a Jew who has been raised on a small farm among Gentiles, who has never studied Torah, and who does not even know how to pray. When he came here and saw the whole congregation in prayer, a great stirring moved his heart, tears filled his eyes, and he cried out, 'O Father of mercy, You are the Master of all prayers. As for me, I only know the twenty-two letters of the alphabet. Let me recite them before You—aleph, bet, gimel, dalet—and You, O Lord, in Your great mercy, join them together into words of prayer.'

"Now," concluded Rabbi Levi Yitzhak, "the Holy One, blessed be He, is busy weaving those letters that came out of the mouth of that Tzaddik into a resplendent tapestry of prayer. And so, we must wait."

One Yom Kippur the Rabbi of Berditchev saw that the darkness of judgment hung over the people of Israel. Then, during the *Neilah* service, he noticed that a new light had burst forth which scattered the darkness. He inquired into the reason for this light, and it was revealed to him from Heaven that in a distant place there was a Minyan of Jewish soldiers and that the soldier who led the service illumined the entire world by means of his prayer.

At that time it was the law in Russia that soldiers serve for a period of at least ten years. Often the Jewish soldiers were treated with extreme cruelty, and were even forced to give up their faith. The Rabbi of Berditchev decided that in the coming year he himself would travel to the place of that soldier's service, which had been shown him from Heaven, that he might see with his own eyes how the prayers were said. So it happened that at the conclusion of the year, after overcoming many difficulties, he did arrive in time to join in the prayers of the soldiers for *Kol Nidre*. He entered the room just before the service began and noticed that a certain soldier stepped down before the Ark and spoke to his fellow soldiers with these words:

"My brothers and friends, on this day all Israel ask for their own needs: one for his livelihood, a second for his wife and family. But it is otherwise with us. Our livelihood is given to us by the Czar, and we have neither wives nor children. What, then, should we pray for? We have but one request: *Yisgadal v'yiskadash shmei raboh*. May His great name be magnified and sanctified!"

"Because of the words of this simple soldier, the hearts of all those who prayed there were touched by the love and fear of God," said the Rabbi of Berditchev. "And then I understood the origin of that great light which I had seen."

Once the Rabbi of Berditchev walked over to a group of his Hasidim after they had completed the *Amidah* prayer, shook hands with them, and greeted them warmly with, "*Sholom aleichem*."

They were taken by surprise since they had neither left the city nor were they visiting strangers.

Seeing their surprise, the rabbi said, "Why are you so astonished? You were far away, were you not? You were in the grain market in Odessa or in the woolen market in Lodz or on a distant ship bound for a port of trade. When the sound of praying ceased, you returned from your long voyage, and I greeted you."

On the eve of one Sabbath, Rabbi Levi Yitzhak prayed before the congregation of a town in which he was passing some time as a guest. As always, he drew out his prayers far beyond their usual length through exclamations and gestures not provided for in the liturgy. When he had finished, the Rav of the town went up to him, offered Sabbath greetings, and asked, "Why are you not more careful not to tire the congregation? Do not our sages relate of Rabbi Akiva that, whenever he prayed with the congregation, he did so quickly, but that when he prayed alone, he abandoned himself to ecstasy, so that frequently he began in one corner of the room and ended up in another?"

The Rabbi of Berditchev replied, "How is it possible to assume that Rabbi Akiva with his countless disciples hastened his prayer in order not to tire the congregation? Surely every member was more than happy to listen to his master hour after hour! The meaning of this Talmudic story is more likely this: When Rabbi Akiva really prayed with the congregation—that is to say, when the congregation felt at heart the same fervor as he—his prayer could well be short, for he had to pray only for himself. But when he prayed alone—that is to say, when he prayed in the congregation, but his was the only fervent heart among them—he had to draw out his prayer to lift their hearts to the level of his."

> **Flaming fervor ["*Hitlahavut*"] should pervade all our prayers. Alas, in this generation, however, our transgressions have so weakened our spirits that we are unable to reach such a rung until half the service is over. But when the Messiah appears—may he come soon!—it is written: "The earth will be filled with the knowledge of the Lord as the waters cover the sea." Then shall we even be able to begin our prayers with *Hitlahavut*.**[15]

Then there was the time when the *Hazzan* of the House of Prayer of Rabbi Levi Yitzhak became hoarse.

The rabbi asked him, "What has happened that your voice has become hoarse?"

The *Hazzan* answered, "It is because I prayed before the Ark."

"Correct," said the rabbi. "He who prays before the Ark, his voice becomes hoarse. But he who prays before the living God, how can his voice become hoarse?"

Prayer should spring from the inner heart of man, and not hang heavy as the burden of duty. Perhaps that is why Levi Yitzhak so loved the *Minhah* prayer.

The morning prayer is called *Shaharit*, which means "dawn," because it refers to the dawn of the day, while the evening prayer is called *Ma'ariv* because it refers to the eventide of the day. Why then is the afternoon prayer called *Minhah*? Some two hundred years ago, Rabbi Yomtov Heller explained that it refers to the repose ["*Menuhah*"] of the sun. But I would like to give a different reason. We are obliged to say the morning prayer because God has returned our souls to us and has brought us the light of the sun and so many other good things. Thus, in the morning service we say, "true and abiding" has been the Lord. We are also obliged to pray the evening prayer because we are giving over our souls to the Lord and trust that He will be faithful to return them to us. Thus, in the evening service, we say, "true and faithful" is He. But we are not at all obliged to pray the afternoon prayer. We offer it to God of our own free will. Therefore do we call it *Minhah*, for that is what it is—a "gift."[16]

One of the favorite stories which the Hasidim would tell about their master relates how Rabbi Levi Yitzhak once came to an inn where many merchants were stopping on the way to market their wares. The place was far from Berditchev, so no one knew the Tzaddik or paid him any attention. He appeared to be only another traveler. In the early morning the guests wanted to pray, but since there was only a single pair of *Tefillin* in the house the guests had to share them. One man after another, all anxious to reach the market, put them on and rattled off his prayer, then handed them on to the next. When all had prayed, the rabbi called two of the young men to him saying that he wanted to ask them something.

When they had come close, he looked gravely into their faces and said, "Ma-ma-ma; va-va-va."

"What do you mean?" cried the young men.

But he only repeated the same meaningless syllables.

They looked at him in amazement and thought; Surely this fellow is a fool.

But now Levi Yitzhak himself returned the look of amazement and said, "How is it you do not understand this language which you yourselves have just used in speaking to God?"

For a moment the young men were taken aback and stood silent. Then one of them said, "Have you never seen a child in the cradle, who does not yet know how to put sounds together into words? Have you not heard him make babbling sounds such as 'ma-ma-ma, va-va-va'? Even if all the wise men from the East and the West were to enter the room and listen, none would understand him. But the moment his father or his mother comes, they know exactly what he means—whether he is hungry or thirsty or in pain."

When the rabbi heard this answer, he began to dance for joy. "He understands, He understands. Our Father in Heaven understands His children."

From that time on, whenever on the Days of Awe he spoke to God in his own fashion in the midst of prayer, he never failed to remind Him of this answer.

SONGS

Among the most beloved folk songs of East European Jewry are those attributed to the Rabbi of Berditchev. These songs are in fact prayers that he wrote and sang (for it is the custom of the people Israel to sing their prayers) in moments when his soul overflowed the bounds of the written text.

Though written in Yiddish and reflecting the inner world of the ghetto Jew, the beauty and power of some of these prayer-songs have made them popular in many parts of the world. The best known is the famous *Kaddish*, which was discussed earlier and which expresses his endless love for Israel.

A second prayer-song said to have been written by Levi Yitzhak mirrors another part of his personality and teaching: the awareness of God's all-pervading presence. God was not in some faraway "there," Levi Yitzhak taught, but in an ever-present "here," as much a part of man as his own breath, as near to him as the innermost star. The verse of Scripture "I shall set the Lord before me at all times" was to be taken quite literally. It was of the immanence of God that the Psalmist sang:

> *Whither shall I go from Thy spirit?*
> *Or whither shall I flee from Thy presence?*
> *If I ascend up into Heaven, Thou art there;*
> *If I make my bed in the netherworld, behold, Thou art there....*
>
> (Psalms 139:7)

and about which the medieval Spanish poet-philosopher, Judah Halevi, wrote:

> *Lord, where shall I find Thee,*
> *High and hidden is Thy place;*
> *And where shall I not find Thee,*
> *The world is full of Thy glory.*
>
> *I have sought Thy nearness,*
> *And with all my heart have I called to Thee;*
> *And going out to meet Thee,*
> *I found Thee coming toward me.*

This indwelling of God, the immanence of the divine in our world and in our lives, is expressed with magical simplicity in the prayer-song of the Rabbi of Berditchev called "The Dudele." The name of this poem is derived from the Yiddish, *Du*, the second-person "you." *Dudele* is the diminutive form of *Du*, and so there is an endearing, informal, and intimate character to the name by which Levi Yitzhak calls God in his song.

THE DUDELE

Master of the Universe,
I will sing a song to Thee.
Where will I find Thee?
And where will I not find Thee?
Where I go, there art Thou,
Where I stay, there art Thou.
Only Thou, Thou alone,
Thou again, and only Thou.

When things go well—Thou,
And, alas, when things go ill—Thou.
Thou art,
Thou wast,
Thou wilt be.
Thou reignest,
Thou didst reign,
Thou wilt reign.

In heaven art Thou,
On earth art Thou,
Above art Thou,
Below art Thou.
Where I turn
And where I stir
Thou,
Thou,
Thou.

Ribono shel olom, Ribono shel olom,
Ich vil dir a dudele zingen.
A-ye emtzo-e-cho? Ve-a-ye lo emtzo-e-cho?
Vo ken man dich yo gefinnen?
Un vo ken man dich nit gefinnen?
Vo ich geh iz doch du,
Un vo ich shteh iz doch du.
Rak du, nor du,
Vieder du, ober du.

Is emitzen gut, iz doch du,
V'choliloh shlecht, oy du.
Atoh du,
Ho-yo du,
Ho-ve du,
Yihye du.
Moloch du,
Melech du,
Yimloch du.

Shomayim du,
Eretz du.
Maloh du,
Matoh du.
Vo ich kehr mich,
Vo ich wend mich,
Du!
Du!
Du!

The early death of his brilliant son, Meir, whose Torah he lovingly quotes in *Kedushat Levi*, deeply pained the Rabbi of Berditchev. The following song, said to have been written by Levi Yitzhak, is a dialogue between them.

> *Meirel my son,*
> *Do you know who you are?*
> > *I am dust and ashes, father.*
>
> *Meirel my son,*
> *Do you know before Whom you stand?*
> > *Before the King of kings, father.*
>
> *Meirel my son,*
> *What do you ask of Him?*
> > *Children, life and food, father.*
>
> *Meirel my son,*
> *What do you mean by "children"?*
> > *Children who study the Torah, father.*
>
> *Meirel my son,*
> *What do you mean by "life"?*
> > *A life which praises the Lord, father.*
>
> *Meirel my son,*
> *What do you mean by "food"?*
> > *"Thou shalt eat, be satisfied and bless the Lord thy God,"*
> > *father.*

In many parts of Eastern Europe, at the close of the Sabbath, before *Havdalah*, it was the custom, especially among women, to chant this Yiddish prayer, set to a beautiful melody. Both words and tune are ascribed to Levi Yitzhak.[17]

> *God of Abraham, of Isaac, and of Jacob,*
> *Protect in love Your dear people Israel.*
> *The holy Sabbath is departing.*
> *Send us a new week marked by*
> *No lack of food,*
> *Deepened faith,*
> *Love for our fellowmen,*
> *And strength to do Your will.*

> *Master of the World,*
> *You Who gives strength to the weak,*
> *Give strength to Your dear Jewish children,*
> *That they may praise You*
> *And serve You alone.*
> *May the days of the oncoming week bring*
> *Strength, health, and blessing,*
> *Children, life, and food*
> *For us and for all Israel.*
> *And let us say, Amen.*[18]

Speaking of this prayer, one of the disciples of Rabbi Levi Yitzhak asked his students, "Have you ever wondered why it is that after the close of the Sabbath we recite the prayer *Got Fun Avrohom* in the Yiddish vernacular and not in Hebrew, the holy tongue? I shall explain the reason to you.

"On the holy Sabbath day, the sages tell us, it is proper to speak in the holy tongue. Only after Sabbath is ended do we use the vernacular. But just as it is hard for the Jew to take leave of the holy day abruptly, going from the sacred to the profane, from Sabbath peace to weekday travail in one moment, so it is with the holy language. Let the change be gradual and gentle. Therefore we recite the prayer, *Got Fun Avrohom* in Yiddish. For while the husk—that is, the language—is common, that which stands within—that is, the meaning—is holy."

If we could ask Rabbi Levi Yitzhak if there could ever be a time when worship would be superfluous, he might answer, to our surprise, in the affirmative. For at the close of the seventy-second Psalm are the words, "And let the whole earth be filled with His glory. Amen and Amen. The prayers of David the son of Jesse are ended."

Concerning this passage, Rabbi Levi Yitzhak said, "All prayers and hymns are a plea to have His glory revealed throughout the world. But if once the whole earth were, indeed, filled with His glory, there would be no further need to pray."

4

Doing the Mitzvot

A MAN'S MOOD, be it ever so ennobling, profound, or praiseworthy, is frail, transient, fickle. The Law tries to guarantee the mood, to lend stability and permanence to what might otherwise fly away. Inward feeling is not enough; outward form is needed to add strength and permanence. The Law is composed of Mitzvot. Indeed, Mitzvah is perhaps the key word in all Jewish literature. Without it one lacks the essential insight into the meaning of the Jewish faith. Yet it is a difficult word to translate, being variously termed "commandment," "good deed," and, sometimes, spoken of by the mystics as that which God and man have in common. As Levi Yitzhak explained:

The word Mitzvah means "to bind," which is to say, he who properly performs a Mitzvah joins himself to the Creator, blessed be His name. [1]

The peculiar genius of Judaism took the teachings of holiness, justice, and mercy which the prophets had proclaimed and formulated from them a system of Mitzvot, both ritual and moral, that resulted in a remarkable discipline which sought to encompass every aspect of life. It was through the regimen of law that the life of man was sanctified and thereby raised up in service of God.

It is written in the Zohar that the Holy One, blessed be He, is glorified by every Mitzvah a man performs. As an earthly father proudly recounts the words of the child he loves, so does our Heavenly Father dwell upon the good deeds of each man, saying: "See what My children have done!" [2]

This day the Lord your God is commanding you
To observe these statutes and ordinances.
You must be careful to observe them
With all your mind and heart.

Concerning the Lord, you have today avowed that
   He is your God
And that you would walk in His ways,
And keep His statutes, commands, and ordinances,
And heed His injunctions.

And the Lord has today avowed concerning you that you
   are a people of His very own,
As He promised you.
And so you are to keep all His commands,
That you may be a people consecrated to the Lord your
   God. . . .

And now, Israel, what does the Lord your God require of you
But to fear the Lord your God,

> *To walk in all His ways and to love Him*
> *And to serve the Lord your God with all your heart*
>   *and with all your soul;*
> *To keep for your good the Mitzvot of the Lord.*
>
>   (Deuteronomy 26:16-19, 10:12-13)

To the Jew, Torah, in both the narrow sense of the Five Books of Moses—the Pentateuch—as well as in the broad sense of the entire religious literature of Israel, is not merely history, theology, or wisdom, but, first and foremost, Mitzvot. Grounded in the Bible but developed by the rabbis of the Talmud into a comprehensive system of daily living, the Mitzvot have become a trustworthy guide to man in his life on earth. They are a means of ennobling Israel; a divine-human method of permitting the One Who dwells on high to reach down into all parts of our lives; a means of sublimating the natural impulses—hunger, sex, power—to higher goals; a way of releasing and drawing to their source the sparks of holiness that lie buried within every man's heart. The Mitzvot are a special complex of laws, difficult to obey, demanding daily sacrifice. Yet if a man gives himself in love to their strict regimen, bending his will to the divine will, they will train him to forsake the ways of pride and temptation and teach him to walk in the ways of the Lord. He learns to hallow the everyday by performing each deed so that it becomes a means of serving God.

But doing the Mitzvah is not enough. Much—sometimes everything—depends upon how the Mitzvah is performed. Because the Mitzvah is law and because the system of Mitzvot comprises a complex code of conduct, it is possible to speak the words or perform the act without engaging heart and mind—simply to "go through the motions." This is a danger that has confronted Jewish life from ancient times. "Mitzvot performed by rote," was how Isaiah put it some twenty-six hundred years ago.

Love without law would waste away; it would have no substance, no reality, no guarantee of performance. But law without love would result in a harsh, officious legalism, gloom, restriction and eventual rebellion. For example, the commandment concerning the observance of the Sabbath is mentioned twice in Scriptures, once in Deuteronomy, where it is written, "*keep* the Sabbath day"—that is, keep its laws and statutes with devotion and loyalty and steadfastness—and once in Exodus where it is written, "*remember* the Sabbath day"—that is, remember it in your heart and soul with joy and love and inner peace. Both versions, "keep" and "remember," are necessary. One without the other is contrary to the Jewish spirit that combines *Halakhah* and *Aggadah*, prose and poetry, remembering and keeping, law and lore, inward devotion and outward form.

There were times in Jewish history when the Law became dry and hard, devoid of inwardness; when the Mitzvah contracted into an end in itself and was no longer a means for cleaving to the Lord; when it became the custom to deliver hair-splitting lectures to demonstrate scholarly prowess instead of teaching the Law and urging its proper fulfillment.

One of the decisive contributions of Hasidism is its re-emphasis of the spirit of inwardness, its "joy in performing the Mitzvah," its insistence on *Kavvanah* ("inner devotion") and even *Hitlahavut* ("ecstasy"). That is why Abraham Heschel can write that "a Mitzvah is performed when a deed is outdone by a sigh." With the rise of Hasidism, much that had become dull and drab took on new life. Rabbi Levi Yitzhak was a glowing example of this Hasidic renewal of the Mitzvot.

Rabbi Levi Yitzhak was always eager to learn how he might better observe the Mitzvot, even if those from whom he learned sometimes seemed a bit strange. On one of his trips to collect charity, his appeals brought little response. Meeting disappointment in village after village, he grew despondent. "Surely I have done the wrong thing," he said to himself, "wasting precious time which might otherwise have been used for prayer and study. It would have been better for me to remain at home. I shall return at once."

Then, while planning to depart, he witnessed the capture of a thief. About to be thrown into prison, the thief was being pummeled by the crowd.

"See, my son," said the Rabbi of Berditchev to the thief, "what you have brought upon yourself. Now you will surely forsake your former ways."

"What do you mean?" answered the thief. "If I have failed today, I shall try again tomorrow."

Levi Yitzhak was stunned by the shameless reply. But then he thought: That fellow has taught me a lesson: to persevere in the doing of a Mitzvah and to have faith that if I fail today, I shall succeed tomorrow.

ITS OWN REWARD

The Mitzvah, Rabbi Levi Yitzhak taught, is its own reward. And the man who fulfills the Mitzvah best is he who considers not the reward he may derive from it but whose heart and soul are so bound up with the Mitzvah that all rewards pale in comparison. To him alone reward may come.

> The general rule is that one must serve the Creator, blessed be He, without any thought of reward. Indeed, in order that he might carry out God's will, he should be ready to relinquish his portion in this world as well as in the world to come.
>
> This was the case with Rachel. On her intended wedding night, Rachel revealed to Leah those secret signs of identity that she and Jacob had agreed upon in order to assure the deception. So she fulfilled the Mitzvah of delivering her sister from a marriage to Esau, but at great personal sacrifice. For Rachel had no knowledge at that time that Jacob would yet marry her. Further, since Leah was now wed, Rachel had reason to fear that Esau's design to marry her might come to pass. Thus she would forfeit her share in both this world and the next. [3]

It is well known that the Mitzvah of the *Etrog* was observed by Rabbi Levi Yitzhak of Berditchev with infinite care and boundless joy. The finest *Etrog* obtainable graced his holiday.

It once happened that because evil winds had delayed the ships and summer rains had washed out the roads, as Sukkot approached, not an *Etrog* was to be found in the whole area of Berditchev. The rabbi was gloomy. His Hasidim, saddened by the sorrow of the rabbi, took to the roads in one final effort to find an *Etrog*, ready to pay any price for it. But Jew after Jew told them the same story: They too had searched but could find no *Etrogim*.

Late one night, however, they came upon a Jew who had a large and lovely *Etrog*.

"We must have it for our rabbi. Name your price."

"It pains me to hear that the holy rabbi may be without an *Etrog*. But I, too, am a Jew and no less duty bound to observe the Mitzvah. All my life I have said the blessing over the *Etrog*, and I have no intention of changing my ways now."

The Hasidim pleaded and offered any price but to no avail. Yet they did persuade the owner of the *Etrog* to travel home by way of Berditchev so that he himself could tell the rabbi that his refusal to sell the *Etrog* was not due to the niggardliness of the Hasidim.

When Levi Yitzhak saw the *Etrog* the Jew carried, his face shone with ecstasy.

"You must remain here for Sukkot," he pleaded, "you and your *Etrog*. Ask what you will. I must have it!"

The Jew thought for a while, then replied, "Very well, I'll stay. And the price is the place next to you in Paradise!"

"Settled and done!" said the rabbi, and they shook hands on the bargain.

The Jew remained in Berditchev for Sukkot and was entertained there in the finest homes in the most gracious manner. Only one courtesy was denied him: He was not permitted to enter a *Sukkah*! Finally, in desperation, he ran to the rabbi, pleading, "How can you refuse to permit a Jew to set foot inside a *Sukkah*? After what I did, is this justice?"

"Do not fret, my son," said the rabbi. "You can observe the Mitzvah. But there is a price you must pay."

"Name it!"

"Very well," replied the rabbi. "You must return that place in Paradise."

The Jew was in a dilemma. Paradise or a Mitzvah, which was he to choose?

He made his decision in this way. "All my life I have performed the Mitzvah of the *Sukkah* because the Torah commands us to. But nowhere does the Torah command us to enter Paradise. Take back your Paradise."

Levi Yitzhak's face lit up. "You have done well, my son," he said. "Paradise cannot be gained through a bargain. It can only be had through the quality of the life you lead. When you were ready to surrender Paradise for a Mitzvah, in that moment you made ready for yourself your rightful place there."

TEXT:
"It shall come to pass if you heed these ordinances and are careful to observe them, . . . that the Lord your God will bless the fruit of your body and the product of your soil, your corn, your wine, your oil, the issue of your cattle . . ." (Deuteronomy 7:12-13).

EXPLANATION:
In truth, however, these rewards are the least of the joys one receives. For, as our sages taught, "the reward of the Mitzvah is the Mitzvah itself." The other benefits which the Lord bestows upon us in this world and in the future world are but the meagerest of pleasures. For the greatest joy is the act of doing the Mitzvah, performing the will of the Creator and bringing Him joy. [4]

For there are two kinds of servants of the Lord: one who serves from fear and one who serves from love. The difference between them is: He who serves from fear is aware that it is "he" who recites his prayers, "he" who fears Heaven. But the one who serves from love—when he prays or performs some other Mitzvah—he is unmindful of himself. While the first troubles his head about rewards and punishments, the second gives them not a thought.[5]

But if it is indeed true that a reward will be given, how can a man *not* give it a thought? Even here, taught Levi Yitzhak, God aids us.

> "How great is Thy goodness, O Lord, which Thou storeth up for those who revere Thee" [Psalms 31:20]. This verse is explained by the Mishnah: "Do not be as servants who serve their master for reward, but be servants who serve their master without reward." For if the Holy One, blessed be He, rewards those who do His will, how should a man perform a Mitzvah without thinking of the reward? But the Holy One, blessed be He, helps His people Israel: at the very moment a man does a Mitzvah, the Holy One, blessed be He, snatches from his mind all thought of reward, so that he might do the Mitzvah only for its own sake. And this is the meaning of the words of the Psalm: "How great is Thy goodness, O Lord, which Thou storeth up for those who revere Thee." The Lord does good to His creatures by "storing up" their reward—that is, He makes them forget all about the reward which the Mitzvah brings. [6]

FROM MITZVAH TO MITZVAH

Just as the power of a sin is great because it may lead to another sin and yet another, so the power of a Mitzvah is great because it may lead to another Mitzvah and yet another. The wisdom of this ancient teaching of the Talmud was clear to the Rabbi of Berditchev.

> When we perform one Mitzvah, the Holy One, blessed be He, plants in our hearts thereby the desire to do another, like a father, observing that his son has learned something new, asks him a further question on the basis of it. [7]

Half the battle is won once a man turns from his past ways and enters the path of the Mitzvot, for the first Mitzvah will surely bring him to the next, as the following story indicates.

The Rabbi of Berditchev became related to Rabbi Shneur Zalman of Ladi through the marriage of their grandchildren. After the wedding, Rabbi Levi Yitzhak said to Rabbi Zalman, "Dear M'huten [Yiddish term for a male in-law], the Almighty has blessed us through the joy of this marriage. Therefore it is only right that to celebrate properly we should engage in some Mitzvah together."

"I quite agree," said Rabbi Zalman.

"I have raised an orphan girl," the Rabbi of Berditchev continued, "who is now of marriageable age but has no money for dowry. Let the two of us go about the city to collect money for her dowry."

Rabbi Zalman agreed to this, even though he was not known in the city. But before they set out, Rabbi Levi Yitzhak made one condition, namely, that whatever amount of money was given to them, they would accept without complaint, even though it was not in accordance with the means of the giver or the honor of the two rabbis.

Now in the city of Berditchev there lived a very wealthy man who was known for his generosity. The Rabbi of Berditchev suggested to Rabbi Zalman that it would be well for them to go to this man first. When they came to his house, he received them politely and heard their story. Then he put his hand in his pocket, took out a halfpenny, and gave it to them. The Rabbi of Berditchev accepted the money without a word and left with Rabbi Zalman.

Once out of earshot, Rabbi Zalman complained angrily, "Is this an example of honor for the Torah? And is it permissible to close one's eyes when such a pittance is given to the rabbi of the community who comes for so worthy a cause as dowering a bride?"

Replied the Rabbi of Berditchev, "Did I not clearly make a condition with you not to complain against any man no matter what he might give? I beg you to be patient, and let us go to another house."

When they had gone a short distance, they heard a voice calling after them to wait a moment. It was the wealthy man who was pursuing them. When he reached them, he asked for forgiveness for his effrontery in offering such a pittance. He then took from his pocket ten small pieces of silver, gave it to them, and left.

At that Rabbi Zalman turned to the Rabbi of Berditchev. "Is it for ten pieces of silver that you made me promise to make up with him?"

"I ask that you be patient."

And so they went on their way. Suddenly they again heard the rich man's voice calling after them. This time he begged forgiveness for giving them only ten pieces of silver and gave them an additional thousand pieces of silver. They forgave him wholeheartedly and asked God to bless him for returning him to his former generosity.

Sometime later Rabbi Levi Yitzhak said to Rabbi Zalman, "I shall explain to you the whole matter regarding the rich man we visited, for in truth he is a generous person, as I told you. Only a week ago a beggar came to his house for a donation, but at that very moment a number of important people were with him so that he was not able to go to his safe. He took what was in his pocket—half a penny—and gave it to the beggar, thinking that he probably did not receive more than that elsewhere in any case. The beggar took the halfpenny and angrily cast it into the face of the rich man so that it struck his eye, nearly blinding him. At this effrontery, the latter swore that he would never again give a poor man more than half a penny. We are taught that one sin leads to another, and so it was. For when beggars would come to his door and ask for money, they would not accept the halfpenny that he gave them because they had been accustomed to receive more generous contributions from him. Thus for several weeks he had not given any charity at all. So it was that when we came to him he gave us also only half a penny. One sin leads to another, for even if he could not help but give the first beggar a halfpenny, nevertheless it was not proper for him to do so with all the other beggars who came afterward. It is not right for a man, because he is angry at one person, to take his wrath out upon all. Therefore it was necessary for me to accept even the halfpenny that he gave us in order that he should be accomplishing at least a small Mitzvah.

For we are also taught that one Mitzvah leads to another. So it was that, later, he found the strength to give us first the ten pieces of silver, which was a greater Mitzvah, and subsequently a thousand pieces of silver, which was a still greater Mitzvah. By means of this, I have been able to do him a good turn in that he has now become a man of generosity once again."

LOVE OF THE MITZVOT

Rabbi Shneur Zalman was a dear friend of Levi Yitzhak's all his life and many stories are related about these two. One of them deals with the former's love of the Mitzvot. At the time Rabbi Shneur Zalman, the great leader of Hasidism in Lithuania, was imprisoned because of the false accusations made against him to the government by the Mitnagdim, messengers were sent to other Hasidic leaders asking them to pray for his deliverance. When a messenger came to Berditchev, Rabbi Levi Yitzhak asked him if Shneur Zalman was alarmed at the time he was imprisoned.

"Yes, quite alarmed," said the messenger.

"Was his alarm only apparent or did he really feel this way in his heart?"

After a moment's reflection, the messenger answered, "It was only apparent."

"And what makes you so certain that it was only apparent?"

"There was a sign. The rabbi—may his light continue to shine!—forgot to buckle his shoes when the soldier came for him. But he did not forget to take his *Tallit* and *Tefillin*."

"That Litvak!" said Rabbi Levi Yitzhak, smiling. [8]

As a young man still living with his father-in-law before he came under the influence of the Maggid, Levi Yitzhak was eager to observe the Mitzvah of caring for travelers. Whenever he noticed strangers arriving in the city, he would run out to the street, buy some straw, put it on his shoulders, carry it home, and prepare beds for the visitors.

Once his father-in-law said to him: "Levi Yitzhak, my dear son, why do you undertake such heavy work? When you pay the peasant for the straw, add a little more to the price, and he will carry it to the house for you."

"What?" asked Rabbi Levi Yitzhak in astonishment. "Should I hand over my Mitzvah to another and pay him for doing it, too?"

Levi Yitzhak's manner of performing the Mitzvot was wonderful to behold. He fulfilled them with a love and a yearning that spread through his whole body like a flaming fire. It was hard for him to sleep at the close of the festivals of Sukkot, Passover, and Shavuot, during which the *Tefillin* are not worn. He would sit up all night and wait for the dawn to appear in order that he might once again be able to put on his *Tefillin*. Then he would seize them in his hand with great joy and kiss them with a heart filled with love. He would conduct himself this way with every Mitzvah, kissing his *Tefillin*, his *Tzitzit* with all his heart, doing the commandments with fear and trembling, and with such holy fervor that it seemed as if he were no longer in this world.

During a visit with the Maggid of Koznitz, Rabbi Levi Yitzhak asked whether he might walk to the *Mikveh* with the Maggid early one morning.

"I do not think it advisable for us to walk together," said the Maggid, "for it is your habit to walk rapidly and excitedly while I walk slowly and quietly."

Rabbi Levi Yitzhak promised that he too would go slowly and quietly. When they approached the Mikveh, however, Rabbi Levi Yitzhak forgot his promise and began to tremble and shake with such fervor that he almost fell into the water!

If matches are made in Heaven, they are prepared for on earth. What a rare Mitzvah to have a share in the planning, especially if it is for an orphan, the child of the Great Maggid, Dov Ber!

After the Maggid died, his disciple, Rabbi Shlomo of Karlin, assumed the responsibility of finding suitable marriages for the young orphaned sons. When the time came for the Maggid's son, Shalom, Rabbi Shlomo took him to Tchernobil, and on the way stopped over night at Berditchev with Rabbi Levi Yitzhak. Levi Yitzhak had a grand feast prepared in their honor. When they departed he sent musicians to accompany them and himself danced before the musicians along the way. Upon returning home, his wife asked why he had shown them so much honor, dancing before the musicians like a young boy. Was the festive meal not enough? "How could I not dance before the groom," he replied, "when I saw Elijah the Prophet dancing before them?" [9]

The inner feeling of drawing close to God through the Mitzvah can be achieved even by the simple and the unlearned. On the first day of *Selihot*, before reading the Psalms, as was his custom, Rabbi Levi Yitzhak told the following story to his congregation.

There was a time when the government, in its desire to destroy our faith and our people, issued a terrible decree to take young Jewish boys into the army—by force, if necessary. So it happened that weeping children were torn from the arms of mothers and fathers and sent into distant and strange provinces of the Empire where they might, it was hoped, forget in time their families and their faith.

With the approach of the New Year in one of these camps, the exiled boys wanted to pray to the Almighty—even though it meant rising while it was still dark and perhaps arousing the ire of the officers and other soldiers who took advantage of every opportunity to harass them—but alas, none of them remembered a single paragraph from the prayer book.

On the first day of the New Year one little soldier finally said to the others in despair, "Jews are accustomed to read the Psalms. Does anyone of us know a Psalm by heart, or even a few lines of one?"

But they were young and had been away too long from home, school, and synagogue. With shamed sadness they shook their heads. And some added, "To think that on this holy day there is not one of us who can at least pray to the One above from the Psalms which our fathers knew by heart!"

At last one of the boys exclaimed, "True, we have forgotten the words of the Psalms. But wait, I remember a melody! Come, let us sing the tune!"

So it was that all of them—still only children, with dirty faces and rumpled uniforms—stood up together and with a solemnity beyond their years, chanted the melody to the Psalm which was led by the one who remembered. And that melody, carrying their prayers, pierced the highest heavens.

Thus it is with us, concluded the rabbi. The words of the Psalms are full of mysteries which are hidden from our understanding. But the melody we know. Come, then, my children, let us sing *Ashrei ha-ish...*

And all the congregation chanted the Psalm according to the melody of Rabbi Levi Yitzhak.

> *Happy is the man that has not walked*
> *In the counsel of the wicked,*
> *Nor stood in the way of sinners,*
> *Nor sat in the seat of the scornful,*
> *But his delight is in the Law of the Lord*
> (Psalms 1:1-2)

It is true that an inner light should shine when a Mitzvah is performed. But what if no light shines? Should one forgo the Mitzvah and do it only when one is aglow with fervor?

It is written in the book *Imrei Tzaddikim*: "I heard from the holy mouth of the Rabbi of Berditchev that a man should not abstain, Heaven forbid, from performing the Mitzvot of the Lord because he lacks fervor. For if a man waits until he possesses *Kavvanah*, the time for doing the Mitzvah may pass, Heaven forbid, and he would not then be a true servant of the Lord. Whenever the occasion arises one must hasten to fulfill the Mitzvah, even though he feels no fervor."

The Mitzvah must be fulfilled in any case. It is the vessel of man's spirit. Sometimes the vessel may be empty, but if there were no vessel at all, how could it ever be filled? Thus there may be times when we perform Mitzvot without *Kavvanah*, but is it not from doing the Mitzvah that *Kavvanah* may arise? The violinist does not reach sublime heights each time he plays, but how can he ever reach them except by playing?

Levi Yitzhak, however, was like a pure flame, leaping ever

higher. He was that rare artist of the soul who fashioned again and again those deeds of holy fervor which marked him as a symbol and a goal to other men.

CHARITY

"How great is the Mitzvah of *Tzedakah*!

"When a man gives charity, he brings joy and gladness to all worlds, to all the holy seraphim, to all the angels, and to all the heavenly souls. And when the spirit of such a man rises upward after his demise, all the angels, seraphim, and heavenly souls of all the worlds gather together to embrace and kiss him, crying aloud with one voice, 'Give honor to this one who has brought joy to the Master by giving gifts to the poor!'"

These are the words of the Rabbi of Berditchev.

Levi Yitzhak tried to fulfill the Mitzvah of *Tzedakah* with all his heart and soul. He would often travel to nearby cities to raise money to dower needy brides, to redeem captives, or simply to meet the needs of the poor. In each place a haunting impression was left of this strange, holy man.

In the course of one such journey the Rabbi of Berditchev stopped in Lvov and went to the house of a man of wealth and esteem. When he was admitted to the master of the house he asked for a day's lodging but did not divulge his name and calling.

The rich man said gruffly, "I have no use for wayfarers. Why don't you go to an inn?"

"I am not a man to stay at an inn," said the rabbi. "Just give me a corner in one of your rooms and I shall not trouble you for anything else."

"Away with you!" cried the other. "If—as you say—you are not a man to stay at an inn, go to the schoolteacher around the corner. He likes to welcome vagrants like you with honor and give them food and drink."

Rabbi Levi Yitzhak went to the schoolteacher where he was warmly received. But on his way there someone had recognized him and soon the whole town buzzed with the news that the holy Rabbi of Berditchev had arrived and taken lodgings in the house of the schoolteacher. Hardly had he rested when a throng of people gathered, desiring to enter and be blessed by the Tzaddik. Among them was the rich man. He fought his way to the rabbi and said, "May the master forgive me and honor my house with his visit! All the Tzaddikim who ever came to Lvov were my guests."

Rabbi Levi Yitzhak turned to those standing around him and said, "Do you know the difference between our father Abraham, peace be with him, and Lot? Why does such a spirit of satisfaction pervade the story of how Abraham set before the angels curd and milk and tender calf? Did not Lot also bake for them and give them to eat? And why is the fact that Abraham received them in his tent regarded as so deserving an action? For Lot also asked them in and gave them shelter. Now this is the truth of the matter: In the case of Lot it is written that angels came to Sodom. But concerning Abraham, the Scriptures say, 'And he lifted up his eyes and looked and lo, three men stood over against him.' Lot saw heavenly angels while Abraham saw poor, dusty wayfarers in need of food and rest."

One Sabbath afternoon in the *Bet ha-Midrash* Rabbi Levi Yitzhak expounded on the verse that Joseph spoke to his brothers in Egypt, "Unless your lesser brother [Benjamin] come with you, you shall not see my face" (Genesis 44:23).

"Let us take this verse out of its context in the story of Joseph," Levi Yitzhak said, "and explain it as if it stood alone and the Lord Himself had spoken it. It would then refer to those of the Children of Israel who selfishly direct all their thoughts to their own welfare. 'It is enough that *my* clothing is good,' they say. 'It is enough that *my* bed is warm. *I* am a kosher Jew. After one hundred and twenty years, when I approach the Heavenly Court, the gates of Paradise will be flung open for *me*. And *him*? I am not concerned about him. Even if he descends into *Gehinnom*.'

"But the Holy One, blessed be He, does not send a blessing to men such as these. For the verse teaches, 'If your lesser brother is not with you, you shall not see My face.'"

What a fine thing it is to train one's young sons and daughters in the way of the Mitzvot by sending them with gifts to the poor. As a child I remember how my father, may he rest in

peace, would send me in place of a servant to bring gifts to the poor, in order to teach me the Mitzvah. It was all done with a full heart, with joy and in confidence, so that the poor would not be ashamed.[10]

When Levi Yitzhak became Rav of Berditchev, he made an agreement with the leaders of the congregation that they were not to ask him to their meetings unless they intended to discuss the introduction of a new usage or a new procedure. One day they did ask him to come to a meeting.

Immediately after greeting them he asked, "What is the new procedure you wish to establish?"

They answered, "From now on we do not want the poor to beg at the threshold. We want to put up a box and all the well-to-do people are to put money into it, each according to his means, and these funds shall be used to provide for the needy."

When the rabbi heard this he said, "My brothers, did I not beg you not to call me away from my studies and summon me to a meeting for the sake of an old usage or an old procedure?"

The leaders were astonished and protested, "But, master, the procedure under discussion today *is* new!"

"You are mistaken," he cried, "it is age old! It is an old, old procedure that dates back to Sodom and Gomorrah. Do you remember what is told about the girl from Sodom who gave a beggar a piece of bread? How they took her and stripped her and smeared her naked body with honey and exposed her for bees to devour, because of the great crime she had committed! Who knows—perhaps they too had a community box into which the well-to-do dropped their alms in order not to be forced to face their poor brothers eye to eye!"[11]

HOLY DAYS

For each of the Holy Days the Hasidim had tales about how the Rabbi of Berditchev fulfilled the Mitzvot in a strange and wonderful manner.

On the Sabbath, a mood of holiness and exultation would come over him. He taught that each week on this day man returns to his true self.[12] He regains for a fleeting moment the original state of wholeness in which he was made, for the taste of Heaven is in his mouth and the future world becomes entwined with the present. He explained the Talmudic passage, "A precious gift the Lord has, and the Sabbath is its name," to mean that on the Sabbath a divine light breaks forth and a new spirit pours down upon man. For this grace of light and spirit one should wait longingly, he said, all during the week. So illumined and ennobled was he on this day that when people compared his weekday manner of expounding the teachings with that of the Sabbath they found them to be as different as a glowing coal from a flaming fire. On the Sabbath he insisted on speaking only the "holy tongue"—Hebrew—in his household. Indeed, according to his grandson, the Rabbi of Neshkhiz, Rabbi Levi Yitzhak was more stringent in observing the laws of the Sabbath than even the laws of the Passover.

The Mitzvah of sounding the *Shofar* on Rosh Hashanah was cherished by Rabbi Levi Yitzhak, for it is a cry of alarm and a summons to battle. It recalls the covenant at Mount Sinai and heralds the end of time, the two poles of Jewish history. "There are those," he would say, "who hear the sound of the *Shofar* of the New Year all year long." He was especially concerned that this Mitzvah be observed with scrupulous care. It is related in the book *Shivhei ha-Besht* that the Great Maggid from Mezritch was not accustomed to sounding the *Shofar* himself. Menahem Mendel, who died in the Holy Land, would blow it as the Maggid called out the blasts. Indeed, even several years before his death during the period when he could not move, he still called out the blasts from his sickroom.

One year, when Menahem Mendel was not present in the congregation for Rosh Hashanah, the Maggid told the young Levi Yitzhak to sound the *Shofar*. Levi Yitzhak made himself ready and stood in fear and trembling as was his custom. When he heard the call *Tekiah*, dazzling lights flashed before him and he fainted.

Later the Maggid said, "We did not know what happened to him, for surely Mendel sees more and is not so frightened."

Several weeks before Rosh Hashanah, when he was rabbi in Berditchev, Levi Yitzhak let it be known that he needed someone to blow the *Shofar* for his *Bet ha-Midrash*. At once there descended upon him all manner of *Shofar*-blowers from the city and even beyond, each anxious to sound the *Shofar* in the *Bet ha-Midrash* of the Rav.

Rabbi Levi Yitzhak tested each applicant with this question, "What goes on in your mind at the very moment of the blast?"

Each one endeavored to prove his mastery of the mystical thoughts relating to the sounding of the *Shofar*, according to the Ari and the other great Kabbalists.

But not one of them pleased Rabbi Levi Yitzhak.

One day a *Shofar*-blower he did not know approached him and said, "My lord, I am one of the common people. I have four daughters, all of whom have reached the age of marriage. At the moment when I sound the *Shofar* there is only this thought in my mind: 'Master of the World, I have bent my will to Yours and fulfilled all Your Mitzvot. You, too, then, bend Your will to mine and help me to find husbands for my daughters.' "

Rabbi Levi Yitzhak's heart filled with great joy, and he said: "Your *Kavvanah* was a true *Kavvanah*. You will blow the *Shofar* in my *Bet ha-Midrash*."

The year that Rabbi Levi Yitzhak spent Yom Kippur in Lvov, the leaders of the community invited him to lead the *Kol Nidre* prayers. When the *Shammash* found him, he was eating the last meal before the fast in the company of some of the town roughnecks. And he was drinking with them, as well. The *Shammash* informed Levi Yitzhak of the request but thought to himself, he will never be able to lead the prayers in such a condition.

At the proper time Levi Yitzhak rose, went to the synagogue, stepped down before the Ark and prayed the entire service. When the service was over he opened the tractate Yoma of the Talmud, which deals with Yom Kippur, and studied all night with unflagging zeal. By morning, when he had gone through the entire tractate, he again stepped down before the Ark, led the congregation in all the prayers of the day and read the Torah as well.

When, at last, Yom Kippur had ended, he went to his inn where a table full of good food and drink had been prepared for him. He sat down, pushed aside the plates and said to the *Shammash*, "Bring me some food for the soul."

The innkeepers thought that he must surely be referring to some special delicacies which they had put away in the cellars, and turned to look there. Yet it was not such food that he sought. He wanted the tractate Sukkah of the Talmud, that deals with the Festival of Sukkot, which was then only five days off. The *Shammash*, amazed but obedient, brought him the tractate Sukkah that he had requested. Levi Yitzhak then proceeded to study throughout the night and all the following day. In this way the Tzaddik fasted two days for Yom Kippur.[13]

The holiday of Sukkot and the Mitzvot attached to it held a special place in the life of the Tzaddik, for this season was named the "time of our rejoicing" by the sages of old.

> The period between Rosh Hashanah and Yom Kippur is called "the Days of Awe" because God's power and majesty and glory is disclosed upon earth. Anyone with eyes and a brain in his head will return then to the Lord with a broken heart. For does not Yom Kippur draw near when He will rise up to judge all creatures? And where is the man who dares proclaim himself righteous in such judgment? Shall he not tremble at the approaching day and mend his ways.
>
> Such repentance is called *repentance-from-fear*.
>
> But after Yom Kippur, with the approach of the Festival of Sukkot, a Jew busies himself with such Mitzvot as building his *Sukkah*, preparing his *Lulav* and *Etrog*, giving *Tzedakah*, and worshiping the Lord with a joyous heart.
>
> Such repentance is called *repentance-from-love*.[14]

We are told that Rabbi Levi Yitzhak of Berditchev used to lead the congregation in prayer during the entire Day of Atonement with all the strength of his soul. One year, at the close of Yom Kippur, after having stood upon his feet from early morning until nightfall, pouring out his heart in marvelous fervor, he fell into such a deep faint that his followers were unable to awaken him with any manner of smelling salts. Finally they brought an *Etrog* and placed it beneath his nose. The love for the Mitzvah stirred within him, and he awoke at once!

He so yearned for the coming of the holiday that he used to remain awake during the whole first night of Sukkot, awaiting the break of dawn, when the time for using the *Lulav* would begin. At the first rays of light he would take the *Lulav* and *Etrog* in his hand and recite the blessing over them with such ecstasy that often he would faint.

Once early in the morning on the first day of Sukkot, Rabbi Levi Yitzhak ran to take the *Lulav* and *Etrog* which were in a chest with a glass lid. He thrust his hand through the glass, shattering it and cutting his hand, and seized the *Etrog*. Several minutes passed before he noticed that he had injured himself.

Stories have been handed down from generation to generation, from father to son, about the way in which Rabbi Levi Yitzhak danced on Simhat Torah, the festival that concludes the Sukkot season. His eyes closed, his face ablaze with a heavenly light, he would hold the Torah pressed to his heart with both hands, and dance on and on with such abandon that his feet almost seemed to be moving in the air, never touching the floor of the synagogue at all, while the congregation stood back and watched with wonder until a holy fear settled upon them.

In that moment, it is told, all the Upper Worlds were silent. Even the angels ceased their singing before the Holy One, blessed be He, for there was no greater joy to Heaven than the dance of Rabbi Levi Yitzhak of Berditchev.

At the Feast of Purim, before the Book of Esther was read, the rabbi danced during the benediction, danced on the *Bimah*— almost on the Scroll itself.

At the Passover *Seder*, when the assemblage reached the part of the Haggadah when the *Matzah* is raised and its meaning given, it was Rabbi Levi Yitzhak's holy way to snatch the *Matzah* and say with great fervor, like a man unable to speak from excitement: "Ah, ah, ah—*Matzah Zu!*"

Soon after Rabbi Levi Yitzhak had been received as Rav by the community of Berditchev, he prayed with great ardor on the first evening of the Feast of Passover, and this lasted so long that the congregation grew tired of waiting, finished their prayers, and went home to partake of the *Seder*. Only one man remained—one of those poor wayfarers from another place who, according to custom, was to take the festive meal at the house of one of the local Jews. He had been told that the Jew leading the prayer was to be his host, and because he was weary from the day's journey he lay down on a bench and was soon fast asleep. Meantime the rabbi had finished the silent *Amidah*. When he saw that all the people had gone home he cried, "O angels, angels on high! Descend on this holy day in praise of the Lord, blessed be He!"

At this the stranger half woke from a deep sleep. Still drowsy and dazed, he heard a rushing sound surge through the building. He was terrified to the core of his being. But the rabbi stood, reciting the hymns in great happiness. Then he caught sight of the stranger and asked him why he alone had remained. The man, who was now fully awake, explained. Thereupon the rabbi invited him to his *Seder*. But the stranger was timid and dared not accept for he feared that—in lieu of food—secret words that work magic would comprise the entire *Seder*.

"Calm yourself," said the rabbi, "You will eat at my house just what you would eat at the table of other Jews!"

To those Jews who felt the holy days a chore, Levi Yitzhak brought a freshness of heart; to those who only managed the outward forms, he revealed the inward spirit; to those who reduced such days to sheer idleness and pleasure-seeking, he was not averse to giving gentle rebuke:

> The miracle of Hanukkah celebrates our deliverance by the Holy One, blessed be He, from the evil decree [of the Syrians] to separate us from our holy Torah. It is proper, therefore, for each Jew to devote himself to the study of

Torah in celebration of this holiday, for on it the divine light which flows from the Torah has the power to brighten our souls.

Surely we should not waste our time on foolishness during the Festival of Hanukkah. I have observed that many have begun to squander these days in the wicked habit of playing cards and see no evil in it. But lay it to your hearts, my brothers: Each card is a tempting devil and all the while you play, you forget to fear the Lord. What is more, I hold that card playing is nothing else than thievery. Therefore, my brothers, I implore you not to take this matter lightly. Would it not be better to spend your hours in the study of God's Torah, or to go to a sage and hear Torah from him? Then the light of Heaven would illumine you and wonders would be yours.[15]

Once, during the Feast of Hanukkah, when Levi Yitzak saw the holy light burning, he was impelled to put his bare hand into the flame, yet felt no pain.

LEGEND AND TESTIMONY

The strange ways of the Rabbi of Berditchev became a legend to his people but, even more, they were a testimony that within this man was hidden an added portion of spirit unknown to other men, as if the *Neshamah Yeterah*—that surplus of soul which each Jew receives on the eve of the Sabbath and loses at the close of the Sabbath—was never taken from him but remained even on weekdays, raising him above the level of others in all his ways, especially when he fulfilled the Mitzvot.

The Seer of Lublin, who marveled at Levi Yitzhak's manner of performing the Mitzvot, used to say, "Every day I put aside a moment to thank God that He has sent into our world a soul as great and as holy as that of Rabbi Levi Yitzhak."[16]

It once happened that Rabbi Levi Yitzhak was journeying toward the city of Lublin. The Seer learned of this and commanded his disciples to put on their Sabbath clothes and go out to meet him. Rabbi Tzvi Hirsh of Zydatchov, then a student of the Seer, hid in one of the rooms to watch his master get ready to receive the Rabbi of Berditchev. And this is what he saw.

The Seer walked from room to room in consternation and spoke aloud to himself, "Master of the World, what shall I say before such a holy Gaon and Tzaddik? Will he not of a certainty know me for what I am? For everyone thinks that I am a Tzaddik, holy in every deed, wise in every word, able to resolve all the problems of the people and to influence the very Heavens. But he will see through all this in a glance and know me for what I truly am. How should I not then be filled with shame in his presence?

"And should you ask, O Master of the World, why is it that I am not filled with such shame in Your Presence? The answer is that, alas, over the years I have learned to be at ease with You ... but with him I have not learned to be at ease."

In the middle of his soliloquy, the Rabbi of Berditchev entered. At once they lost themselves in discussing the mysteries of the Torah.

5

The Messiah

ALL HIS LIFE Rabbi Levi Yitzhak awaited the coming of the Messiah. Out of his great love for the people Israel, his heart was always filled with hope for their final redemption. He even kept his Sabbath clothes constantly in readiness so that he could prepare himself at any moment to receive the long-expected one in proper dress.

According to an old tradition, the Messiah will be born on the day commemorating the destruction of the Temple—Tishah b'Av, the ninth day of the month of Av. The Hasidim tell how one year on the day before Tishah b'Av, after the final meal before the fast, Rabbi Levi Yitzhak stood at the window of his house anxiously looking out. At the slightest noise from the street he strained his eyes and ears to learn the cause. The sun was setting and the congregation had begun to gather in the synagogue to pray the evening prayers and to chant the Book of Lamentations, which is recited on this day in an eerie and melancholy melody. Since the hour was late and the Rabbi had not yet arrived, the *Shammash* hurried to his home.

"Rabbi, everyone is waiting for you."

As Levi Yitzhak slowly prepared to leave he muttered, almost to himself: "Alas! It is time to say *Eikhah* ("Book of Lamentations") once again and still the Messiah has not come!"

The Hasidim tell how, at the engagement party for his granddaughter, Levi Yitzhak took the betrothal agreement in his hand to examine it and began to read it slowly and carefully. Suddenly he stopped and tore it to pieces.

"Surely," he said, "you believe that the Messiah will come and we shall no longer be in exile next year! Then how could you put down 'Berditchev' as the location of the wedding?"

He asked for a pen and rewrote the agreement, changing the wording slightly:

"... the wedding will take place, God willing, in Jerusalem, The Holy City. If, however, the Messiah should not come during the coming year, God forbid, it will take place in Berditchev."

Rabbi Levi Yitzhak met several students from his *Yeshivah* walking down the street during the first days of the month of Av, that most mournful period in the Jewish calendar which culminates on Tishah b'Av. He asked them, "Where do you eat?"

"We 'eat days,'" they replied, using the Yiddish expression *essen teg*, which referred to the meal provisions commonly made for students—one day with one family, the next day with another.

"My children," said Rabbi Levi Yitzhak jokingly, "if it is true that you 'eat days,' would that you might devour once and for all the nine days of Av and receive a blessing from the whole people of Israel!"

But in his jest there was a sigh, and in his smile there was a tear. For there were times when the glory of Israel that was in exile, the pain and the humiliation his people suffered, so filled him with anguish that he could not abide even the innocent rejoicing of others. When Rabbi Levi Yitzhak came to a gathering of his friends and found them drinking wine and making merry without words of Torah in their mouth, he turned and said to them, "I am astonished that you are able to drink wine at a time when our holy Temple lies in ruins!"

Why is Israel hated by the nations?

> It is written in the Midrash that the Holy One, blessed be He, went about with the Torah to the nations of the world, offering it to each of them in turn, but none would accept. Only Israel took the Torah, and for this they received an added measure of God's love. And because God's love was upon them for accepting the Torah, so were they hated by the other nations. "Therefore," say the sages, "the mountain upon which the Torah was given is called *Sinai* for through what transpired on that mountain, *Sina* [Hebrew for 'hatred'] came to the nations." [1]

According to Levi Yitzhak, exile entails more than the wandering of an afflicted people among the other nations. It encompasses God as well as people, the divine along with the human. Had not the prophets daringly taught that the fate of God was bound up with that of Israel? "In all their afflictions He was afflicted" (Isaiah 63:9). And the wise men of the Talmud and the *Kabbalah*, meditating upon this teaching, declared that when Israel went into darkest exile as an oppressed and vagabond people, God's presence, the *Shekhinah*, descended into exile with them. It is the exile of the *Shekhinah* that is to be grieved over even more than the exile of Israel.

This is how the Rabbi of Berditchev expounded on the verse, "Remember what Amalek did unto thee" (Deuteronomy 25:17).

"Because you are a man," he said, "you first are permitted to remember what the power of evil has done 'to you.' But when you ascend to the rung of the Tzaddikim and your heart has rest from all your enemies round about, then you will 'blot out the remembrance of Amalek from *under* Heaven' (Exodus 17:14) and will remember only what the power of evil has done to Heaven itself; how it set up a wall between God and Israel, and drove into exile the *Shekhinah*."

When will the Messiah come? That is a secret hidden from man. But it is also revealed to him, because the coming of the Messiah depends not only on God's grace but also on man's deeds. "If all Israel would keep two Sabbaths," the Talmud says, "the Messiah would come." Therefore the coming of the Messiah is delayed because we are not ready for him, because we have not yet prepared ourselves for his coming. Our task is to bend our will to God's will in order that we might heal those breaches that separate a man from his fellowman and that rend a man within himself.

While sitting at table with his disciples, Rabbi Levi Yitzhak said, "Let us try to understand that puzzling passage in the Talmud where the Messiah is asked when he will come, and replies with a verse from the Psalms: 'Today, if you will hearken to God's voice.' Now what makes that passage puzzling is this: How could the Messiah come 'today' even if we were to hearken to God's voice, seeing that Elijah did not come yesterday? For it is surely written, 'Behold, I will send to you Elijah the Prophet *before* the coming of the day of the Lord.'

"And do you know, my brothers," he continued, "why it is really necessary for Elijah to come before the Messiah? Because men are devoured by vanities and are consumed by the search for vanities. One frets over a new house, another over his crops, and still another over the price his cows will bring. For the Messiah to come to such people, Elijah would surely have to precede him by at least a day to proclaim his advent, so that we might shake ourselves loose from our dull habits and make ready to receive him. But if the day will ever come when we shall truly hearken to His voice—that is, a day when we shall completely turn away from the vanities of the world and toward the Messiah's coming—then there will be no need of Elijah's visit. Do you understand now, my friends?"

> The secret of the exile is only this: that we might herein raise up the sparks which have fallen because of Adam. And Israel bears the sufferings of exile until the time when all evil will be overcome and every spark will rise to its source. The redemption will surely come and all the dwellers of earth will know that the earth is the Lord's and the fullness thereof, and His great name will be magnified. [2]

During the long wait for the Messiah there have been a host of false messiahs, impostors and charlatans of every sort who, searching for personal glory or suffering from delusions of grandeur, have arisen from time to time in Jewish history. Like blazing meteors they have flashed across the sky for a moment in full splendor, only to disappear as quickly as they came. But how could such men have gained acceptance in the first place? And what purpose, if any, did they serve?

An unbeliever once pointed out to the Rabbi of Berditchev that even the great masters of old had erred gravely—that Rabbi Akiva, for instance, had taken Bar Kokhba, the rebel, for the Messiah and honored him accordingly.

The Rabbi of Berditchev replied, "There was an emperor whose only son fell ill. One physician advised that an acrid salve be spread on a piece of linen and wrapped around the bare body of the patient. Another contradicted him saying that the boy was too weak to bear the pain the salve would cause. A third prescribed a large cup of sleeping potion. A fourth feared this might prove injurious to the patient's heart. Then the fifth physician suggested one final solution: that the linen upon which the salve had been spread should be put around the prince, who should be given but a small spoonful of the sleeping potion so that he would wake up from time to time and not harm his heart. And so it was done.

"When God saw that the soul of Israel had sickened, He wrapped it in the acrid linen of the exile and, that the soul might bear it, He swathed it in numbing sleep. But, lest this destroy it, He wakens it from time to time with hope in a false messiah and then lulls it to rest again until the night is past and the true Messiah appears.

"And for the sake of this, even the eyes of sages are sometimes blinded." [3]

DO NOT DESPAIR

"Jews do not despair!" These words are seen on the walls of some Hasidic houses of prayer even today.

Levi Yitzhak feared that the burden of Israel's suffering, each year heavier and each year more unbearable, might turn them from the true service of God to such sorrow, such weariness, such self-mortification, that despair would distort their service beyond recognition. "And all these curses shall come upon thee," Scripture declares, "because thou didst not serve the Lord thy God with joyfulness and with gladness of heart" (Deuteronomy 28:47). Notice that Scripture does not say that the curse would come because Israel would not serve God—that is, keep the Sabbath and festivals and observe the many Mitzvot—but because they would not serve Him "with joyfulness and with gladness of heart."

"Rabbi," a simple Jew asked, "during the 'three weeks' before Tishah b'Av, the saddest period of our entire year, when we abstain from rejoicing in mourning for the Temple and when, accordingly, we read during those weeks three *Haftarot* of rebuke and calamity, is it not strange that on one of those three Sabbaths we always read *Pinhas*, the portion of the Torah which contains most of the laws dealing with the festivals, wherein we are commanded to rejoice? Is it not strange, Rabbi, this mixing of joy and sorrow?"

"My son," replied the Tzaddik of Berditchev, "at that time of the year the hearts of all Israel, the holy people, are rent in two for the holy city that was destroyed, for the holy Temple that was burned, and for the countless tragedies that befell us century after century, in city after city. Because the memory of those miseries are once again recalled and recounted, drawing fresh blood from old wounds, it is possible, God forbid, that the people might topple into the abyss of despair.

"Therefore we are commanded by the sages of old to take

heart, to read from the Torah during those 'three weeks' precisely that portion which deals with our festivals, so that the spirit of rejoicing which breathes within them may ease our bitterness."

Yet there were times of exaltation when Levi Yitzhak felt the hand of the Lord so strong upon him that bodily wounds were hardly sensed at all.

> How pleasant, how sweet and how good are the wounds we Jews bear and the pains we suffer, for it is through them that His great name is exalted and magnified in our world. [4]

But the question is: Is God's name magnified through Israel's suffering? Even a saint such as Rabbi Levi Yitzhak, though he believed that Israel was a "kingdom of priests and a holy people," had agonizing moments of doubt when he saw the web of misery in which his people were caught. We are told that whenever Rabbi Levi Yitzhak came to that passage in the Haggadah of Passover dealing with the four sons and read about the fourth son—about him "who knows not how to ask"—he would say:

"The one who knows not how to ask—that is myself, Levi Yitzhak of Berditchev. I do not know how to ask You, Lord of the World. And even if I did know, I could not bear to do it. How could I venture to ask You why everything happens as it does, why we are driven from one exile into another, why our foes are allowed to torment us so. But in the Haggadah the father of him 'who knows not how to ask' is told, 'It is for you to disclose it to him.' The Haggadah refers to the Scriptures in which it is written, 'And thou shalt tell thy son.'

"Lord of the World, am I not Your son? I do not beg You to reveal to me the secret of Your ways—I could not bear it! But show me one thing. Show it to me more clearly and more deeply. Show me what this, which is happening at this very moment, means to me—what it demands of me—what You, Lord of the World, are telling me by way of it.

"Ah, it is not *why* I suffer that I wish to know, but only whether or not I suffer for *Your* sake." [5]

WHY THE MESSIAH HAS NOT COME

The Rabbi of Apt, Abraham Joshua Heschel, used to say that Rabbi Levi Yitzhak's love for Israel and his compassion for their suffering in exile did not cease when he died, for the Tzaddik of Berditchev had promised that even when he reached the future world he would not rest until the Messiah would come and bring deliverance for all Israel.

But the heavenly angels, knowing Levi Yitzhak's love of song and prayer, went out to greet him and diverted his attention through their wondrous chants, and have continued to distract him until this very day. That is why he is unable to turn his mind to the needs of our world.

And it is for this reason that the Messiah has not yet come—concluded the Rabbi of Apt—and Israel still suffers.

6

Day-to-Day

BECAUSE OF RABBI LEVI YITZHAK'S love for his people, he preferred to speak of the good that Israel did and to excuse their misdeeds. From this endless love for the Children of Israel have come some of the most memorable stories of the saint of Berditchev. But this does not mean that Levi Yitzhak was ignorant of his people's errors. He was by no means what some writers have pictured him to be: a precious simpleton, amusing and even attractive at times, but hardly to be taken seriously as one of the great leaders of Israel. Quite the contrary. Although a guileless man whose naïvete was legendary, Rabbi Levi Yitzhak was at the same time one of the wisest of his generation. His head touched the Heavens, but his feet were quite firmly planted on the earth;

and his life, far from being removed from the community, was its very heart.

Once he discovered that the girls who kneaded the dough for the Passover *Matzah* drudged from early morning until late at night. Then he cried aloud to the congregation gathered in the House of Prayer, "Those who hate Israel accuse us of baking the unleavened bread with the blood of Christians. But no—we bake it with the blood of Jews!"

A TOPSY-TURVY WORLD

Levi Yitzhak knew his people as a father knows his children, as a shepherd knows his flock. There were occasions, nevertheless, when what he saw of Israel puzzled him and made him sad. The search for material gain was an example. God had given His children so much to wonder at and so many things to sing songs of gratitude for—a child's kiss, the stars in the sky, the Sabbath day, the hand of a friend, the mysteries of Torah. It was difficult for Levi Yitzhak to fathom how men could turn away from the true joys of living in order to sink all their powers into acquiring wealth. What a misuse of precious time! What a loss! he thought. I feel sorry for the rich. Their lives are nothing but worry and anxiety, as is plain to see. They know so little of the real pleasures of this world!

There were times when the sight of the holy people becoming "like unto all the peoples" made him cry out in pain and dismay. The world of "getting and spending" did not exempt the Jew from temptation and corruption. The struggle to gain a livelihood can lead easily to cruelty, exploitation, deceit, and idolatry—the replacing of the old God with a new one.

"What I see before me is a topsy-turvy world," he said to his disciples in a disheartened moment. "Once the whole truth could be found in the alleys and marketplaces of Israel. But when the people came to the House of Prayer on Yom Kippur, they told lies. Now it is just the other way around. In the streets and in the squares they speak falsehoods, but when they enter the House of Prayer on Yom Kippur they confess the truth.

"For once it was thus in Israel: Truth and faithfulness were the lamps lighting their steps and when they went to the marketplace and into the world of trade, with their souls they proved the words, 'Let your "yes" be true and your "no" be true,' and all their trading was done in good faith. But when they came to the House of Prayer they beat their breasts and said, 'We have trespassed!' 'We have dealt treacherously!' 'We have robbed!' And all this was a lie because they had kept faith before God and man. Today the reverse takes place: In trading many lie and cheat; in their prayers they profess the truth." [1]

The love of money above righteousness is also the theme of this tale:

It once happened that Rabbi Levi Yitzhak met a villager and did not tell him who he was. The villager thought that he was a Shohet ("ritual slaughterer") and said to him, "I believe that you are a *Shohet*. Would you be so kind as to do some work for me and I will pay you well for it."

Rabbi Levi Yitzhak, who did not like the easy way in which the man had approached him without inquiring into his credentials for such holy labor, answered the villager, "Yes, I will do it for you. However, would you lend me twenty rubles, which I will repay after a few days?"

The villager replied in surprise, "Shall I lend money to a stranger whom I do not even know?"

Said Rabbi Levi Yitzhak, "Let your ears hear what your mouth has said: Over the small sum of twenty rubles you are afraid to trust me because you do not know me well enough, but over the laws of the Torah you are willing to trust me regardless!"

The race for success often makes men forget their family and faith in the effort to push ahead.

One day Levi Yitzhak saw a man hurrying along the street looking neither right nor left.

"Why are you rushing so?" he asked the man.

"After my livelihood."

"And how do you know," asked the rabbi, "that your

livelihood is running on before you so that you have to rush after it? Perhaps it is behind you and all you need do to encounter it is to stand still. In that case, you are running away from it!"

Another time he was at a great fair and saw the people rushing back and forth, caught up in the race for business. He went up to the roof of one of the nearby houses and shouted at the mob, "My children! You are forgetting God!"

THE PEOPLE'S MISERY

Words of condemnation did not come easily from the Rabbi of Berditchev. He did not berate his people from some lofty vantage point, immune to their concerns. Levi Yitzhak knew only too well the misery of his people. They struggled against cruel laws that prevented them from living where they wished and trading as others could, that squeezed from them heavy taxes and often turned them into pawns of the local princes. He suffered in his people's suffering and he understood their physical needs as well as their spiritual needs.

> TEXT:
> "Not for us, not for us, O Lord, but for Thy great name give glory" [Psalms 115:1].
>
> EXPLANATION:
> Even in this world we seek good things from the Lord, that is to say, our daily bread and the like. And we do so with justice. I shall tell you why. We would happily endure poverty in this world if, instead of cursing us for it, the nations would understand that our portion is reserved for the future world. But this is not the way of the nations. When they behold the privations of Israel, they continue to blaspheme, saying, "Where is their God?" Therefore do we seek the good things of this world. For even though by right we have no share in them, You should give them to us, O Lord, in order that Your name be not profaned.
> And this is the meaning of the verse: "Not for us, O

Lord." That is to say, not for our sake do we seek these good things. "But for Your name give glory." That is to say, why should the nations cry, "Where is their God?" For Your own sake You should help us with the good things of this world, so that Your name be not cursed, Heaven forbid, but sanctified. [2]

A miraculous tale is told about Levi Yitzhak at the time of the fair in Berditchev. Among the farmers and traders who came to this fair were many pious Jews and students of the Torah. During one unfortunate year all the days of the fair passed and they had still not sold their merchandise. They went to the rabbi and lamented their lot, for now they would not be able to pay their debts.

The rabbi cried out, "Master of the World, why do we need a livelihood? Only because You chose to put our soul into a body that requires food and clothing and housing. If there are no buyers, then You should send them angels who will buy!"

The next day, according to the story, a number of men came whose destination and origin were unknown and bought up all the goods.

The Mitzvot of the Torah are meant to ennoble man and raise him up. But do they help if a man is no longer a man, if he is reduced to a haggard beast scurrying in search of scraps of food to keep body and soul together? Of what use is it to welcome the Sabbath if the winter wind causes frail bodies to shiver, or if there is not enough food on the table to stop the pangs of hunger? Man is not an angel who soars aloft without needs or wants; man is flesh and blood, and to be a man the blood must be red and the flesh must be firm.

Such were the thoughts in the mind of Levi Yitzhak when he proclaimed, "Jacob our Father said, 'If God will be with me and will give me bread to eat and clothing to wear, then the Lord "shall be" my God' " (Genesis 28:20).

"Now the verb 'shall be' [Hebrew: *V'hayah*] is commonly used in Scripture to imply rejoicing and, according to the rabbis, it is surely used so in this verse. For would there not be great rejoicing in all the world if all Jews had bread to eat and clothing to wear, so they might be able more easily to fulfill the words, 'Serve the Lord with joy,' which is the essence of the service of God?"

The Rabbi of Berditchev saluted those who withstood temptation in earning their daily bread, for he was well acquainted with the countless pitfalls along the way.

The wife of Rabbi Levi Yitzhak, it is said, once came before the court in Berditchev with a complaint and a claim. She said, "My husband, Levi Yitzhak, does not provide for the needs of our house. He is not fulfilling the promise which is written in our *Ketubah* ["marriage contract"] 'to provide for her [his wife] in the manner of Jewish husbands!' "

Rabbi Levi Yitzhak was called to the court and informed of what his wife had said.

What did Rabbi Levi Yitzhak do? He brought the *Ketubah*, unrolled it before the court, put his finger upon the words to which his wife referred and explained: "Look, immediately after the words 'to provide for her in the manner of Jewish husbands,' it is written 'who provide for their wives *in truth*,' that is, with complete honesty, without falseness or deceit.

"Money such as this is not easily come by!"[3]

HALLOWING THE EVERYDAY

The teaching of the *Kabbalists* that only the soul was precious while the body was the source of sin and should therefore be disparaged, was not the way of normative Judaism and was opposed from the beginning by the Baal Shem and his followers. The Rabbi of Berditchev joined this fight and waged a vigorous battle.

"Do we not pray," he said, " 'the soul which Thou hast given me is pure?' But did the Almighty not also give us the body? How then is it possible to slander the body? Who puts on *Tefillin* each day? The body. Who gives power to the soul? The body. Who fulfills the Mitzvot, builds the *Sukkah*, eats *Matzot*, keeps the Sabbath? The body. The body learns Torah, prays, and recites,

'Hear, O Israel, the Lord is our God, the Lord is One.' Heaven forbid that we should despise the body!

"We must not mortify our flesh! It is nothing but the tempting of the Evil Urge who delights in weakening our spirit in order to keep us from serving God rightly.

"Once two strong men were struggling with each other and neither could prevail over his opponent. Then one of them had an idea. 'Instead of striking wildly and hitting first one limb and then another,' he said, 'I shall take care and strike his head, for if I do that all of his limbs will be weakened and I shall be victorious.'

"That is just what the Evil Urge wants to do when it tempts us to mortify our flesh."

The verse which best sums up Judaism's attitude toward wordly matters is "Know Him in *all* thy ways" (Proverbs 3:6). This verse, to which the Talmud refers as the fundamental teaching of the Torah, reveals something so obvious and yet so radical, that most religions have never understood it. Instead they choose to pit soul against body, spirit against matter, heaven against earth. God, the verse says, can be known—that is, served and loved—in all our deeds, not only through prayer and Torah study, but through each of our acts—through the most ordinary and common deeds. It is not so much what we do as how we do it.

> **Everything that the Holy One, blessed be He, created in this world was created only for His glory—even material things. For example, when a man sits down to eat and drink, let his mind dwell upon the thought that he nourishes his body in order that it might better serve his Creator in strength and health; or when he performs his marital duties, let him understand that he is fulfilling the commandment of the Lord. And so it is with all matters of the flesh. For in this way he is able to raise up the hidden holy sparks to their divine source. When you desire to eat and drink or to perform other wordly desires, and you keep in mind the thought that it is for the love of God that you do this, then you elevate physical desire into spiritual desire, and consequently, you are able to draw out the holy spark that dwells within it.**

> And this is the mystery of the blessing over the washing of the hands, *N'tilat Yadayim*, for *N'tilah* means "raising up." And this too is the secret of the blessing over the bread, "... Who brings forth bread from the earth," for "bread" is a mystical symbol of holiness, and "earth" refers to earthy, material qualities, thus implying that one "brings forth" the holy hidden sparks [bread] from the material world [the earth]. When a man walks in this path, he gives evidence of the deep and abiding love that dwells within him for the Holy One, blessed be He, and there is no path greater than this. For in every place that a man walks and in everything that a man does—even seemingly unimportant things of this world—he is able to serve the Creator, blessed be He.[4]

The purpose of the Torah and the Mitzvot, if we understand them correctly, is to help us learn how to raise up all of life—not only the so-called spiritual aspects of it—to God. The task of man is to sanctify his entire existence.

Levi Yitzhak liked to express this thought very simply, with parables and striking explanations of Biblical verses. He taught that while those scholars whose learning made them arrogant and aloof traveled a perilous path to the divine, the simple man, though not learned and so pressed by his work that only scant time could he find for Torah and prayer, might find a way to God through his daily deeds.

> When a man fulfills a wordly act, let his desire be to thereby serve God. That is to say, for example, when he is threshing his wheat or hoeing his crops his intent should be to thresh or hoe in order that from his labor he will derive the food from whose eating he will be enabled to study Torah and to obey the Lord.[5]
>
> How wretched is the privation of the people Israel. There are those whose search for sustenance gives them little leisure for the study of the Torah. Yet even for them there is a way. As King Solomon said, "Know the Lord in all your ways." Thus at the very moment when one is immersed in worldly affairs

he may study Torah. For example, if a man goes to the market and meets a woman but determines not to look at her or at her garments [because he remembers the law that forbids one to look at the garments of woman], then it is as if he were studying that particular law of the Torah.

Or if in the market where men conduct themselves without restraint it would be easy for him to tell a falsehood but he does not do so [because he remembers the verse, "Thou shalt not bear false witness against thy neighbor"], it is as though he were studying that verse.

And when a shopkeeper sells his merchandise according to the proper weight [because he remembers the verse, "An honest weight shall there be for you"], it is as if he were studying that particular verse.[6]

"Since a portion of God is in all things, and all things exist through God," Rabbi Levi Yitzhak taught, "it follows that one can serve God by means of all things—not only prayer and Torah study—but at all times, no matter what one is doing."

A poor wagon-driver came to Rabbi Levi Yitzhak with a question. He explained that while he faithfully recited the morning and evening prayers himself, the hours of his work prevented him from attending the synagogue service. From early morning until after sunset he traveled with his horse and wagon up and down the countryside, and so he could not pray daily with a *Minyan*, as is proper. He wondered whether in view of this violation he should not give up his work and seek another occupation, and this was the question he put to the rabbi.

Rabbi Levi Yitzhak replied with another question, "Tell me, when you meet someone walking along the road, do you take him into your wagon without payment?"

"Certainly," answered the driver, "Can a Jew do otherwise?"

"If so," concluded Rabbi Levi Yitzhak, "you should not change your livelihood, for what you are now doing is precious in the eyes of God."

How can one serve God except by first serving man? And how can one understand God except by first understanding man?

Secluding oneself from life's challenges is no guarantee of divine grace. Perhaps the reverse is the way. Perhaps the path to the divine is through the path to the human. To brighten Heaven, lights must be kindled along all the streets of earth, even the humblest.

As head of the Jewish court in Berditchev, problems of every sort came before Levi Yitzhak. Once two wealthy merchants, who owned forests and dealt in lumber, arrived with a dispute which involved an exceptionally large sum of money. As the case proceeded and evidence was presented, one of the litigants, realizing that the judgment would go against him, began to cast about with various arguments in an effort to extricate himself. In desperation he said at last, "Perhaps the holy Rabbi of Berditchev is unfamiliar with such mundane matters as business contracts and lumber prices and the like."

With a smile Levi Yitzhak replied, "Were we dealing with Heavenly matters you might be right. In Torah perhaps you exceed me, and in piety you surely do. But we are dealing now with wordly matters—with business transactions—and I am quite at home in the affairs of men. I understand them better than you do."

At the close of the Day of Atonement the Rabbi of Berditchev said to one of his Hasidim: "I know what you prayed for this day! On the eve you begged God to give you the thousand rubles—which you need to live on during the entire year—all at once, now, at the beginning of the year, so that the toil and trouble of business may not distract you from learning and prayer. But in the morning you thought better of it and decided that if you had the thousand rubles all at once you would probably launch a new and bigger business enterprise which would take up even more of your time. And so you begged to receive half the amount every half year. And before *Neilah*, the Closing Prayer, this too seemed precarious to you, and you expressed the wish for quarterly installments, so you might learn and pray quite undisturbed. But what makes you think that your learning and praying is needed in Heaven? Perhaps what is needed there is that you toil and rack your brains."

SUBLIMATION

Sublimation, that miraculous inner transformation which has been explored and described by modern psychologists, was long a part of the program of spiritual health which Levi Yitzhak held to be fundamental to Hasidism.

"What should one do," he asked, "if he is seized by a fierce love for one of the vanities of the world of which he is not able to rid himself, despite the anguish it causes him?

"The matter is thus," he said, answering his own question. "There are times when a man is unable to drive out of his heart a 'lower' love which he feels. The solution to the problem is neither to make it flee from him nor for him to flee from it, lest it follow after him or he follow after it, but to raise it to a higher level. That is to say, you must think of what the source of all love is—the Creator, the Life of all life. Then you will say to yourself, 'Why have I been so foolishly drawn after this or that love, which has only a spark of the great fire which nourishes all love? Is it not better to turn and attach my love to the cause and source of all love, the Holy One, blessed be He?' Therefore not only will you not feel shame after having stopped up your 'lower' love for whatever it was directed to, but your love will be elevated to a higher and mightier level of love. Thus, by joining your love to God, you will have redeemed it, purifying it from its dross and leaving only the good and pure. It is like a coat to which thorns and thistles and dust cling. Do not throw the coat away. Shake it until it is clean."

> There is love that is private and there is love that is public.
>
> Private love is the love between husband and wife, for it is expressed behind closed doors.
>
> Public love is the love between brother and sister, for it may be expressed before the eyes of others. Out of affection they may kiss one another openly, and there is no shame in this.
>
> We should understand the verse—"O that your love for me was that of a brother" [Song of Songs 8:10]—as if the Lord

were pleading with us, "O that your love for *Me* was that of a brother!" That is, even when you find My holy sparks in wordly and seemingly unimportant matters, even there will you raise them to their source.

And this is the mystery of the kiss.[7]

IDLE CHATTER

"It was the custom of Levi Yitzhak" writes his disciple, Rabbi Israel of Koznitz, "while garbed in his *Tallit* and crowned with his *Tefillin*, to discuss all manner of wordly matters with people. [Let this not serve as an example for others to freely follow!] On so exalted a rung did he stand, that while in conversation with simple men he could raise their words up to their higher source."[8]

When Rabbi Levi Yitzhak came to Nikolsburg to visit Rabbi Shmelke, who had taught him the way of serving God when he was young and whom he had not seen in several years, he went on the very first morning wrapped in his *Tallit* and wearing double *Tefillin* on his forehead, into the kitchen and asked Rabbi Shmelke's wife what dishes were being prepared for the noonday meal. Although she was surprised, she answered his question. Then he went on to ask whether the cooks had really mastered their art and other questions similar in nature. Rabbi Shmelke's disciples, who heard of this, took him for a veritable glutton. Next he entered the House of Prayer and, while the congregation prayed, began to talk to an utterly worthless fellow, despised by all, about quite unimportant wordly subjects.

One of the disciples could not bear to observe this behavior any longer and said roughly to the stranger, "Silence! Idle chatter is forbidden here!"

But the Rabbi of Berditchev paid no attention to him and continued his conversation.

At the midday meal Rabbi Shmelke greeted Levi Yitzhak joyfully, bade him sit at his side, and ate from the same bowl while his disciples, who had heard of the curious manners of the visitor, marked these signs of favor and friendship with sullen surprise. When the meal was over, one of them could no longer suppress his annoyance and asked his master why he showered honors on so empty-headed and impudent a man.

The Tzaddik replied, "In the Talmud we read, 'Rav, during all the days of his life, never spoke of worldly matters.' Is this praise not strange? Does it indicate that the other masters spent their time in worldly talk? Can nothing worthier be told of Rav? The meaning is this: Whatever worldly affairs he discussed with people in the course of the day, each of his words was, in reality, filled with deeper significance and purpose in an attempt to hallow even the most common acts of this world; and his spirit remained steadfast in such service all day long. That is why our sages have accorded him praise of which none other was found worthy. What others could do for only three hours—after which they sank from this level—he could do throughout the day.

"And the same is true of Rabbi Levi Yitzhak. What I can do for only three hours, he can do the whole day through. He concentrates his spirit so that even the talk which men consider idle makes itself felt in the world of Heaven."

7

Humility

RABBI LEVI YITZHAK of Berditchev was among the humblest men of his generation.

In Warsaw he met a Jew, a coarse, common fellow by the name of Beinush.

"Beinush, my brother," said the rabbi, "pay attention to what I say. Cling with love to the Higher Source, to the Merciful One, Beinush, my brother, and you will see that there is nothing more precious than this."[1]

Thus would he enter into conversation with the lowliest of people and thereby draw them to the Torah and its observance. He never raised himself above them or looked down on them. "Even if pride were commanded in the Torah," he said, "I still could not believe it possible, for man is but 'dust and ashes.' How then should he be proud?"

When the news became known that he had been appointed rabbi of the city of Berditchev, Levi Yitzhak said, "Woe to the generation if such as the likes of me can become its leader!"

It was Levi Yitzhak's custom to invite to his *Sukkah* simple unlearned men.

"Our master," his disciples asked, "why do you ask these men to be here with us each year?"

"I shall explain it to you," replied Rabbi Levi Yitzhak. "In the world to come, when the Tzaddikim are sitting at the holy feast in the heavenly *Sukkah*, I shall come there and seek to be admitted. But they will refuse me. For who am I that I should sit among true Tzaddikim? Then I shall present my case: that I too invited simple and unlearned men into my *Sukkah*."[2]

He who causes pride to enter his heart, Rabbi Levi Yitzhak used to say, transgresses a law of the Torah: "Thou shalt not bring an abomination into thy house" (Deuteronomy 7:26). For there is no abomination greater than the abomination of pride. And there is a verse to indicate this: "An abomination of the Lord is every lofty heart" (Proverbs 16:5). If one who causes pride to enter his house sins, how much the more so one who causes it to enter his heart!

Because Levi Yitzhak lived in the presence of God and because God, not his own interests, was the center of his life, he was neither flattered by praise nor offended by scorn. Before he came to Berditchev, while walking through the street of one of the communities where he served as rabbi and was bitterly persecuted by the Mitnagdim, he passed the wife of one of those who disliked him. She spat upon him and cursed him. Without so much as turning his head, he hastened to the *Bet ha-Midrash*, approached the Holy Ark and said, "Master of all worlds, do not punish this woman. She is a good woman and only does the will of her husband."

When God is truly the center of a man's life, taught the Tzaddik of Berditchev, that man is not jealous of his neighbor's success, for the main thing is to love God and to serve Him and further His kingdom. It matters not who serves God best, only that He be served.

"Whether a man really loves God," Levi Yitzhak said, "can be determined by the love he bears his fellowmen, which, in turn, depends on his selflessness. I shall give you a parable:

"Once upon a time a country was suffering from the ravages of war. The army which had been sent against the enemy was defeated. The king discharged the general of the army and put in his place another who succeeded in driving out the invader. The first general was suspected of having betrayed his country. The king wondered how he could find out whether he was loyal or not. He decided that if the man about whom he was in doubt showed friendship for his rival and expressed true joy at his success, he might be regarded as trustworthy. But if he grew jealous and plotted against his rival, this would prove his guilt.

"God created man to strive against the evil in his soul. There is many a man who does indeed love God but is defeated in that bitter struggle. He can be recognized by his ability to share wholeheartedly and without reservation in the happiness of his victorious fellowman."

When a Jew studies Torah or performs a Mitzvah he must do so for the sake of God. And even after he has done so, the thought must not arise in his heart, Heaven forbid, that he has already fulfilled the will of the Creator. He who thinks thus—his deeds are not accepted, for he has not even reached the threshold of true service. But the true servant of God, although he has performed a Mitzvah with all his heart, remains humble in the awareness that he has still not served the Lord, for the awe of Heaven is upon him.

A parable: Once there was a man who wanted to enter the palace of the king. The closer he came into the inner chambers of the palace, the more he saw of the treasures and the glory of the king and the smaller he felt.

So it is with the Mitzvot. The greater the love and fear

with which one fulfills a Mitzvah, the deeper he merits to penetrate into the inner recesses of the temple of the King; and the more he beholds of the majesty of the King, blessed be His name, the more unworthy he knows himself to be.

Thus the man whose pride stirs him to think that his deeds have satisfied the Creator, he is not even upon the threshold of service.

But the Tzaddik is as nothing in his own eyes, believing that he has still not begun to serve the Lord, Whom he beseeches to open a way for him that he might enter and serve. And this is the meaning of the verse, "Open to me the gates of righteousness.... This is the gate of the Lord; let the Tzaddikim enter into it" [Psalms 118:19-20].

All the while [such] a man cleaves to the holiness of the Creator, blessed be He, he imagines himself to be far away.

How then should he know when he is near to the holiness of the Creator?

When he believes he is distant, this is the sign that he is near.[3]

Once Rabbi Levi Yitzhak celebrated the *Seder* of the first night of Passover so devoutly that every word and every rite at the Tzaddik's table glowed with all the holiness of its secret significance. Afterward he sat in his room, joyful and proud that he had performed so successful a service. Suddenly he heard a voice saying, "More pleasing to me than your *Seder* is that of Hayim the water-carrier."

The rabbi trembled. He summoned his disciples and the people in his house and inquired about the man whose name he had heard. Nobody knew him. At the Tzaddik's bidding, some of his disciples went in search of Hayim. They asked around a long time before, at the outskirts of the city, where only the poor families lived, they were shown the house of Hayim the water-carrier. They knocked at the door. A woman came out and asked what they wanted. When they told her, she was amazed.

"Yes," she said, "Hayim the water-carrier is my husband. But he cannot go with you because he drank a lot yesterday and is sleeping it off now. If you wake him, you will find that he cannot manage to lift his feet."

All they said in reply was, "It is the rabbi's order."

They went and shook Hayim from his sleep. He only blinked at them, could not understand what they wanted him for, and tried to turn over and go back to sleep. But they raised him from his bed, took hold of him and brought him, all but carrying him on their shoulders, to the Tzaddik. The rabbi had Hayim put in a chair near him and when he was seated, silent and bewildered, Levi Yitzhak leaned toward him and spoke as one friend to another, "Hayim, dear heart, what mystic intention was in your mind when you gathered the *Hametz*?"

The water-carrier looked at him dully, shook his head, and replied, "Master, I just looked into every corner and gathered it together."

The astonished Tzaddik continued questioning him. "And what *Kavvanah* did you have in your mind when you burned it?"

The man pondered, looked distressed, and said hesitatingly, "Master, I forgot to burn it. And now I remember—it is all still lying on the shelf."

When Rabbi Levi Yitzhak heard this, he grew more and more uncertain, but he continued his questions.

"And tell me, Reb Hayim, how did you celebrate the *Seder*?"

"I shall tell you the truth," answered Hayim, hanging his head in guilt. "You see, I always heard that it is forbidden to drink brandy the eight days of the festival, so yesterday morning I drank enough to last me eight days. Before I knew it I got tired and fell asleep. When it was evening my wife woke me angrily. 'You sot!' she cried. 'Why don't you celebrate the *Seder* like all other Jews?'

"Said I, 'What do you want from me? I am an ignorant man and my father was an ignorant man, and I don't know what to do and what not to do. One thing, however, I know: Our fathers and mothers were slaves in the land of the Gypsies [Egypt]. But we have a God and He took them out and into freedom. And now—may the Lord pardon me for saying it—we are again slaves. But I tell you that God will lead us to freedom, too!'

"And then I saw before me a table and the cloth gleamed like the sun, and on it were platters with Matzot and eggs and other dishes and bottles of red wine. I ate of the Matzot and eggs and drank of the wine and gave my wife to eat and to drink. And then I was overcome with joy and lifted my cup to God and said, 'See, God, I drink this cup to You! Now You lean down to us and make us free!' So we sat and drank and rejoiced before God. And then I felt tired, lay down, and fell asleep."

"Take this good man to his house," Rabbi Levi Yitzhak said to his *Shammash*.

Later he told his disciples, "Now I understand why the Lord preferred Hayim the water-carrier's *Seder* to mine."[4]

Levi Yitzhak believed that man should always be generous toward others but critical of himself. "To search out transgressions and to speak words of praise," he wrote, "are two good qualities which every Jew is obliged to possess. However, it is necessary to understand in what manner they should be used.

"Transgressions, a man should search out in himself. Praise, however, he should speak in regard to others. And not the reverse."

But it seems that he himself sometimes forgot this good advice. He writes of an early period of his life: "When I saw that the people of my city did not heed me, I began to examine my deeds. Soon I discovered that the members of my own household did not respect me, and so I looked further into my ways. At last the Almighty opened my eyes so that I realized the error was in myself, in that I failed to conduct myself as I should have. I determined to improve myself. When the members of my household noticed this, they began to listen to me and, soon after, the people of the city stopped criticizing me and no longer refused to accept my opinions."

The problem of pride is eternal, and the battle against it is never ending. The Tzaddik knows that man is the least static of creatures, that love of self is always present in him and must be met and defeated through self-judgment and sublimation of self-love to the love of God.

Once Levi Yitzhak asked his friend, Rabbi Shneur Zalman, "What counsel can you give to the man who struggles mightily to subdue his ego?"

Replied Shneur Zalman, "If possible, drive it away. And if not, then at least be consoled by the fact that the Almighty, of Whom it is written, 'He made everything for His own glory,' was also touched by self-interest during the creation of the world."

"Consolation!" said Levi Yitzhak. "But all these acts of self-interest which the Holy One, blessed be He, did, were done for the sake of Heaven!"

No man, even the Tzaddik, can destroy the Evil Urge within. It is our constant companion, tempting, trying and following after us wherever we go, always surprising us just when we think it is defeated. But to be aware of this fact and not fool ourselves is half the battle.

As has already been told, Levi Yitzhak, while still quite young, was known far and wide as a brilliant student of the Talmud and Codes. One of the wealthiest Jews of Libertov, Israel Peretz, heard of his achievements and chose him as husband for his daughter. It was arranged for Levi Yitzhak to live with his wife's family and spend his time in the study of Torah as was the custom. The young man's good fortune—to be a noted scholar married to the daughter of a wealthy man—was the talk of the town.

As a mark of respect for his prominent father-in-law, the congregants honored Levi Yitzhak on Simhat Torah in the first year of his marriage by asking him to recite the passage *Atah Hareita* before the congregation in the House of Prayer. The *Shammash* called him to the pulpit in a voice so loud, and marked by so many trills, that everyone's eyes were upon him. Levi Yitzhak went to the pulpit and for a while stood motionless. Then he put out his hand to take his *Tallit* but laid it down again and stood without moving, as before. The heads of the community bade the beadle whisper to him not to weary the assemblage, but to begin. "Very well," Levi Yitzhak said and took the *Tallit* in his hand. But when he had almost covered his shoulders, he laid it back. His father-in-law was ashamed before the congregation, especially since he had often boasted of the excellent young man he had gained for his house. Angrily he sent Levi Yitzhak a message that he should either begin the prayer or leave the pulpit. But before the message could be delivered Levi Yitzhak's voice suddenly rang through the hall. "If you are versed in the teachings, if you are a Hasid, then *you* speak the prayer!" And with this he returned to his place.

His father-in-law said nothing. But when they were at home and Levi Yitzhak sat opposite him at the festive table, his face bright with the joy befitting the day, his father-in-law could contain himself no longer and shouted, "Why did you bring this disgrace upon me?"

The young man replied, "When I first put out my hand to draw the *Tallit* over my head, the Evil Urge came and whispered in my ear, 'I want to say *Atah Hareita* with you!'

"I asked, 'Who are you that you regard yourself worthy of this?'

"And he answered, 'Who are you that you regard yourself worthy to do this?'

" 'I am versed in the teachings.'

" 'I, too am versed in the teachings.'

"I thought to put an end to this idle talk and said contemptuously, 'Where did you study?'

" 'Where did *you* study?' he countered.

"I told him.

" 'But I was right there with you!' he murmured laughingly. 'I studied there in your company!'

"I pondered for a moment. 'I am a Hasid!' I informed him triumphantly.

"And he, unperturbed, said, 'I, too, am a Hasid.'

"I asked, 'To what Tzaddik did you travel?'

"And he replied, again echoing me, 'To whom did *you* travel?'

" 'To the holy Maggid of Mezritch,' I replied.

"Whereupon he laughed again. 'But I tell you that I was there with you and became a Hasid just as you did. And that is why I want to say with you *Atah Hareita*.'

"Then I had had enough of it. 'If you are versed in the teachings,' I said, 'if you are a Hasid, then *you* speak the prayer.'

"At that I left him. What else could I have done?"[5]

There is no final conquest of self. The ego is too elusive, subtle, and deceiving. It is an eternal struggle demanding eternal vigilance.

Each evening before he went to sleep it was the custom of Rabbi Levi Yitzhak to take a *Heshbon ha-Nefesh*—that is, to examine his thoughts and deeds for that day. If he found a blemish in them, he would say to himself, "Levi Yitzhak will not do that again."

Then he would chide himself, "Levi Yitzhak, you said the same thing yesterday."

Then he would reply, "Yesterday Levi Yitzhak did not speak the truth. Today he speaks the truth."

Sometimes the study of Torah can lead to the pride of superior knowledge, and such pride was characteristic of many of the scholars of the time. The writings of the early Hasidic leaders warned against this danger. Rabbi Levi Yitzhak taught that the Torah requires humility of Israel.

Once he was asked the question, "How is it that Moses, who humbly had implored God not to send him to Pharaoh, did not hesitate for a single instant on his mission to receive the Torah?"

"He had seen the tall mountains come before God," said the rabbi, "and each beg the privilege of being the one on which the revelation should come to pass. But God chose little Mount Sinai. That is why, when he saw that he, too, was chosen, Moses did not resist but followed the call."[6]

Rabbi Levi Yitzhak asked his disciples, "Why is it that the tractates of the Talmud are printed in a manner different from ordinary books? For each book of the Talmud begins on page two instead of page one."

When no one replied, he answered his own question, "In order that one should know that no matter how much he has learned, he has still not even begun."

TEXT:
"If one should sin through error by doing any of the Mitzvot which the Lord has forbidden to be done . . ." [Leviticus 4:2].

EXPLANATION:
Why in this verse does the Torah use the word "Mitzvah" in reference to a sinful act? To teach that the Lord detests pride. The more one serves the Lord, the more humbled he ought to be before the awesomeness of the Creator. But the Mitzvah which is performed with the vanity that God's very will is being done is accounted for naught; while the one who performs it thus has, in truth, sinned.[7]

Beware, however, of overmuch humility!

That man must strive for meekness in all his ways is axiomatic. Heaven forbid, however, that this should affect his service to God! For if a man would think, "Of what value are the deeds of such a clod of dirt as I to the Lord of all the worlds?" and thereupon perform the Mitzvot hesitantly—he would be denying the Creator Himself! Rather should each one say to himself, "The Mitzvot I do are dear, very dear, to God."[8]

The truly humble know that words, miraculous mirrors though they may be, are but clumsy tools; the hidden depths of the soul remain inaccessible to even the most eloquent poems. This is why the Hasidim so loved to sing songs without words, because their yearning for God soared beyond any text. This, too, is why there were times when Tzaddikim could meet and communicate with one another without uttering a single syllable. It is told that when Rabbi Levi Yitzhak served as Rabbi of Pinsk, Rabbi Shlomo was a poor *Melammed* in the nearby city of Karlin. Once Rabbi Levi Yitzhak sent his *Shammash* to Karlin to find Rabbi Shlomo and bring him to Pinsk. The messenger searched for days until he located someone who could tell him where the poor *Melammed* lived. When he had found him at last and told him of his master's request, Rabbi Shlomo said, "Good, I shall go."

As he entered Levi Yitzhak's house, the rabbi rose from his seat and said, "*Barukh ha-Ba*. Welcome, Rabbi Shlomo of Karlin. Let the honorable Rabbi Shlomo of Karlin be seated."

Then both sat down. But not one word escaped their lips. After some time they suddenly rose and each smiled at the other. Rabbi Shlomo departed from Rabbi Levi Yitzhak in silence. Neither those of the household nor the others who were nearby understood the meaning of that smile.

8

Between God and Man

WHEN SPEAKING ABOUT the Rabbi of Berditchev to his Hasidim, Rabbi Barukh of Mezibosh, the aloof grandson of the Baal Shem who frequently criticized the Tzaddikim, said, "The very angels of Heaven envy his marvelous love and fear of God." [1]

Rabbi Elimelekh testified to the Rabbi of Zanz that just as a man trembles who is suddenly surrounded by robbers while walking through a forest, so did the heart of Rabbi Levi Yitzhak beat within him out of fear of God, even when he was asleep.

BEYOND ALL BOUNDS

Where does God dwell? is a question that Rabbi Levi Yitzhak pondered.

Where is God? He is beyond all bounds. With all our philosophy, He continues to elude us; with all our mental searching, He is always yonder.

> The voice that came to Job out of the whirlwind cried:
> "Who is this that darkeneth counsel by words without
>   knowledge?
> Gird up now thy loins like a man;
> For I will demand of thee.
>
> Where wast thou when I laid the foundations of the earth?
> Declare, if thou hast understanding.
> Who determined the measures thereof if thou knowest?
> Or who laid the cornerstone thereof?
> When the morning stars sang together
> And all the sons of God shouted for joy? . . . "
>
> For My thoughts are not your thoughts,
> Neither are your ways My ways, saith the Lord.
> For as the Heavens are higher than the earth,
> So are My ways higher than your ways,
> And My thoughts than your thoughts.
>
> (Job 38:1-7, Isaiah 55:8-9)

When Rabbi Shneur Zalman of Ladi—the *Rav* as he was called—had written his celebrated work, the *Tanya*, it was received by the Hasidim of that generation with honor and awe. As soon as the book reached the hands of Rabbi Levi Yitzhak of Berditchev, he studied it thoroughly from beginning to end.

After he had completed his examinations he said, "How noble is the achievement of Rabbi Shneur Zalman that he is able to contract the glory of God, Who is beyond all bounds, into one small thin book!"

Rabbi Elimelekh once said, "Rabbi Levi Yitzhak of Berditchev's way in Hasidism was opposite to the way of Rabbi Shneur Zalman. The latter built his way on the foundations of HaBaD:

Hokhmah ["wisdom"], *Binah* ["understanding"] and *Da'at* ["knowledge"].

"The way of Rabbi Levi Yitzhak was different. He built on the feeling of the heart which burns, without reflection or inquiry, with such love and fear of the Almighty that nothing else matters: 'The Merciful One desires the heart.'"

God dwells in the Heavens, Creator and Lord over all, infinite, majestic, beyond all imagination. Finite man ever yearns to draw the Infinite One down to earth.

"There are worlds," said Levi Yitzhak, "in which one is able to see the *Shekhinah* and these are the Upper Worlds, for in them the love and fear of God is revealed. However, in our world His dominion is hidden and His ways are covered over. Now all the worlds—from that of the Heavenly Throne down to the one which is below—yearn to serve the Lord, the living God, for it is He Who sustains them. Those who live in the lower world, the world of man, desire that God illumine it as He has already illumined the Upper World—that His ways and His kingdom be made manifest and that all may serve Him. Like the pauper who dreams of wealth, so does the lower world yearn to have His ways and His kingdom revealed for they are poor in the knowledge of God."

IN TORAH

Where is God?

He can be found in the Torah. And since He dwells in the Torah, when Israel studies Torah they are not only learning, a discipline of the mind, but they are also communing with the Infinite One, an activity of the soul. For Torah-study is, in truth, a form of prayer wherein the student is caught up in a divine world of holiness which the glory of God inhabits. "When three sit and study Torah," the Mishnah teaches, "the *Shekhinah* dwells among them."

"It is written in the Book of Isaiah [51:4]: 'For Torah shall go forth from Me.' How shall we interpret this?" asked Levi Yitzhak. "For we believe with perfect faith that the Torah which Moses received on Mount Sinai cannot be changed, that none other will be given, and that we are forbidden to question even one of its letters. The answer is that we comprehend only the meaning of the black letters but not the white gaps between the letters. There will come a time, Isaiah foretells, when God will reveal even the white hiddenness of the Torah."

The Baal Shem explained the verse of the Psalms, "The Torah of the Lord is perfect," to mean that the Torah is still quite perfect: even after generations of study, we have not yet begun to fathom it.

IN MIRACLES

Should we look for God in miracles?

God brought ten plagues upon the Egyptians; He split the Sea of Reeds before the Israelites; He made the sun stand still for Joshua; He brought miraculous healing for Elisha; He gave Israel victories against enemies greater in number and better armed. God is to be found in such miracles. Indeed, Levi Yitzhak warns, that is the very danger; in perceiving the miraculous, we may forget God.

> When the Holy One, blessed be He, works wonders for us—for all Israel or for one man alone—let not the source of our joy derive from the miracle itself—that is from the benefit we derive from it—but rather from the fact that through the wonder we are able to perceive the love of the Lord. And this is what King David said:
>
> "This was the *Lord's* doing; it is marvelous in our eyes. This is the day which the *Lord* has made; we will rejoice and be glad thereon" [Psalms 118:23-4].[2]

What is a miracle? Must the sea split, the sun halt in its course, or a river turn to blood for men to know God's glory? Can He not be found elsewhere? This finding of God elsewhere, Levi Yitzhak claims, is a difference between Israel and the nations, for

> the nations are able to perceive God through His miracles in the world of nature. Israel, however, is able to perceive even that which surpasses nature.[3]

There are two ways to faith in God.

One way is through believing in the wonders of old.

The other way is by understanding that each moment God renews our lives through the bounty of His blessing.[4]

IN MAN

Where is God?

He is present within each of His creatures. God is both Creator and Revealer, both transcendent beyond the heavens of the heavens and immanent within man himself. Man possesses a "portion of the divine above." By the very fact of his creation, he is not a separate, autonomous creature. Man's life partakes in the life of God. Just as he is a part of nature and subject to its laws, he is bound to the divine and part of its being. "The Holy One, blessed be He, is the Creator of everything and dwells in all things," said the Rabbi of Berditchev. "Therefore, no one may say 'I' to another, for this implies that he is self-sufficient, quite complete in himself. But the truth is that the 'I' of man is not only his own self but also the divine within him.

"And Moses rose up early in the morning, and went up unto Mount Sinai, as the Lord commanded him, and took in his hands two tablets of stone. . . . And the Lord passed by before him and cried out, 'the Lord, the Lord, merciful and gracious, long-suffering, abundant in goodness and truth . . .'" (Exodus 34:4, 6).

Why is it written, "the Lord, the Lord"? Why is "the Lord" repeated twice? Would once not be enough? Rabbi Levi Yitzhak puzzled over this question until he found an answer by reading the words differently: "The Lord cried out, 'O Lord. . . . [*Vayikra Adonai, Adonai*].'"

"It is the *Neshamah* ['man's soul']," he explained, "calling to the Holy One, blessed be He. For the soul of man is a divine portion from above. Thus when 'the Lord passed by,' that is, when the feeling of love and awe for Heaven overwhelms one, the divine within—'the Lord'—cries out to the divine above, 'O Lord!'"[5]

To wait for the Lord and to worship Him alone, with no curtain between us, to be worthy of becoming the dwelling

place of the *Shekhinah* ["Divine Presence"]—this is our heart's desire and our soul's delight. So it is that the word *Shekhinah* derives from *Shokhen*, which means "to dwell," for He dwells in our midst because we do crown Him King over us. For the true goal of man is that he might become a vessel worthy of receiving the yoke of God's kingdom, as the Talmud says, "It is you who must enthrone Me over you." [6]

Because the divine image resides in him, the sufferings of man are sufferings for God as well. Rabbi Levi Yitzhak of Berditchev once explained the verse, "As a man chasteneth his son, so the Lord thy God chasteneth thee."

"When a human father chastens his son and strikes him, his own heart aches, and it is as if he had struck his own flesh. So it is with the Holy One, blessed be He. As it is written in the Talmud, 'When a man is sorely troubled, the *Shekhinah* says, "How heavy is my head, how heavy is my arm."' If God suffers so much for the blood of the wicked, how much more for the blood of the righteous!"

Where is God? And where is He not? Rabbi Levi Yitzhak, in "The Dudele," proclaims:

> *Master of the Universe,*
> *I will sing a song to Thee.*
> *Where will I find Thee?*
> *And where will I not find Thee?*
> *Where I go, there art Thou,*
> *Where I stay, there art Thou.*
> *Only Thou, Thou alone,*
> *Thou again, and only Thou....*

THE GLORY OF MAN

If God is Creator, Revealer, and Redeemer, beyond all and within all, then man, who is the creature fashioned to rule the universe, to receive the revelation and advance the redemption, is a sacred vessel. "We are forbidden to think evil thoughts," taught Levi Yitzhak, "for the mind of man is the holy of holies, and in it is the Ark with the Tablets of the Law. If he permits evil thoughts to arise within him, he is setting an idol up in the Temple. But when, in the midst of praying, the Tzaddik is seized with great fervor, when he kindles with flame and lifts his hands, it is as once when—in the Holy of Holies—the cherubim pointed upward their wings." [7]

As a sacred vessel, it is the purpose of man to know and serve God.

> It may seem to man that he was created in order to do the business of this world. But that is not so. The purpose of man's creation was that he should understand the unity of God. And when the Redeemer comes—may it be speedily—then the true purpose of the creation of man will be revealed. [8]

Man's power is great.

TEXT:
"The earth was void and without form" [Genesis 1:2].

EXPLANATION:
All the worlds were created only for the sake of Israel and for the sake of the earth wherein man might serve his Creator. Man must ever be aware of this: that for his sake the world and all the angels were created. Thus he will rouse himself to serve the Creator, blessed be His name, with fervor, since everything depends upon him. So we understand the verse, "And the earth was void and without form." That is to say, the lower world was unfinished because it waited for man to dwell thereon and serve his Creator. And it was for this reason that even the Upper Worlds were created. [9]

There are two ways to serve the Creator, blessed be His name. One way is: When a man reflects on the grandeur of the Creator, blessed be He, and on his own frailties, then such an inexpressible awe falls upon him that he is as nothing in his own eyes.

The second way is: When a man considers that all the worlds and all the angels are dependent upon him, upon his Mitzvot and Torah—for it is through him that joy and blessing flow to all the worlds—then he rises in stature and understands the solemn duty he has to take care that his every deed be in the service of the Holy One, blessed be His name.

And this is the difference between Passover and Shavuot. On Passover we are bidden to eat *Matzah*, which is unleavened bread that does not rise, symbolizing humility and selflessness. But with the giving of the Torah, it was revealed that all the worlds are dependent upon our deeds. Then all Israel rose in eminence, and man began to learn to elevate himself through all his actions. For is there anything nobler than the one upon whose deeds all the world depends? And this is why it was commanded that bread be offered in the Temple on Shavuot, for it is the nature of yeast to rise higher and higher.[10]

If man's greatness is so solemn—holy vessel! servant of God! supporter of all worlds!—then what extraordinary tasks must be expected of him each day and how impossibly overwhelming must his burden be. "Nonsense!" said the Rabbi of Berditchev. "We should work for God the same way in which we work for our wives and children."

LOVE OR FEAR

Is it all the same whether one serves out of love or out of fear?

There is a difference between the man who serves God out of fear and the man who serves Him out of love.

He who serves God from fear is aware of his own existence; that it is *he* who serves God.

But he who serves God from love loses all awareness of himself, his love for God encompassing all.[11]

To truly love God means to strip oneself of all accustomed habits and to work only for the Lord with every deed and every limb. This is the meaning of *tzimtzum*, to withdraw out of oneself into love for the Creator. And this is the secret of becoming a chariot for the Divine Presence.[12]

There are two kinds of men who serve the Creator, blessed be He. The one serves the Lord in order to receive a reward, because he knows that He has the power to supply every creature's needs. The other serves the Creator, blessed be He, not to receive a reward but only because of His glory: how the Lord rules over all the angels who stand before Him in fear and trembling, singing praises and serving Him in joy and holiness.

And this is the difference between these two servants: He who serves the Creator in order to receive a reward is always lacking something; his eyes are never satisfied. Not so he who serves the Creator out of reverence. For, knowing that the Creator rules all the heavenly creatures who sing praises before Him, a holy reverence falls upon him, and he says in his heart, "If even the angels serve God, how much the more so a clod of earth such as I!" Then does he experience sweet bliss, for the Creator has revealed to him His majesty and His power, and more glowing still is the fervor with which he serves Him. To such a man nothing is lacking, "for there is no lack to those who revere Him."

So do we explain the words of Scripture, "Perfect you shall be with the Lord your God." He who only pursues his material desires lacks something, while he who serves God out of awe for His glory lacks nothing. Each day his service to the Holy One rises in joy, for from awe comes joy. And this is what is explained in the writings of the Ari: "Before performing each Mitzvah we are bidden to say, 'I do this for the sake of the unity of the Holy One, blessed be He, in awe and in love.' "

Notice that we we first say "in awe," then "in love." For at the beginning a man serves the Lord in fearful trembling for the glory of the Creator which descends upon him, but afterward rejoicing rouses him so that he merits to be a [true] servant to the Creator. Likewise, in Scriptures, the order is first *"to fear* the Lord thy God" [Deuteronomy 5:26], and later, *"Thou shalt love* the Lord thy God with all thy heart and all thy soul and all thy might" [Deuteronomy 6:5].

The service of the Lord rests upon the foundations of awe and love. Of the two, awe should precede love. One begins in awe of the Lord, for the majesty of His splendor. My master, Dov Ber, taught that a man should prepare himself for the fear of Heaven and then, of itself, love will come. For love seeks out him who truly fears the Lord.

There are 365 negative commandments in the Torah; they are performed through awe. There are 248 positive commandments; they are performed through love. The positive commandments are more difficult to keep than the negative ones. For example, one is able to fulfill the negative commandments even in an unclean place, such as a bathhouse or a toilet, but not the positive commandments such as putting on *Tefillin*.

As mentioned above, there is the Tzaddik who serves the Lord to receive a reward, and there is the Tzaddik who serves the Lord out of love for the Creator—how the angels and all the holy creatures stand in dread and serve Heaven in loving joy. The Tzaddik who serves out of fear desires vengeance against those who hate him; but the Tzaddik who serves out of love is long-suffering.[13]

SORROW OR JOY

When he was asked which was the right way—that of sorrow or that of joy—the Rabbi of Berditchev said, "There are two kinds of sorrow and two kinds of joy. When a man broods over the misfortunes that have come upon him, cowers in a corner, and despairs of help—that is a bad kind of sorrow, concerning which it is said, 'The Divine Presence does not dwell in a place of dejection.' The other kind is the honest grief of a man who knows what he lacks.

"The same is true of joy. He is a fool who is devoid of inner substance but consumed with empty pleasures and who neither feels nor tries to fill his lack. But the truly joyful man is like one whose house has burned down; struck by his loss, he begins to build anew. Over every stone that is laid, his heart rejoices."

THE TURNING

Even though man is a holy vessel of the Divine, created to serve God with all his heart and all his might, he may lose his way, distort the image in which he was made, and listen to the voice of Satan instead of God. He may surrender to the Evil Urge—that devil within, which, though subdued or sublimated, is never destroyed. He may give way to passion, envy, sin. What then? Is man, once shattered, never to be mended? No. Because he is a vessel of God, man may always immerse himself in holy and pure waters by turning back toward Him from Whom he strayed. God stands ready to receive and forgive and mend. This is the meaning of repentance.

In those days of skepticism, when the winds of modern thought blew over their land and caused many to question the validity of their faith, Rabbi Levi Yitzhak of Berditchev sent messengers to various communities with a proclamation to be uttered in his name:

"Behold, I, Levi Yitzhak of Berditchev, proclaim to each and every one:

"There is a God in the world."

Repentance requires a broken heart, the honest feeling that what was before was wrong and must be made right.

A man came to Rabbi Levi Yitzhak and complained, "Rabbi,

what shall I do with the lie that keeps sneaking into my heart?" He stopped and then cried aloud, "Oh, and even what I just said was not said truthfully! I shall never find truth!"

Then, in despair, he threw himself on the ground.

"How fervently this man seeks the truth!" said the rabbi.

With a gentle hand he raised the man from the ground and said, "It is written in Scripture, 'The truth will grow out of the ground.' "

A disciple questioned the Rabbi of Berditchev. "The Talmud teaches that those who are perfect in righteousness are not worthy to stand in that place where repentant sinners stand. According to this, one who has been innocent from youth comes after one who has transgressed against God many times and cannot attain to his rung. Why?"

The Tzaddik replied, "He who sees a new light every day—light he did not see the day before—if he wishes truly to serve, must condemn his imperfect service of yesterday, atone for it, and start afresh. The innocent one who believes he has rendered perfect service and persists in it, does not accept the light and comes after him who ever turns anew."[14]

> There are two kinds of servants: one who sees the face of the king each day and therefore obeys him; another who rarely sees the face of the king but of a sudden rouses himself from his lethargy to obey the king. Thus each day as he toils to eke out his livelihood, this latter asks the king nothing for himself. His only wish is that he might turn from all other concerns and serve the king. Mighty is the Lord's joy with such a man. "See this man who was a sinner," He says, "but has now chosen to serve Me, for he was brutish and went in the way of the fool but now is filled with fervor for the service of the Lord." And this is the meaning of the Talmudic passage: "In the place of repentant sinners, the righteous are not worthy to stand."[15]

Thus the story is told of how Rabbi Levi Yitzhak was walking along the streets of his city and met a man known for his wickedness, for his sins against God and man.

Rabbi Levi Yitzhak seized him by his coat and said to him, "Why do you not repent? For if you would only repent, I would be envious of you. Because if you do *Teshuvah*, you would turn all of your sins into Mitzvot, and therefore your power for good would be greater than mine. Repent, I tell you!"

Those who tell the story say that soon after his meeting with the rabbi that man repented all and became one of Levi Yitzhak's Hasidim.[16]

Sometimes evil may be the occasion for great good, and the wickedness of a man can even bring about virtue in others. "I envy Pharaoh!" said Levi Yitzhak. "What glorification of the name of God did his stubbornness beget!"

9

Days of Awe

THE DAYS OF AWE, the period in the Jewish calendar starting with Rosh Hashanah, are the holiest of the entire year. In Elul, one month before Rosh Hashanah, the *Shofar* is sounded each day in the synagogue after morning services. During this month a mood of holy fear comes over the people as they prepare their souls for *Yom ha-Din* ("Day of Judgment"), Rosh Hashanah, when man is bidden to take stock of himself for the year which has passed and to seek renewal for the year to come. From the Sunday morning before Rosh Hashanah until Yom Kippur, *Selihot*, special prayers of confession and remorse, are recited in the early hours of the morning. The Ten Days of Penitence (the Days of Awe) culminate in the most solemn day of the year: a twenty-four hour fast marked by a magnificent cycle of confession and reconciliation—Yom Kippur—when all Israel, garbed in white, the color of the angels, pours out its heart to God.

It is during this season of the Jewish year that many of the stories told about Levi Yitzhak are supposed to have taken place. It is not difficult to fathom why this was so, for the solemn holiness of the season moved the Rabbi of Berditchev to intense fervor, and the themes of judgment and forgiveness gave him an opportune moment to seek both favorable judgment and gracious forgiveness for his people.

ROSH HASHANAH

It is told that before the Holy Days, on the first of the month of Elul, Rabbi Levi Yitzhak was standing at his window when a Gentile cobbler came by looking for work.

Spying the rabbi, he called, "Have you nothing that needs mending?"

"Have I nothing that needs mending?" Levi Yitzhak echoed reflectively.

Then his heart contracted within him, he sank to the floor, and he wept. "Woe is me, the Day of Judgment is approaching and still I have not mended myself."

On Rosh Hashanah when the Rabbi of Berditchev was near the end of the *Zikhronot* part of the *Musaf* service and came to the words:

> *I will remember My covenant with you in the days of your youth;*
> *And I will establish unto you an everlasting covenant*

he would pause and sing a curious melody:

> *My father, of blessed memory, once said, "A woman came to me once, just before New Year's Day, and cried and cried.*
> *"I asked her, 'Why are you crying?'*
> *"She said, 'Why shouldn't I cry? My head hurts! My head hurts!'*

> "I said to her, 'Don't cry. If you cry, your head will only hurt more.'
>
> "She answered, 'Why shouldn't I cry? I have an only son, and now that holy and awesome day is coming and I don't know whether my son will pass when God makes His judgment.'
>
> "I said to her again, 'Don't cry! He will surely pass when God makes judgment. For look, it is written [and here Levi Yitzhak continued the service]:
>
> "Is not Ephraim a precious son unto Me?
> Is he not a child of delight?
> For as often as I speak against him,
> I do earnestly remember him still.
> Therefore My heart yearneth for him.
> I will surely have compassion upon him, saith the Lord."

Even today the Hasidim tell this story in the same sweet melody and with the same movements.

On Rosh Hashanah eve, after *Kiddush* had been recited, Rabbi David Moshe of Tchortkov would relate how it was the custom of Rabbi Levi Yitzhak always to entreat the Lord in behalf of Israel, saying, "Master of the World, all the good fortune of Israel is spent only for Your sake. For what does Israel do when there is plenty? They spend more to have their children taught Torah, or make a finer Sabbath, or contribute more generously to charity. Thus the substance of their spending goes for Your Mitzvot.

"Why then do You not deliver Israel?"

One year, before the sounding of the *Shofar*, the Tzaddik hesitated and then said, "Master of the World, do You think I shall sound the *Shofar* before You this year? Let the evil kingdoms to whom You have given power and who issue harsh decrees against us sound it!

"Yet, Master of the World, do I not love You with an eternal love? Therefore, I shall bend my will to Your will, and, in spite of all, I shall cry out *Tekiah*!"

Another time, before sounding the *Shofar*, Levi Yitzhak recited the verse, "With trumpets and sound of the horn shout ye before the King, the Lord," and then he told the following story:

There was once a king who went hunting in the forest. He penetrated so deep into the forest that he could not find the highway that would lead him back to his palace. He finally met some countrymen and asked them the way, but they could not show it to him, for they did not know it either. At last he found a wise man and asked him the way. The wise man, realizing who the king was, trembled, but showed him to the highway, for he knew the way, and led the king back to his kingdom. For this, the wise man found great favor in the eyes of the king, who lifted him up above the lords of the realm, clothing him in costly garments, and ordering his old clothes to be laid in the king's treasure house.

Some time afterward, the wise man sinned against the king, who grew angry and commanded the lords who stood highest in his kingdom to judge the man as a transgressor against the king's commandment. The wise man was in sad straits, for he knew that they would decide against him. He fell on his face before the king and pleaded for his life, asking also to be allowed, before the verdict was reached, to put on the same clothes he had been wearing when he had led the king out of the forest. The king acceded to this request.

It came to pass that when the wise man had put on his old clothes, the king recalled the great kindness the wise man had done him by returning him to his palace and to his royal throne, and the king's compassion was kindled. He allowed the wise man's sin to pass unpunished and returned him to his former high position.

"So it is with us, the people of Israel!" concluded Levi Yitzhak. "When the Torah was about to be given, the Holy One, blessed be He, went from nation to nation, asking them to accept the Torah, but they would not. We received it with such joy and delight that we said, 'We will do,' before 'We will hear' [Exodus 24:7]. We took the yoke of the Kingdom of Heaven upon ourselves and made Him King over us, and accepted His commandments and His sacred Torah. But now we have transgressed and rebelled against Him, and on Rosh Hashanah we are fearful of the Day of

Judgment, when He weighs all the hidden things and pronounces the verdict of every man according to his deeds. Therefore we sound the ram's horn and put on the same dress we were wearing at the time of the giving of the Torah, when we accepted the Torah and crowned Him King with the *Shofar*, as it is written, 'When the sound of the horn waxed louder and louder' [Exodus 19:19]. This is so He may remember our merit and forgive us our iniquities and willful transgressions and vindicate us in judgment and inscribe us at once for a long and happy life. Amen. So be His will!"

> Among the prayers for Rosh Hashanah there is one that begins, "Thou, O Lord, rememberest the ways of man."
> Now this can be explained by a parable.
> Despite his superior wisdom, the father delights in the clever sayings of his child. So from time to time does he abridge his wisdom and descend into the mental world of the child in order to play with him. And this is what is meant by the above passage, "Thou rememberest the ways of man": God dwells upon the good deeds of His people Israel, even though in comparison to the Lord Himself they are as naught. [1]

Rabbi Levi Yitzhak was always happy when he had an opportunity to come before the Lord with a claim on behalf of Israel. For example, when he taught that passage of the Mishnah that begins, "When the holiday of Rosh Hashanah falls on the Sabbath," his face would radiate with happiness, and he would expound on these words.

"Which is the choicest of days for Rosh Hashanah? The Sabbath. For on that day, although the angels may seek to judge every man according to his deeds, Rabbi Levi Yitzhak can turn to the Lord and say, 'Master of the World, on Rosh Hashanah some are written down for life and some for death. But this year Rosh Hashanah falls on the Sabbath, and writing is forbidden on the Sabbath! How, then, can You carry out the words of our prayers, "On Rosh Hashanah they are inscribed"?

" 'However, there is the principle, "The saving of a life takes precedence over the Sabbath." Thus, Master of the World, only if You write us down for *life* will the Sabbath not be violated, since the saving of a life takes precedence even over the Sabbath!

" 'Moreover, the law is clear when it states that, "When one must violate the Sabbath to save a human life, this should be done neither by non-Jews nor by minors nor by servants nor by women . . . but it should be done by the leaders and wise men of Israel." This law should apply to the Heavenly Court too. It must be carried out not by the angels but only by the Holy One, blessed be He, Himself.' "

And Rabbi Levi Yitzhak concluded his explanation exultantly. "Therefore, I say that the choicest of days for Rosh Hashanah is the Sabbath!"

An old Hasid from Berditchev told the following story:

Once, when the power of Satan and the fear of judgment were strong over the people of Israel, Rabbi Levi Yitzhak prepared himself to do battle. It was his holy custom not to debate that other one with words but with deeds. First he would permit Satan and all his followers to level their accusations against Israel before the Heavenly Court; afterward he would enter, carrying upon his back a heavy bundle containing the records in Israel's favor, and place them before the Throne of Glory, saying, "Behold, our Father in Heaven, I shall not plead for Israel; here are their deeds. Let them speak, not my mouth!"

And, if we may use such language, the Holy One Himself would take the package, open it up, and all the good deeds of Israel would fly up and surround the Throne of Glory like so many white doves. Then Satan, confused and distraught, would hasten away with lowered head.

But one year, during the days of *Selihot*, the old Hasid continued, the gates of Heaven were closed tight before Rabbi Levi Yitzhak. He struggled with the Adversary, but it seemed that he would not prevail this time. The hand of Satan was so strong that the Tzaddik of Berditchev needed to find some unusual merit to offset the claims and accusations that had been made. So he began to search.

After he had recited the *Selihot*, he departed from the synagogue and walked quietly through the dark streets and alleyways in the poorest section of the city. Suddenly he saw a light coming from a small old house, and his heart told him that there he would find what he sought. He entered without knocking and saw a young woman sitting on a chair, her head covered with a scarf. She was reciting *Tehinot* (prayers in Yiddish, recited by women). The woman recognized the Tzaddik and was startled. She knew that it was Rabbi Levi Yitzhak's custom to rise early and to remain awake late during the days of *Selihot*, spending much time visiting the homes of sinners, speaking to their hearts, and urging them to repent. And since he had come to her house, the meaning of his visit seemed clear.

She began to weep. "I have sinned, my holy rabbi, but I have already repented; I have done everything possible to blot out my transgression."

The Tzaddik said to her, "Weep not, my daughter, you are not a sinner; indeed, you have been accorded great merit in Heaven. Sit down, be at ease, and tell me everything that has happened to you."

The woman spoke. "My father and mother lived not far from Berditchev in a small village where they managed to eke out a modest livelihood selling the milk that came from the farm of the duke. When both my parents died, I was seventeen years old and an orphan. I went to the duke to ask that he permit me to keep the rights of my parents so that I too might have a livelihood. When the duke saw me, he began to speak vile words and tried to lay his hands upon me. I pushed him away and tried to flee.

"Then he changed his manner and said gently, 'It would be a shame if any harm should come to you. I will give you the same rights as your parents, for three years and for half the price. In return I have but one request—permit me to kiss your hair.' And before I could protest, he did so.

"When I returned to my house, I found no peace. My heart cried out within me that I had somehow permitted this evil man to defile me. All that night I could not sleep. In the morning I took the scissors and cut off my hair; the next morning I left the village and my livelihood and settled in the city. Here I worked as a servant in the house of a wealthy family for some years until I was married. After several happy years my husband died and I have lived in poverty and despair ever since. I fear that he died because of my sin."

"Where is the hair you cut off?" asked Rabbi Levi Yitzhak.

"I have kept only one lock as a remembrance." The woman moaned as she took it from a box and brought it to him. "When my heart is filled with anguish over my misery, I gaze upon this curl and remember the sin of my youth and understand the justice of my judgment."

Tears gathered in the eyes of Rabbi Levi Yitzhak as, with a blessing, he took leave of her.

The day of Rosh Hashanah came. Rabbi Levi Yitzhak sat and studied the tractate Rosh Hashanah of the Talmud until midnight. With the break of the dawn he went to the *Mikveh*, put on his white *Kittel* and his *Tallit*, and entered the synagogue. The synagogue was filled with worshipers, all clothed in their *Talleitim* and praying the morning service. When they reached the part of the service that begins with the word *Ha-Melekh*, all eyes were raised to the holy Tzaddik. He pulled his *Tallit*, adorned with silver braid, over his head and his face, and soon his strong voice was heard, "*Ha-Melekh!*" He approached the Ark, singing the well-known melody, and as the congregation answered him—"Ay ya'i ya'i ya'i!"—all the voices seemed to merge into one great voice flowing from one great heart.

Later, during the prayer, "*Avinu Malkeinu*" ("Our Father, Our King"), the tearful cries seemed to pierce the very Heavens, and the congregants felt that the power of the Berditchever would surely bring their prayers before the Divine Throne. Who knew, they thought, how many adversaries there were in the heavenly heights who sought to prevent the prayers of Israel from entering and being joined as crowns of glory around the head of their Creator? In fear and trembling they recited the prayer, "Our Father, Our King, annul all evil decrees against us and close up the mouth of all those who attack us."

Then, finally, it was time for the sounding of the *Shofar*. Impatiently the worshipers awaited the return of their holy master from the *Mikveh*, where he had gone to purify himself for this moment. His delay, they thought, must be a result of some dreadful accusation in Heaven against the Children of Israel. At last the Tzaddik, dressed all in white, entered and slowly ascended the *Bimah*. There he bowed and again put his *Tallit* over his face, lowering his head upon his arms on the table.

Suddenly he lifted his head, raised his eyes to Heaven, and began to speak. "Master of the World, if our transgressions weigh the scale in favor of guilt, take, I beseech You, the lock of hair of this forsaken woman and place it on the other side of the scale. Surely this lock of hair will outweigh all our sins!"

So Rabbi Levi Yitzhak began to plead before his Creator while standing before the congregation.

He related the tragic story of this woman: how, left an orphan by her parents in her youth, she had gone to the duke to ask that he not deny her livelihood; how he sought to molest her and how she resisted him; how the duke promised to guarantee her the livelihood of her parents, if she would only permit a kiss on her hair; how this poor orphan, able to change her entire position for one kiss, refused, so pure and righteous a Jewish soul was she; how the duke seized her nonetheless and kissed her hair; and how she fled in shame to a strange city, afflicting herself for a sin she had not committed by cutting off her lovely tresses, and was forced to work for crusts of bread; how she failed to find peace, believing that she was somehow involved in the sin of the duke; and how she married and yet, after a few years her husband died and she again remained alone, poverty stricken, distressed, broken-hearted, and remorseful; how she still did not complain against the harsh judgment of Heaven but placed the blame on herself, even preserving the lock of hair she had cut off as a remembrance of her "transgression."

"Now, I, Levi Yitzhak, Your servant, turn to You, O God of mercy and compassion, and ask You: Is not this lock of hair a symbol of the difference between a pure daughter of the people of Israel and a corrupt duke of the nations of the world? Does not this lock of hair set apart those who each day declare the unity of Your name in love, from the others, with all their pomp and power? Is not this lock of hair worthy of weighting the scale in favor of the Children of Israel?"

A mighty thundering burst forth from the heavenly chambers. The Holy One, blessed be He, descended in all His glory from the Throne of Justice and sat upon the Throne of Mercy. The complaints of Satan were halted, and the gates of Heaven opened wide. The face of the Tzaddik shone with joy and light.

And that year was a year of blessing and success for all Jews.

Thus the old Hasid of Berditchev concluded his story.

YOM KIPPUR

The love for Israel that each day burned in the heart of Rabbi Levi Yitzhak flamed even higher during the Days of Awe, reaching its climax on the Day of Atonement. During this period of mercy, when he would come before the Ark, dressed in a white *Kittel* and covered with his *Tallit*, and look out upon the faces of his people, tired from overwork, humbled from suffering, standing in trepidation before the Throne of Judgment, his heart would melt with compassion for each and every member of the household of Israel. As a son speaking to his father, so Rabbi Levi Yitzhak would speak to the Lord. He would ask and plead—sometimes, demand and insist—that the Father in Heaven take mercy upon His children—the children of Abraham, Isaac, and Jacob—a mercy of deliverance and redemption.

"Each of us," he once said, "is like a woman who suffers terrible pain in childbirth and swears she will never lie with her husband again—and yet forgets her oath. So on every Day of Atonement we confess our faults and promise to repent, and yet we go on sinning. And You go on forgiving us."

"Rabbi Levi Yitzhak's mood was always a happy one," related his grandson, Rabbi Yitzhak of Neshkhiz, "for he believed in serving God in holy joy. One year, on the day before Yom Kippur, I was with him at the last meal before the fast, and I noticed how radiantly joyous was the movement of his lips. A little later two tears—only two—rolled down his cheeks." [2]

Once, when he came to the passage, "We are filled with sin, and You are filled with mercy," Levi Yitzhak said, " 'We are filled with sin.' That is, alas, true. But how great, after all, is Levi Yitzhak, and how great, after all, could his sins be even if he is filled with them? But 'You are filled with mercy.' That is, indeed, also true. And You are the *Ein Sof*—the Infinite One. Therefore, there must be no end to Your mercy."

Another Yom Kippur eve, the Rabbi of Berditchev waited for a while before going to the pulpit to lead the prayers, and walked back and forth in the House of Prayer. In a corner he found a man crouched on the floor and weeping.

The man explained in answer to his questions, "Up to a short time ago I had all good things and now I am wretched. Rabbi, I lived in a village where no hungry man went from my door unfed. My wife used to bring home poor wayfarers she met on the road and see to their needs. And then He comes along"—here the man pointed toward the sky—"and takes first my wife and then my house. There I was with six small children, without a wife, without a house! And I had a thick prayer book, and all the prayers were in it in just the right order—you didn't have to hunt around—and that burned up along with everything else. Now you tell me, Rabbi, can I forgive Him?"

The Tzaddik had the worshipers look for a prayer book like the one the man described. When it was brought, the man began to turn the pages to see if everything was in the correct sequence.

The Rabbi of Berditchev waited for a while, then finally asked, "Do you forgive Him now?"

"Yes," said the man.

Then the Rabbi went to the pulpit and began to chant the *Kol Nidre*.

On still another occasion, just before sunset, when the entire congregation had gathered in the synagogue awaiting the start of *Kol Nidre*, Rabbi Levi Yitzhak took a candle in his hand and went from bench to bench, bending and searching.

"Our master," his followers asked him, "for what are you searching?"

"I am searching," replied Levi Yitzhak, "for one drunken Jew. But I do not find him."

Immediately he stepped down before the Ark and began, as was his custom, to plead with the Almighty in defense of Israel. "Master of the World, look down from Heaven and see who is like unto Your people Israel, 'a kingdom of priests and a holy nation.' You have commanded us to eat and drink today before the fast. Indeed, is it not written, 'All who eat and drink on the ninth of Tishri will be counted as if they had fasted on the ninth and tenth'? If a commandment such as this had been given to the other nations of the world, by the time evening came, many would be drunk, many would be rolling in the gutters, many would have bruises and pains. Not so Israel. This day they fulfilled Your command to eat and drink at specially prepared tables. And now, while the sun still shines, they have all hastened here to the synagogue, and none is drunk or asleep. They stand upon their feet, all holy, all pure, all prepared to take upon themselves the hardships of the holy day, to confess before You, and to turn to You in truth and with a full heart.

"Surely, Your children are deserving of forgiveness for all their sins, of being inscribed and sealed for life, and of being granted a good year, a year of redemption." [3]

There was one woman who came to Berditchev every year for the Day of Atonement to pray with the congregation of Rabbi Levi Yitzhak. Once she was delayed, and by the time she reached the House of Prayer, night had already fallen. The woman was vexed and sorrowful, for she was certain the evening service must be over. But she found that the rabbi had not even begun. He had waited—and his astonished congregation with him—for the woman to come.

When she became aware that he had not yet recited *Kol Nidre*, the woman was filled with great joy and said to God, "Lord of the World, what shall I wish You in return for the good You have vouchsafed me? I wish You may have as much joy of Your children as You have just now granted me!"

Then, even while she was speaking, an hour replete with the grace of God came upon the world.

"Why is it," asked the Rabbi of Berditchev, "that on Yom Kippur we recite in our prayers the blessing, 'Blessed art Thou, O Lord, King Who pardonest and forgivest our transgressions'? Are we so certain that the Almighty is going to pardon and forgive our sins? Perhaps—Heaven forbid—He will not forgive us, and we will have recited the blessing in vain.

"But," Levi Yitzhak added in explanation, "just the contrary is true. Let me give you an example of what I mean. It is like a clever child who sees an apple in his father's hand and wants it very badly. If he asks for the apple, perhaps his father will give it to him—and perhaps he will not. What should the child do? He snatches the apple from his father's hand and says the blessing, 'Blessed art Thou, O Lord, King of the Universe, Who createst the fruit of the tree.' Once he has said these words he knows that his father must give him the apple, for he would not want his son to recite a blessing in vain!"

Once, on the Day of Atonement, the Rabbi of Berditchev was praying in the synagogue of Rabbi Jacob Orenstein of Lvov. In the middle of the *Musaf* prayer he suddenly stopped, and the people heard him say in Polish, in a threatening voice, "I'll show you."

During the evening meal, the son of the Rabbi of Lvov said to the Rabbi of Berditchev, "I shall not take the liberty of criticizing your manner of praying. But may I ask you one thing? How could you interrupt your prayer, and with Polish words at that?"

The Rabbi of Berditchev replied, "I managed to down my other enemies, but this was the only way I could get the better of the Prince-Demon of Poland!"[4]

Rabbi Yitzhak of Neshkhiz reported the following incident about his grandfather:

Once, on Yom Kippur, the Rabbi of Berditchev said, "Master of the World, we do not have the strength to say the words of the *Mahzor*, 'And the Lord said, "I have forgiven!"' '

"*You* say"—here he paused for what seemed an eternity, lost in holy fervor, then bestirred himself—" 'I have forgiven!' "[5]

In the synagogue of Berditchev during a year especially marked by poverty, persecution, and hardship for Israel, toward the end of Yom Kippur, when the shadows were falling and hearts were weak from fasting, the rabbi turned to the *Hazzan* and said, "It is time for the *Neilah* prayer. Why do you not begin?"

"I can pray no more today," replied the *Hazzan*. "I am unworthy to lead the congregation."

"Pray *Neilah!*" said Rabbi Levi Yitzhak.

"No, Rabbi, I cannot."

"Then I shall pray in your stead."

A few moments later, in the middle of the prayer, the rabbi cried out, "I propose a trade, O Master of the World! Sins and transgressions from us to You, and pardon and forgiveness from You to us! A fair exchange, You will say. Not so! You must add further: children, life and food.

"What do I mean by 'children'? Children who study Torah, O Merciful Father!

"What do I mean by 'life'? Life that praises and adores You, O Merciful Father!

"What do I mean by 'food'? Food by which we may fulfill the verse, 'Thou shalt eat, be satisfied, and bless the Lord,' O Merciful Father!"

On one Day of Atonement, when the Rabbi of Berditchev recited the *Musaf* service and came to the place where, in recalling the Temple service, the High Priest sprinkles the atoning drops of blood and says the words, "And thus did he count: 'One; one and one; one and two; one and three;' " he was so overwhelmed with fervor that when he had said "one" for the second time, he fell to the floor and lay as one dead. The congregation was not greatly upset, since it often happened that their rabbi fainted because of the ardor of his prayer.

When some time had passed, however, and Levi Yitzhak had still not regained consciousness, those standing near sought to revive him. But in vain. Doctors were called, yet their efforts met with no greater success. Several of the Hasidim lifted him from the floor and carried him to his room, and there laid him on his bed. Then the Hasidim, who knew very well that this was a state that had to do with the soul and not a sickness of the body, continued in prayer. Much later, when they had just begun to recite *Neilah*, the rabbi rushed in and over to the pulpit, shouting "and one!"

Then he completed his worship.

It was times such as these (so Hasidic tradition has it) that the angels of mercy would open a special entrance below the Throne of Glory so that all the rejected prayers of Israel might then ascend together with the prayers of the holy one of Berditchev.

Rabbi Levi Yitzhak once spent Yom Kippur in Brody, where the noted Rabbi Ephraim Zalman Margolis resided. He ate a hurried meal at the inn where he was staying, hastened to the synagogue while it was yet day, put on his *Kittel* and *Tallit*, and went down and stood before the Ark.

As the sun was setting, the congregation began to assemble in the *Bet ha-Midrash*. Each one found his place, put on his *Kittel* and *Tallit*, and made ready to welcome the holy day. Then it was time for *Kol Nidre*. The *Hazzan* was about to step down before the Ark when he noticed that someone else was already there—a stranger, who stood with his *Tallit* over his face and refused to move. The *Parnas* sent the *Shammash* to tell the stranger to make room for the *Hazzan*, but when he approached Levi Yitzhak, such a fear seized him that he began to stammer and tremble. The *Parnas* himself now came, but he too was startled by what he saw. After a hurried consultation, it was decided that the *Shammash* would call the congregation to order and announce that it was time for *Kol Nidre*; then the stranger would surely find another place for himself.

In a loud voice the *Shammash* called the congregation to order, announcing that it was time for *Kol Nidre*. But the stranger, instead of leaving the pulpit, began to chant the *Kol Nidre* prayer, and continued to lead the service with great fervor through the *Shema* and the *Amidah*. When the evening service was over, the stranger still did not move from before the Ark, but chanted first the *Shir ha-Yihud* (Song of God's Unity), and then, with a fiery chant, began to recite *Tehillim*, the Psalms. The hour of midnight arrived. Most of the congregation began to leave for their homes, while some sat down in the corners to take short naps. But still the stranger had not stirred from his place. No one yet knew who he was or from where he had come. Finally it was time for the morning prayers, and the stranger, still standing in the same spot, chanted the *Shema* and *Shaharit*, and, through the rest of the day, *Musaf, Minhah, Neilah,* and even *Ma'ariv.*

The congregation was astonished.

When, after the final service the stranger removed his *Tallit*, Rabbi Ephraim Zalman learned to his surprise who it was. A number of the leading members of the congregation hastened to invite him to their homes to break the fast. But Rabbi Ephraim Zalman claimed Levi Yitzhak for himself.

Immediately after *Havdalah* at Rabbi Ephraim's home Rabbi Levi Yitzhak began to shout, "Woe is me! My heart is aflame within me!"

His host ordered a doctor but the Rabbi of Berditchev would not permit it. Instead he asked for the tractate Sukkah of the Talmud, placed it on the table, opened it and immersed himself in study all that night.

When morning came, Rabbi Ephraim Zalman found him still sitting at the table and inquired how he felt. "My heart still gives me pain," Levi Yitzhak replied, "but thanks to God, I have only eight more pages left."[6]

One year when the Day of Atonement was but shortly over, Shmuel, the Rabbi of Berditchev's favorite disciple, came into his master's room to see how he had withstood the long fast and the flaming fervor with which he had invested the day's service. The Tzaddik was seated at the table, but though the night was well advanced, his glass of tea still stood before him untasted.

When he saw his disciple he raised his head and said, "Good that you have come, Shmuel. Now I can tell it. For you must know that today Satan preferred charges against the judgment of Heaven.

" 'You men of the court of justice,' Satan said, 'tell me why it is that when a man steals a ruble from his fellow you weigh the coin in order to measure his sin and pay no attention to those who have been robbed and have thereby suffered. But if a man gives his fellow a ruble out of charity, you weigh the recipient and all the persons in his house who have been benefited by the gift. Why do you not merely weigh the coin in this instance too? Or why, in the first instance, do you not put on the scales the man who has been robbed and all those who have suffered because of the robbery?'

"Then," continued the rabbi, "I came forward and explained. 'A benefactor wishes to preserve the lives of people, and so the people must be weighed. But the robber wants only the money; he does not even think of the people he is taking it from, and that is why, in this instance, the coin alone need be weighed.'

"That was how I silenced the plaintiff!"

At the close of yet another Day of Atonement, Rabbi Levi Yitzhak sent for one of the most successful brokers in the city.

"Are you familiar," the rabbi asked him, "with the art of negotiation?"

"Of course, Rabbi," replied the broker. "That is my business."

"Have you ever negotiated an agreement," asked Levi Yitzhak further, "that involved a large amount?"

"Certainly, Rabbi," answered the broker. "I have successfully negotiated business dealings that have amounted to tens of thousands of rubles and more."

"If so," said Rabbi Levi Yitzhak, "then I should like you to tell me what my fee should be for my negotiations. For today I have been an agent between the Lord and Israel, and I have successfully completed a negotiation of tremendous consequences—a negotiation of transfer. I have exchanged sins and transgressions for forgiveness and pardon. What should my fee be?"

"Rabbi," said the astounded broker, "I know nothing of such dealings."

"So!" replied Rabbi Levi Yitzhak. "Then I am compelled to determine my own fee. I shall ask that all Israel be granted children, health, and food. Is that not a fair price?"

10

Death of the Rebbe

THE HOLY RAV, Rabbi Levi Yitzhak of Berditchev, always led the congregation in prayer during the *Neilah* service of Yom Kippur, as was the custom of rabbis from times of old. He always took care, out of consideration for the people who had by then already fasted twenty-four hours, not to lengthen the service unduly. But in the last year of his life, he stood before the Ark during the silent prayer of *Neilah* long after the rest of the congregation had finished.

The people were surprised at this, for they had prayed with him year after year and knew that it was unusual for him arbitrarily to alter his established pattern. Though some among his followers were eager to learn why the rabbi had, in contrast to past years, so drawn out the *Neilah* prayer, none dared to ask the reason.

After the close of Yom Kippur, however, when the holy Rav had already gone home and put the first pole of the *Sukkah* into the ground—even before he broke his fast—he said to those who had accompanied him, "You should know, dear ones, that today my end has been decreed; the time has come for me to depart from this world. As I stood before the Ark during *Neilah*, offering my silent prayer to the Creator that He should 'seal' me for a good life in the year to come, I saw the Angel of Death standing before me.

"I said to him, 'Why have you come?'

"And he replied, 'I have come for you.'

"Believe me, dear hearts, I felt no fear when I heard his words, for is there not an end to every man's life? But it was hard for me to leave the world just at this time, for there are two Mitzvot— *Sukkah* and *Etrog*—that have always been especially dear to me, which I knew I would soon have the opportunity to fulfill.

" 'Two precious Mitzvot has the Holy One, blessed be He, given us,' I said to the Angel of Death, 'with which the Children of Israel begin to busy themselves in the days between Yom Kippur and Sukkot. Even now my thoughts are filled with them, and I yearn to observe them once more. Do let me remain until after the Sukkot holiday. Then you may take my soul.'

"The Angel of Death stared at me for a moment and then said, 'Rabbi of Israel, is this matter in my jurisdiction? I am but a messenger from on high, and my task is to carry out the command of the One who sent me.'

" 'Messenger from on high,' I replied, 'your words are true. There is but one small request I wish to make. Permit me to recite the *Viddui* [the "last confession"] before I die.'

"He answered, 'Have you not been confessing your sins throughout this Day of Atonement? Between last night and today you have said the *Viddui* nine times!'

"I asked, 'Can you compare the confession made in life with the one made before death?'

"He smiled, thought for a moment, and then agreed. 'You are right. It is customary for all those who are about to die to confess their sins. Do so, if you wish.'

"I recited the *Viddui* with a broken heart, and without intending to—for the words came forth more of themselves than from any direct act of my will—I implored the Almighty to delay my death until the days of Sukkot had passed, for the reason I have already mentioned. When I finished my prayer, I opened my eyes and saw that the Angel of Death was gone. I looked about, here and there, but he was nowhere to be seen. Then I knew that He who dwells in Heaven had heard my prayer, and my request had been accepted. I was to be granted a few more days in order to fulfill the two Mitzvot, *Sukkah* and *Etrog*.

"And now, therefore, since Heaven has taken mercy on me and added several days to my life because of these Mitzvot, let us fix this pole firmly into the ground as a sign that here we shall begin to rebuild the fallen *Sukkah* of King David."

The people heard the words of the holy rabbi and a terrible trembling passed over their bodies. Out of the great fear they felt, they stood transfixed, no one uttering a word. Meanwhile, the rabbi made sure the pole was fixed firmly in the ground and then went into his house. The people who had accompanied him dispersed.

It was not long before the rabbi's words were known to all the Jews of the city. But if their hearts were filled with dread, the rabbi was at peace with himself and revealed no sign of anguish. He welcomed the holiday with gladness, and spent all the days of Sukkot in rejoicing, as is proper on that festival which is known as the "time of our rejoicing." He sat in study in the *Sukkah* during the day and even slept there at night, as the law requires. Frequently he would lift the *Etrog* to smell and kiss it, and gaze lovingly at the walls of the *Sukkah*, as was his custom.

On Simhat Torah he danced and sang with abandon, being called to the Torah on that day as *Hatan Torah*—the Bridegroom of the Torah—and himself read the last portion of the year.

When he came to the words, "And Moses went up to Mount Nebo from the plains of Moab at the top of Pisgah which is before Jericho," he raised his voice in a manner at once sweet and sad. And when he reached the verse, "And Moses, the servant of the Lord, died there in the land of Moab, according to the word of the

Lord," he could contain himself no longer. But he was unaware whether the one for whom he wept, the one who was going to his eternal home without seeing the Promised Land except from afar, was Moses or Levi Yitzhak.

Long after the Simhat Torah service had ended, he continued to dance and rejoice in the Torah together with the congregation. On the following day, however, he took ill, feeling a pain in his head and fell upon his bed. A doctor was brought at once who examined Levi Yitzhak and said that the rabbi's life was in danger and in need of Heaven's mercies.

The news of his illness spread like fire through the city, and within what seemed a moment, all the houses of prayer and study, great and small, were filled with men and women who came to pour out their souls before the Healer of all souls, asking Him to take mercy on the pure soul of Levi Yitzhak. Though they prayed day and night, the gates of Heaven remained sealed.

Thus, on the twenty-fifth day of Tishri, in the year 5570 (1809), the angels gathered up the Holy Ark which was Rabbi Levi Yitzhak, and brought him to eternal peace in Heaven. His people gave him an honorable resting place in the city of Berditchev and he is revered as the Rabbi of Berditchev to this very day.

LIGHT AND DARKNESS

The death of the Tzaddik Levi Yitzhak plunged vast areas of the Jewish world throughout the Ukraine and beyond into mourning. Everywhere among scholars of the Torah and simple people alike, there was weeping and lamentation—a feeling that there had been taken from them the very ark of the Lord. Both men and women, young and old, wept that the holy one of Berditchev was no longer.

Those Hasidim who lived in Berditchev or journeyed there—as great numbers did to be present at the funeral procession—claimed that they saw a pillar of fire going before the coffin.

When Rabbi Nahman of Bratzlav, who referred to the Rabbi of Berditchev as "the glory of Israel," heard of the Tzaddik's death and funeral, he said, "Surely it is possible that there was a pillar of light going before his coffin, for the true leader of Israel has died.

He who has eyes in his head knows that the light has gone from the world and darkness has enveloped us all."[1]

Indeed, it is told that at the very hour Rabbi Levi Yitzhak died, a Tzaddik teaching in a distant city suddenly interrupted his discourse, in which he was trying to fuse the power of doctrine with that of worship, and said to his disciples, "I cannot go on. Everything has become dark before my eyes. The gates of prayer are closing. Something must have happened to the great worshiper—to Rabbi Levi Yitzhak."

During Rabbi Levi Yitzhak's time there was a holy man who lived in his city of Berditchev. He was called the Rabbi of Morchov because he had grown up in Morchov, in the Ukraine. The friendship between these two was such that reproof was open and love hidden. When Levi Yitzhak died, the Rabbi of Morchov came to walk behind his bier. As they carried the body out of the house, he went close up to it, leaned down, and whispered something, of which only the last words were audible: "as it is written, 'Seven weeks you shall count.'"

Seven weeks later the Rabbi of Morchov died.[2]

Shortly after Levi Yitzhak's funeral, Rabbi Yitzhak of Neshkhiz, the husband of the dead Tzaddik's granddaughter, said to a group of friends, "When I married our master's granddaughter, he told me that he could not promise to keep me in his house for longer than four years."

"How could he make such a condition?" the friends asked.

"I asked myself that same question," the young Hasid replied, "but I have never understood the answer until today. You see, it is now just four years since I came to his house!"[3]

Some time later, when Rabbi Moshe Yakhnash was called to his heavenly abode, Rabbi Yisrael, the son of Rabbi Levi Yitzhak, requested that Rabbi Moshe be buried at the side of his father. Zelig, Rabbi Levi Yitzhak's *Shammash*, who was present at the time, interrupted their conversation with this story:

"Once Rabbi Moshe Yakhnash came to visit Rabbi Levi Yitzhak. They were alone together for a long time. I looked through a crack in the door and saw them standing close to one another, each with his hand on the other's head.

"'Moshe, my friend,' said Rabbi Levi Yitzhak, 'bless me.'

" 'No, Levi Yitzhak,' said Rabbi Moshe, '*you* bless *me*.'

" 'Moshe,' said Rabbi Levi Yitzhak, 'it is my wish that after one hundred and twenty years, your body will lie next to mine.'

" 'No, Levi Yitzhak,' said Rabbi Moshe, 'it will be enough if I lie at your feet.' "

And so it was that they buried him at the foot of Rabbi Levi Yitzhak's grave.

During the weeks following his death eulogies were delivered for Levi Yitzhak in many communities by the Tzaddikim of that time. Some said that while the loss of the great luminary had brought darkness and misery to all Israel, it had brought light and gladness to the Upper Worlds. They explained this by referring to the verse in the Book of Ecclesiastes, "A time for mourning and a time for dancing." For in truth, light and darkness, mourning and rejoicing, were intermingled at that moment.

Mourning in the lower world. Dancing in the Upper World.

Since the death of Levi Yitzhak, Berditchev has had no rabbi. No one could be found to take his place.

Epilogue

SOMETIME AGO one of the foremost historians of philosophy passed away. He was a German Jew who had fled to America in the 1930s and spent his remaining years in this country. First his student and later his friend, I was impressed by his reverence for Judaism. Though not a Hebrew scholar, he had read widely in Jewish literature and knew the Bible intimately. He attended the synagogue with regularity, participating in its weekly Talmud class, and observed some of the traditions in his home as well. At times he even spoke of the works he planned to write dealing with Judaism. I was aware that he had been raised in an assimilated German-Jewish home, that in his youth he had known little more of Jewishness than the fact that he was a Jew, and that as a university student, like his contemporary, Franz Rosenzweig, he had seriously considered conversion to Christianity.

One evening several years ago, lamenting my friend's death with a colleague of his, I raised the question of his return to Judaism and was told how it came about.

During World War I he was stationed for the fall and winter of one year in the city of Berditchev in the Ukraine as an officer of the German army. The day before Rosh Hashanah his commanding officer ordered him to oversee the Jewish soldiers who were to attend services in the local synagogue. For the first time in his life, he entered an East European synagogue and observed the manner of prayer there. He was confused by what he saw and heard and yet was strangely drawn to it, as if something buried within him were tugging at his heart—deep calling to deep. As he came to know some of the local Jews and sought to learn more about the mysterious power which the service seemed to possess, he heard mentioned again and again the name of one who had lived in Berditchev more than a hundred years before, a certain Rabbi Levi Yitzhak.

He observed how often the people referred to this man in tones of respect and reverence. In a store, while making a purchase, in a home over a cup of tea, at the Sabbath table—everywhere he turned—he listened to tales about Levi Yitzhak. The people sang songs they claimed had sprung full-blown from Levi Yitzhak's soul and delighted in recounting how he had spoken and prayed and performed wondrous deeds. These stories were marvelously strange, full of tears and laughter, sadness and love, all at once. Never had my friend heard their like. And remarkable as the stories themselves was the way in which the spirit of Levi Yitzhak, through these stories, lived on amidst the people so many years after his death. It was as though he were still present among them and had not died at all. For the tales were not told in sadness but with a sense of joy and consolation and hope. It was as if these people were communing with one who was very much present and whose presence gave light to the world without and to the spirit within, bringing new meaning to ordinary deeds and new strength to even plain men.

It gradually became clear to my friend that Levi Yitzhak was, in truth, still present. The image of the Rabbi of Berditchev was still before the people. Those whose eyes had seen him perform deeds of kindness had handed down this vision to the next generation. Those whose ears had heard him raise his voice in prayer passed on to their children the memory of that sound. Those whose feet had joined in the master's dance lightened the step of others. Those whose hands had given *Shalom* to the rabbi never lost the touch of his grasp. The words Levi Yitzhak had spoken and the songs he had sung had become part of the people's life not only in his own community but far beyond. The remembrance of the Rebbe was precious to almost every Jew in Eastern Europe. But in Berditchev, his home, where day by day he had worked miracles for man and performed sublime service to God, there was a special love for him. This love, with its sweetness, tenderness, and perhaps fierceness, too, affected the very houses of the city and the streets that joined them—even the air one breathed. Levi Yitzhak's memory was an intangible yet compelling influence upon the daily lives of the plain people. He was a part of their conversation, referred to and remembered on countless occasions. Something like a spell had been cast. Berditchev was no longer a city like other cities; a saint had sanctified it, and it had become a sanctuary.

The young German officer was caught up in the spell of the Rabbi of Berditchev. First it was by the tales he heard about him, then by Levi Yitzhak's power to live on in the memories of others after death. Later he felt the wonder of the man himself, and ultimately of the spiritual world from which Levi Yitzhak emerged. Each revelation amazed the young man as it opened into yet another and a deeper revelation, until at last he realized that he had discovered not only the Rabbi of Berditchev but—what was equally important—his own identity. For the first time in his life he understood how, as a Jew, he was bound up in a bond, mysterious and manifest, of centuries of holiness, wisdom and courage. It was Rabbi Levi Yitzhak of Berditchev, dead for more than a hundred years, who returned an assimilated Jew to the faith of his people.

Berditchev—at least "Jewish" Berditchev—no longer exists. Indeed, all of East European Jewry is now gone. That monumental center of Jewish piety and learning, which for four centuries sent a constant stream of lifeblood into the distant limbs of the body of Israel, has now vanished forever. But the memories remain.

Over the vast graveyard left by the Nazi horror stands the monument of human recollection on which is inscribed the glory of Israel's existence in the lands of Eastern Europe. And, at the very least, the memory of what was must not be allowed to fade. If we permit this memory to disappear, then the murderers, even though defeated in war, will emerge as victors and the holocaust will be complete. The time has come to recount, to assemble, and to record in order to prevent such a victory—to provide at least a measure of consolation through the quickening power of memory, and even more, loyalty to that memory. It is thus that ever and again Israel has healed its wounds and made its way across the centuries.

The Rabbi of Berditchev lived on in the spirits of the people of that city long after his death. Here, in another language, on another continent, but where outer changes have not altered the perennial inner problems of man, Levi Yitzhak may yet possess the power to speak to our souls and kindle once more the spark of faith which smolders there.

Chronology

1700 (?)	Birth of Baal Shem Tov
1740	Birth of Rabbi Levi Yitzhak
1757	Marriage of Rabbi Levi Yitzhak
1760	Death of Baal Shem Tov
1771	Levi Yitzhak becomes rabbi of Zholikhov
1772	First "ban" from Vilna against the Hasidim
1772	Death of Rabbi Dov Ber, the Maggid of Mezritch
1775	Levi Yitzhak becomes rabbi of Pinsk
1780	Publication of the first Hasidic book, *Toldot Ya'akov Yosef*
1780 (?)	Debate between Rabbi Levi Yitzhak and Rabbi Katzenellenbogen of Brisk in Warsaw
1781	"Ban" against Hasidim signed by the Gaon of Vilna
1784	Letter from the Gaon and other leaders of Vilna to leaders of Pinsk urging dismissal of Rabbi Levi Yitzhak
1785	Levi Yitzhak becomes rabbi of Berditchev
1798	Publication of *Kedushat Levi*
1803-06	Publication of *Keter Torah* by Meir, the son of Rabbi Levi Yitzhak
1806	Death of Rabbi Meir
1809	Death of Rabbi Levi Yitzhak

Notes

Prologue: THE HASIDIC WORLD

1. Shimshon of Shpetivka, *Divrei Noam* (Warsaw, 1892), p. 12.
2. S. Dresner, *The Zaddik* (New York: Schocken Books, 1974).
3. M. Buber, *Hasidism* (New York: Philosophical Library, 1945), Foreword.
4. See pages 92-93.

Chapter 1: THE LIFE OF A TZADDIK

1. See A. Waldman, *Shem ha-Gedolim he-Hadash* (Jerusalem, 1965), p. 88, No. 21; S. Gutman, *Tiferet Bet Levi* (Yasi, 1909), pp. 2, 3. Levi Yitzhak's son, Meir, also quotes the teachings of his grandfather, Meir, in *Keter Torah* (Mezirov, 1803).
2. J. Tumim, *Rav Peninim* (Frankfurt, 1782), Introduction, quoted in M. Gutman, *Migiborei ha-Hasidut* (Tel Aviv: Mosad Harav Kook, 1953), p. 78.
3. S. Horodetzky, *ha-Hasidut v'ha-Hasidim* (Tel Aviv: Dvir, 1928), Vol. 2, p. 74.
4. G. Scholem, *Major Trends in Jewish Mysticism* (New York: Schocken, 1946), p. 343.
5. *Kedushat Levi* (hereafter referred to as *K. L.*) (Jerusalem: Mosad l'Hotzaat Sifrei Musar v'Hasidut, 1958), p. 60.
6. *K. L.*, pp. 8-9.
7. *K. L.*, p. 25.
8. According to Dubnow, among all the disciples and later followers of the Maggid, only Levi Yitzhak achieved the Maggid's fame (S. Dubnow, *Toldot ha-Hasidut*, [Tel Aviv: Dvir, 1960], p. 194). The first encomium to appear on the Maggid's initial book, *Likutei Amarim*, was by Rabbi Levi Yitzhak. Also noteworthy is the fact that his contemporary, Rabbi Abraham Joshua Heschel of Apt, who was held in highest esteem among the Tzaddikim themselves and to whom they turned most often for encomia for their books, described the author of *Kedushat Levi* in his own encomium to that volume as *Rabban Shel Kol B'nei ha-Golah*, "Leader of all the children of the exile," a term I have not found him use for any other contemporary.
9. Central Zholikhover Landsmanschaft in Chicago (Chicago: 1953), Yiddish.

10. Elimelekh of Lizhensk, *Noam Elimelekh* (New York: Shulsinger, 1942), p. 224.
11. The chronology of Rabbi Levi Yitzhak in Zholikhov and Pinsk has been clarified by Hayim Lieberman in *Yivo Bletter* (New York, 1937), Vol. 11, pp. 92-93, and in *Sepher ha-Yovel to Alexander Marx*, edited by David Frankel (New York, 1943), pp. 15-17. For a review of the arguments and further evidence, see M. Wilensky, *Hasidim u-Mitnagdim* (Jerusalem: Mosad Bialik, 1970), Vol. 1, p. 116, note 4 and Vol. 2, p. 358. See note 27.
12. Aaron of Zhitomir, *Toldot Aharon* (Lemberg, 1864), p. 12b; cf. Yitzhak of Neshkhiz, *Toldot Yitzhak* (Pietrokov, 1928), p. 25.
13. In an anti-Hasidic polemic, *Zemir Aritzim*, while acknowledging that Rabbi Levi Yitzhak is "filled with Torah" and referring to him as "leader of this sect," *i.e.* the Hasidim, the author complains that "he wastes his time with the common folk." See M. Wilensky, *Hasidim u-Mitnagdim*, Vol. 2, p. 49 and p. 244.
14. Yosef of Nemirov, *Vikuha Rabba* (Warsaw, 1913), pp. 43-44.
15. Mordecai Nadav, "Rabbi Avigdor ben Hayim and His Struggle with Hasidism in Pinsk and Lithuania" (Hebrew), *Zion* (Jerusalem, 1971), Vol. 36, pp. 200-219.
16. S. Dubnow, *Kitvei Hitnagdut Al Kat ha-Hasidim* (Berlin: Dvir, 1923), p. 304.
17. In 1784 Rabbi Katzenellenbogen wrote Rabbi Levi Yitzhak a letter which purports to review the arguments which Levi Yitzhak advanced in the Warsaw debate. See M. Wilensky, *Hasidim u-Mitnagdim*, Vol. 1, pp. 122-31 and Vol. 2, pp. 127-30.

In *Vikuha Rabba* (Warsaw, 1913, pp. 37-39) by Rabbi Yosef of Nemirov, who was a student of Rabbi Levi Yitzhak and composed his book in the form of a debate between a Hasid and a Mitnaged, we find that he deals with the matter of delayed prayer at length. "In regard to your question about Hasidim delaying their prayers beyond their prescribed times, I would suggest that you not generalize. The leader of all the Tzaddikim, the Besht—may his merit be a shield for us—would say his morning prayers with the break of dawn as did his disciple after him, our Teacher and Master, the Maggid, Dov Ber of Mezritch—may his merit be a shield for us—on most occasions. In any case, when serious illness compelled him to delay, he would not postpone the prayers of the congregation. Furthermore, I can testify that most of the Tzaddikim of our generation do not delay the time of prayer. Only certain Tzaddikim, such as the noted Tzaddik, Rabbi Mikhal Zlotchover—may his merit be a shield for us—and the Rav and Gaon, our Master and Teacher, the Tzaddik, Levi Yitzhak—may his light continue to shine—do, in fact, delay their prayers, relying upon the *Shema* which they had already recited upon rising. But surely they also have a private reason for this custom which we must not question. ... Further, the time of prayer is an injunction that comes from the Rabbis of the Talmud and not the Torah." Cf. pp. 16-17, 93.

See this entire work for issues which separated the Hasidim from Mitnagdim, the exposition of which may reflect some of the views of the author's teacher, Rabbi Levi Yitzhak.

18. M. Wilensky, *Hasidim u-Mitnagdim*, Vol. 1, pp. 132-36. While Dubnow (*Toldot ha-Hasidut*, pp. 479-81) had questions as to whether the letter did indeed refer to Rabbi Levi Yitzhak, Lieberman and Wilensky have adequately clarified and sustained this assumption. See note 11 above.

On the title page of the first edition of *Kedushat Levi* (Slavita, 1798), which was published during the author's lifetime, he refers to himself as "head of the Court of Berditchev, Zholikhov, and Ritchivol." He does not mention his residence in Pinsk!

Nadav concludes that "there is no doubt that only the full weight of the personal influence of the Gaon was in the end able to turn the balance of the scales against the Hasidim of Pinsk and against its rabbi, Levi Yitzhak" (M. Nadav, "Hasidism and Its Opponents in the Communities of Pinsk—Karlin" [Hebrew], *Zion* [Jerusalem, 1969], Vol. 34, p. 100).

19. Rabbi Shneur Zalman of Ladi told the following: "Once when I was in Mezritch with my holy master, the Maggid, there were gathered there over one Sabbath nine disciples of the master. Rabbi Shmelke and his brother Rabbi Pinhas, Rabbi Nahum of Tchernobil, Rabbi Levi Yitzhak of Berditchev, who was then the head of the court in Pinsk, Rabbi Zev Wolf of Zhitomir, the brothers Elimelekh and Zusya, Rabbi Leib, and Shlomo of Karlin. I was the youngest of them, for they were already rabbis of communities.

"During our stay a letter arrived from Pinsk to the holy rabbi Levi Yitzhak that the Mitnagdim were so harassing his family and the Hasidim in the community, that it had become unbearable. The letter spelled out the miserable details. Taking counsel together, the rabbis decided to read the letter before their master, the Maggid, when they sat together at the Sabbath table, for 'to save a life one may violate the Sabbath,' and this was surely such a case. They asked Rabbi Levi Yitzhak to read the letter before the Maggid, since he was the concerned party..." (Y. M. Kleinbaum, *Shema Shlomo* [Pietrokov, 1928], Part 2, p. 33, No. 64).

20. S. Vednik, *Sefer Baal Shem Tov* (Jerusalem: Horev, 1962), Vol. 2, p. 136, No. 6 and note 5.

21. He also applied to himself the words *V'nahnu Mah* "and what are we?" (Exodus 16:7), the numerical sum of "*Mah*" being 45 (*Mem* = 40 + *Hei* = 5).

22. "The fullness of joy is found only where anguish once prevailed. This is hinted at in the verse, 'I will give thanks to Thee for having afflicted me, for Thou art become my salvation' [Psalms 118:21]. That is, afflictions came for the sake of salvation. And this is the intent of the next verse, 'The stone which the builders rejected is become [afterward] the chief cornerstone.' 'From the Lord is this' [*ibid.*, 22], that it was all providential. This is not so when the Lord showers one from his youth on only with good things, all of which appear accidental. However, when first evil befalls a man and then the Creator delivers him from his anguish

in joy, it is clear that all was planned by the Lord from the start. Therefore, the Psalm continues, 'This is the Lord's doing; it is marvelous in our eyes. This is the day which the Lord has made; let us rejoice and be glad in it' [*ibid.*, 23-24]." *K. L.*, p. 31.

A reading of the entire Psalm will suggest Levi Yitzhak's identification with it.

23. Yissakhar Ber, *Introduction to Sefer ha-Z'khirah*, by Levi Yitzhak (Vilna-Horadna, 1835), p. 2b.

This statement seems to indicate that Rabbi Levi Yitzhak became the official head of the Berditchev community in 1794, though we know he arrived there in 1785. M. Shulvass suggests that he may have served in a less than official capacity before 1794. (See page 42.)

24. *K. L.*, p. 310.

25. Yitzhak of Kamarna, *Heikhal ha-B'rakhah* (Lemberg, 1865), Vol. 1, *B'reishit*, introduction, and Vol. 3, *Vayikra*, p. 281. See S. Vednik, *Sefer Baal Shem Tov*, Vol. 2, p. 136, No. 6 and note 5.

26. Meir ben Levi Yitzhak, *Keter Torah* (Mezirov, 1803), Preface. The full text of the preface reads as follows:

"One young in years writes: All my life I have been reared in the presence of my lord and teacher, my father, the glory of Israel and its holy light, our teacher, Levi Yitzhak—may he be blessed with many years of life! It is well known to all that my father and master raised up many thousands of students, whom he taught Talmud and Codes, and whose hearts were inflamed by his service of God. When they heard his teachings of Torah and experienced his holy way of service, even the least among them, as myself, learned from his wisdom according to the limits of their knowledge. Therefore I have not sought encomia from the rabbis or Tzaddikim of our time. For I have trusted that since all that I have written is taken from the light of the wisdom of my honored father, surely all would give their assent. I ask from the Lord of all, may He be blessed and His name be blessed, my Father in Heaven, that the words of my mouth be acceptable before You and bring You joy. [This book] is a humble gift, the gift of one humble in knowledge. For those whom You show compassion, O Lord, are marked by compassion. The words of him who dwells in the dust, Meir, the son of our master and father, Levi Yitzhak, may his light ever shine." See *K. L.* p. 371.

Meir, whose Talmudic mastery is evidenced in his book, *Keter Torah* (Genesis: Mezirov, 1803; Exodus: Zhitomir, 1803), died in 1806, while his father was still living. Of him his father wrote, "I have returned his soul pure, as I received it." See *K. L.* p. 77.

In *Kedushat Levi* (1798), Levi Yitzhak acknowledges his son, Meir, as the source for some of his teachings (*e.g., K. L.* p. 77). At the close of one section of the book some of the writings of Meir are added which the latter introduces with the following words:

"One young in years and the least of the fellowship speaks. Since the holy words of my honored father, the Gaon and Hasid, our master and teacher, Levi Yitzhak—may he be blessed with many years of life—are now in the press about to be published and will be called *Kedushat Levi*, and since it is known to the whole house of Israel that the words of my father inhabit the loftiest heights, for the divine spirit speaks in them, and thousands of Jews who have listened to him have been moved to serve God more devoutly, and from then until this day they have established a mighty center of Torah in which they have learned with his students *Hiddushei Halakhot* and *Hiddushei Oraita*—because of all this I have decided to provide a branch to his holy words, that my memory should be joined with his holy memory by adding two or three minor explanations of *Aggadot* and two or three minor explanations of *Halakhot*. May my words be accepted before the Lord of all" (K. L. p. 371).

In 1811, after the death of Levi Yitzhak, his second son, Israel, wrote in the preface to his book, *Toldot Yitzhak ben Levi* (Berditchev, 1811):
"Behold the very truth. I am the least of men, lacking the wisdom with which to write words of holy Torah. But what I understand of the words of the holy Gaon, my father—may he rest in Paradise—I have sought to record. I have likewise recorded teachings that I have understood from my late brother [Meir], holy and learned light—may his memory live on in the world to come! May their merit and the merit of all Tzaddikim be a shield for Israel, for us and for all our children."

Among Rabbi Levi Yitzhak's best known students were Aaron of Zhitomir, Avraham David of Butchatch, Israel of Koznitz, Avraham Mordecai of Pintchov, Moshe of Savran, Yosef of Nemirov, Yissakhar Dov-Ber (author of *Sefer ha-Z'khirah*), Hayim Yosef of Pistin, Tzvi Hirsh of Yampla, and Aaron Arush.

27. Before his encomium to *Meir Netivim* by Rabbi Meir Margolis (Polonoye, 1791), Levi Yitzhak is described as "the distinguished Gaon and Hasid, master of the *Halakhah* [*Harif Ubaki*], our master and teacher, Levi Yitzhak—may his light continue to shine—head of the court and the Yeshivah in the holy community of Pinsk and environs, and now head of the court in the holy community of Berditchev." Note the emphasis here on his *Halakhic* mastery and the precedence of his rabbinate in Lithuanian Pinsk over Berditchev, where he had already settled for more than five years. The term *Reish Metivta* ("Head of the Yeshivah"), was rarely—if ever elsewhere—used to describe the classic Hasidic rabbis.

28. The first edition (Slavita, 1798), contains discourses on Hanukkah and Purim, and includes *Divrei Torah* in his father's name as well as selections from his sons, Israel and Meir, about whom see note 26 above.

Rabbi Levi Yitzhak played an important role in Hebrew publishing. He was instrumental in establishing the first Hebrew press in the Ukraine. The first Hebrew printer in Berditchev was Samuel the son of Yissakhar Segal, whose work was made possible through Levi Yitzhak's aid. All the Hebrew books that came from this press (some twenty-eight over a thirteen year period) had the encomia either of Levi Yitzhak himself or of one of his sons. Publication of the Talmud was begun, but only one volume appeared. These books were not limited to Hasidic literature. Their variety represents the wide concern of the Rabbi of Berditchev. Of

the twenty-eight, nine were Hasidic, two Kabbalistic, four Halakhic, four liturgical, and three were in Yiddish for the unlearned. See A. Yaari, "The Hebrew Press in Berditchev" (Hebrew) (Jerusalem: Kiryat Sefer, 1944), Vol. 21, pp. 100—24. More books contain encomia by Rabbi Levi Yitzhak than from any other Hasidic leader but Rabbi Abraham Joshua Heschel of Apt.
29. M. Gutman, *Migiborei ha-Hasidut*, p. 111.
30. A. B. Gottlober, "Memories from My Youth" (Hebrew), *Ha-Boker Or* (Lemberg—Warsaw, 1880), p. 383, quoted by Dubnow, *Toldot ha-Hasidut*, pp. 194-95. Gottlober was born in 1811, shortly after Levi Yitzhak's death. Though raised in the Hasidic way, he later turned against it. His Hasidic father-in-law compelled Gottlober's wife to divorce him and forced him to leave the community. Consequently, he devoted much of his talent to satire of the Hasidim. For a selection from his writings in English, see L. Davidowicz, *The Golden Tradition* (New York: Holt, Rinehart & Winston, 1967), pp. 113-19.

Chapter 2: LOVE OF ISRAEL

1. *K. L.*, p. 225. Compare the following: " . . . the anger of the Lord was kindled greatly; and Moses was displeased" (Numbers 11:10).
    "Do you know why 'the anger of the Lord was kindled greatly'?" asked Rabbi Levi Yitzhak. "Because 'Moses was displeased.' That is, because Moses, may he rest in peace, did not defend the people of Israel."
2. *K. L.*, p. 111.
3. *K. L.*, p. 237.
4. *K. L.*, p. 232.
5. "Rabbi Levi Yitzhak of Berditchev and the Royal Edicts of His Times," in *Jews and Judaism in Eastern Europe* by Israel Halperin, (Jerusalem: Magnes Press, 1969) (Hebrew), pp. 340-48.
6. A. B. Gottlober, *Ha-Boker Or*, V, pp. 383-85. Quoted by Halperin, pp. 343-45.
7. Mendel Levin, *Essai d'un plan reforme ayant pour objet d'éclairer la Nation Juive en Pologne et de redresser par la fes moers* (Warsaw). Though no date is given, Halperin, from another Levin document, determines it as 1791; see Halperin, p. 342, n. 13. Halperin (pp. 342-43) identifies the reference in Levin's work as Rabbi Levi Yitzhak. E. Ringelblum (*Yivo Bletter*, New York, 1938, p. 125), however, disagrees; see Halperin, p. 343, n. 15.
8. E. Ringelblum, "Hasidism and Haskala in Warsaw in the 18th Century," (Yiddish) (*Yivo Bletter*, 1938, p. 126). Quoted by Halperin, p. 343, n. 15.
9. *K. L.*, p. 75.
10. *K. L.*, p. 213. See also p. 133.
11. *K. L.*, pp. 205-06.
12. *K. L.*, p. 335.

13. *K. L.*, p. 306. Compare p. 134.
14. I. Berger, *Eser Orot* (Pietrokov, 1907), p. 59.
15. Leonard Bernstein's 1964 symphony, *Kaddish*, faces "man's possible imminent suicide," and contains a "particularly anguished outburst by the speaker in the middle of the *Din Torah* (trial scene) in which he accuses God of a breach of faith with man, concluding with the theme, 'We are in this thing together, You and I.' " The program notes indicate the direct influence of the Kaddish of Rabbi Levi Yitzhak of Berditchev upon the form and content of this work.

    Other creative works portraying Rabbi Levi Yitzhak as the Defender of Israel are: *Plays*: "The Third Cry" by Yaakov Cohen in *Kol Kitvei Yaakov Cohen* (Tel Aviv: Dvir, 1945); "Three Crowns" by Tzvi Cohen (Tel Aviv: 1954); "The Great Defender" by Yitzhak Sela (1958); *Poems*: "A New Din Torah of Rabbi Levi Yitzhak" by Zalman Shneur in *Shirim*, Part 1, (1951); "At the End of the Road Stands Rabbi Levi Yitzhak Seeking an Answer from Heaven" by Uri Tzvi Greenberg (1951); *Ballad*: "Din Torah" in *Or Zarua* (1959) by S. Meltzer.

Chapter 3: PRAYER

1. *K. L.*, p. 83.
2. *K. L.*, p. 281.
3. *K. L.*, p. 244.
4. Aaron of Zhitomir, *Toldot Aharon* (Lemberg, 1864), Part 2, p. 35a.
5. H. Deutschesman, *Sh'muot Tovot* (Warsaw, 1896), p. 22. Cf. pp. 16-17, 32-33, and p. 209, No. 17.
6. S. Kaminker, *Sh'nei ha-M'orot* (Kishinev, 1896), p. 96.
7. M. M. Bodek, *Seder ha-Dorot he-Hadash* (Warsaw, 1882), p.35.
8. *K. L.*, p. 215. Whatever the communities Rabbi Levi Yitzhak visited and prayed in, the memories of his visit and his prayers were treasured up by the people. Dr. Shlomo Novle informed me that as a child in Sanok, Galicia, his grandfather showed him in the old *Pinkas* book, which recorded the history of the community, that once the Berditchever prayed in their synagogue before the pulpit, a massive wooden structure, reaching almost to the ceiling and embellished with elaborate trestle-work which at one point gave the appearance of two handles, one on each side. In the fervor of his worship, he grasped these handles and broke one. It was never repaired thereafter in loving remembrance. According to a further tradition, while visiting the synagogue of another community, he held on to the sides of the pulpit so fiercely during the ecstasy of his prayer that, though it had been painted several days before, the imprints of his fingers were left upon it and preserved ever afterward.
9. I. Berger, *Eser Orot*, pp. 45-46.
10. David Moshe of Tchortkov, *Divrei David* (Husiatin, Galicia, 1904), pp. 15-17.
11. *K. L.*, p. 52.
12. *K. L.*, p. 193.

13. *K. L.*, pp. 300-01.
14. *K. L.*, p. 269.
15. *K. L.*, p. 290.
16. *K. L.*, p. 40.
17. The text was first published in the name of Rabbi Levi Yitzhak in a book by one of his students, Shmuel Kaminker, *Sh'nei ha-M'orot* (Kishinev, 1896), p. 103. The book's editor, Joshua Pickman, claims to have found a copy of a manuscript of Levi Yitzhak in which the song is written. Horodetzky (*ha-Hasidut v'ha-Hasidim*, p. 82, n. 16), however, questions the authorship, since he claims a similar version of the song was already in use in Germany and Alsace, from where it may have found its way to the Ukraine.
18. Famed though he was for his songs, Rabbi Levi Yitzhak was careful not to substitute music for prayer. His disciple, Rabbi Aaron of Zhitomir, quotes his master to this effect:

    "There are those who select a certain melody for one prayer and another melody for the next prayer, believing that this is the proper manner of worship, through which they will come to *Hitlahavut* and bring joy to the Lord. However, this is not the true way of prayer, and those who pursue it are fools. They walk in darkness and have not even begun to understand the proper manner of worship—which is the following:

    "One should divest oneself of all worldliness, until he has reached the stage where he is no longer aware of this world. He should recite the letters and words aloud in a simple, clear voice, in order that he might be able to join his mind to the holy letters and to understand the meaning of the holy words. Then, of itself, he will begin to burn with an overwhelming fear of God.

    "I have received this holy way of worship from my teacher [Rabbi Levi Yitzhak]. And he received it from his teacher, the Maggid. And he received it from the Baal Shem Tov. And he received it from his teacher, Ahiya Hashiloni. For this is the true manner of serving the Holy One, blessed be He." (*Pitgamim Kadishin* [Warsaw, 1886], p. 17.)

Chapter 4: DOING THE MITZVOT

1. *K. L.*, p. 33.
2. *K. L.*, p. 306.
3. *K. L.*, pp. 53-54.
4. *K. L.*, p. 253.
5. *K. L.*, p. 14.
6. *K. L.*, p. 54.
7. *K. L.*, p. 6.
8. Levi Yitzhak was the first person to whom Rabbi Shneur Zalman wrote after his deliverance from prison in Petersburg in 1798. See N. Mindel, *Rabbi Shneur Zalman of Ladi* (New York: Kehot, 1969), p. 184; cf. pp. 48, 228, 230, 232 and 303; M. Teitelbaum, *Ha-Rav mi-Ladi* (Warsaw:

Tushiah, 1914), Vol. 1, pp. 23, 72, 78, 142, 144; Vol. 2, pp. 57, 58; M. Wilensky, *Hasidim u-Mitnagdim*, Vol. 1, p. 302.
9. Y. M. Kleinbaum, *Shema Shlomo* (Pietrokov, 1928), Part 2, p. 31.
10. *K. L.*, p. 353.
11. Gutman, S., *Tiferet Bet Levi* (Yasi, 1909), p. 12.
12. He derives the Hebrew word *Shabbat* from *shuv* "return." *K. L.*, p. 5.
13. See pp. 193-94 for another version of this story. A. Markus, *ha-Hasidut* (Tel Aviv: Netzah, 1944), p. 122, observes that Rabbi Levi Yitzhak's *Neilah* prayers and his custom of studying the tractate Sukkah of the Talmud before breaking his Yom Kippur fast, so impressed Jacob Orenstein (d. 1839), the Rabbi of Lvov and one of the leading rabbinic figures of his time, that his anti-Hasidic position was softened. Meir Vunder in his article "Rabbi Zekharia Mendel of Yaruslav" (*Sinai*, 1973, Vol. 73, p. 83) notes that Levi Yitzhak came frequently to visit his father's grave in Yaruslav, where he once spent Yom Kippur, and it was there that Rabbi Orenstein learned of his habit. Cf. p. 191.
14. *K. L.*, p. 282.
15. *K. L.*, p. 70.
16. Y. Moshe of Kamaravke, *Derekh Emunah u-Ma'aseh Rav* (Warsaw, 1849), p. 87.

Chapter 5: THE MESSIAH

1. *K. L.*, p. 283.
2. *K. L.*, p. 80.
3. M. Buber, *Tales of the Hasidim* (New York: Schocken, 1947), Vol. 1, p. 229.
4. *K. L.*, p. 88.
5. M. Buber, *Tales*, p. 212-13.

Chapter 6: DAY-TO-DAY

1. S. Gutman, *Tiferet Bet Levi* (Yasi, 1909), pp. 11-12; M. Buber, *Tales*, pp. 229-30.
2. *K. L.*, p. 235.
3. H. Deutschesman, *Sh'muot Tovot*, p. 26.
4. *K. L.*, p. 61.
5. *K. L.*, p. 286.
6. *K. L.*, p. 303.
7. *K. L.*, p. 61.
8. Rabbi Moshe of Koznitz, *B'er Moshe* (Lemberg, 1858), p. 70.

Chapter 7: HUMILITY

1. Yitzhak of Kamarna, *N'tiv Mitzvotekha* (Jerusalem, 1948), "Sh'vil ha-Torah" pp. 104–05. The passage continues: "Such behavior seemed

foolish to others, even to some Tzaddikim. But the true Tzaddik, whose soul is aflame with love and joy and who sees no evil in his fellow, wishes to share this light with every man. For he holds each Jew as precious as the apple of his eye. There are Tzaddikim, however, whose love of Israel does not reach so high a rung since they serve God out of fear, and who may consequently, from time to time, look askance at the ways of this beloved Tzaddik."
2. H. Deutschesman, *Sh'muot Tovot*, pp. 22-23.
3. *K. L.*, pp. 33, 274, and 292.
4. M. Buber, *Tales*, p. 219.
5. M. Citron, *Shivhei Tzaddikim* (Warsaw, 1883), pp. 9-10.
6. Aaron of Zhitomir, *Toldot Aharon* (Lemberg, 1864), *B'shalah*, p. 33a.
7. *K. L.*, p. 177.
8. *K. L.*, p. 256.

Chapter 8: BETWEEN GOD AND MAN

1. David Moshe of Tchortkov, *Divrei David*, p. 15-17.
2. *K. L.*, p. 296.
3. *K. L.*, p. 104.
4. *K. L.*, p. 193.
5. Pinhas of Dinovitz, *Siftei Tzaddikim* (Lemberg, 1863), pp. 32b-33a, Beshalah.
6. *K. L.*, p. 297.
7. M. Buber, *Tales*, p. 230.
8. *K. L.*, p. 220.
9. *K. L.*, p. 3.
10. *K. L.*, p. 302.
11. *K. L.*, p. 14.
12. *K. L.*, p. 11.
13. *K. L.*, pp. 308-09.
14. Yissakhar Dov Ber, *M'vaser Tzedek* (Dubno, 1798), pp. 27b-28a; M. Buber, *Tales*, pp. 218-19.
15. *K. L.*, pp. 263-64.
16. I. Berger, *Eser Orot*, p. 53.

Chapter 9: DAYS OF AWE

1. *K. L.*, p. 278.
2. I. Berger, *Eser Orot*, p. 51.
3. *Ibid.*, p. 48.
4. S. Gutman, *Tiferet Bet Levi*, p. 15; M. Buber, *Tales*, p. 210.
5. I. Berger, *Eser Orot*, p. 51.
6. Rabbi Ephraim Zalman Margolis (1762-1828), the author of a number of important Halakhic works, was one of the most noted rabbinic figures of the time. (See J. E., Vol. 8 and Gelber, *Brody* (Jerusalem: Mosad Harav Kook, 1956) (Hebrew). In his book *Tiv Gittin* (Koretz, 1819), letter

Yod, he writes: "I have heard from my honored relative, the Gaon and Hasid, our teacher, Rabbi Levi Yitzhak, may his memory be a blessing...."

A responsum to Rabbi Levi Yitzhak is contained in the volume *Rabbenu Ya'akov mi-Smela* (Jerusalem, 1968) *Even ha-Ezer*, 3. The responsum, which is dated 1808, begins: "May the Lord grant peace to our honored Master, the distinguished Rav, Gaon, and Hasid, the glory of Israel, whose name is extolled, Rabbi Levi Yitzhak—may his light continue to shine forever—and to all who take shelter under the shade of his wisdom." The responsum concludes with: "...these are the words of the least of his [Levi Yitzhak's] students, who awaits his wise reply...."

This volume, which was first published in 1904, contains several responsa to Rabbi Ephraim Zalman Margolis.

Chapter 10: DEATH OF THE REBBE

1. *Sihot ha-Ran*, No. 196-97, in *Shivhei ha-Ran*, Nahman of Bratzlav, New York, 1972.

    "On the fifth day of the week, the twenty-fifth of Tishri, the honored Rav and Gaon, the holy light, the distinguished Hasid, our Master, Rabbi Levi Yitzhak, the Head of the Court of Berditchev, died—may the memory of the righteous be for a blessing. [Two days later] On *Shabbat B'reishit*, the Sabbath following, our Master [Rabbi Nahman] dealt with the theme of the departure of the Tzaddik, the glory of Israel, from this world (cf. *Likutei Moharan T'nina*, No. 67, 68). When first we heard them, we did not understand for whom our Master's words were intended, for news of the death of Rabbi Levi Yitzhak did not reach us until the second day of the next week. When, however, the sorrow of all Israel became manifest because of the death of that great Tzaddik, we knew that our Master [Rabbi Nahman] had meant Rabbi Levi Yitzhak when he spoke of the disappearance of the "glory of Israel." For the *Tefillin* are called "the glory of Israel," and that is the way he used to refer to Rabbi Levi Yitzhak, as is explained elsewhere. Furthermore, in that year there had been a scarcity of *Etrogim*. Later, as if by a miracle, *Etrogim* arrived just in time. Our Master had said that he relied on the Tzaddikim of the time, and especially on that Tzaddik [Rabbi Levi Yitzhak], who was the "glory of the community," for the arrival of the *Etrogim*. Thus we clearly see that our Master had revealed [to us] through his holy spirit the death of that Tzaddik."

    The complete address of Rabbi Nahman given on the Sabbath of B'reishit (*Likutei Moharan T'nina*, No. 67, 68), which his scribe refers to above, should be studied.
2. I. Berger, *Eser Orot*, p. 57.
3. I. Berger, *Eser Orot*, p. 51.

Glossary

Aggadah—That part of Jewish literature which is non-legal
Amidah—The main part of the three daily prayers, to be said standing
Amkha Yidn—The common people
Ark—Synagogue shrine in which the Torah Scrolls are kept
Ashrei ha-Ish—First two words of the first Psalm
Besht—Baal Shem Tov, "Master of the Good Name" (1700-1760); the founder of Hasidism
Bet Din—Jewish court of law
Bet ha-Midrash—Place for study and prayer
Bimah—An elevated platform in the synagogue where the Torah is read
B'rit Milah—The act and ceremony of circumcision
Codes—Compendiums of Jewish law based upon the Talmud
Dayyenu—Hymn in the Haggadah
Dukhenen—Blessing pronounced in the synagogue by the *Kohanim*, the descendants of Aaron
Ein Sof—The Infinite One; a *Kabbalistic* name for God
Etrog—Citron used for the ritual of the Sukkot festival
Gan Eden—Paradise, Garden of Eden
Geninnom—Hell
Haftarah (*pl.* **Haftarot**)—Selections from the Prophets read on Sabbaths and festivals
Haggadah—The order of the service read at the *Seder* on the first and second evenings of Passover
Halakhah—That part of Jewish literature which deals with religious, ethical, civil and criminal law
Hanukkah—Holiday commemorating the victory of the Maccabees
Hasid (*pl.* **Hasidim**)—Follower of the Hasidic movement initiated by Israel Ben Eliezer, known as the Baal Shem Tov, in eighteenth-century Eastern Europe

Hatan—Bridegroom
Havdalah—Ceremony marking the separation between the holiness of the Sabbath and the profanity of the week
Hazzan—Cantor; leader of synagogue service
Herem—Excommunication
Heshbon ha-Nefesh—Introspection
Hevrah—Fellowship
Hitlahavut—Enthusiasm, inspiration
Hoshana Rabbah—The seventh day of the holiday of Sukkot
Kabbalah—Jewish mystical literature
Kabbalists—Mystics
Kavvanah—Devotion, sincerity
Ketubah—Marriage contract
Kiddush—Blessing generally recited over a cup of wine at home and in the synagogue to welcome the Sabbath or a festival
Kittel—The white garment worn by some during prayers on the High Holy Days
Kol Nidre—The first prayer recited in the synagogue on the eve of Yom Kippur
Lamnatzeiah—Psalm 47, recited before blowing the Shofar on Rosh Hashanah
Lulav—Palm branches used for Sukkot ritual
Ma'ariv—Evening service
Maggid (*pl.* **Maggidim**)—Preacher spreading the teachings of the Torah
Mahzor—Holiday prayer book
Maskil (*pl.* **Maskilim**)—Wise, enlightened; follower of the *Haskalah* movement of eighteenth-century Europe, spreading modern culture among Jews
Matzah (*pl.* **Matzot**)—Unleavened bread eaten during Passover
Melammed—Teacher
Menuhah—Peace, rest
Mikveh—Bath for ritual immersion
Min ha-Meitzar—Prayer before blowing the *Shofar* on Rosh Hashanah
Minhah—Afternoon prayer
Minyan—Minimum quorum of ten adult males required for worship service

Mitnaged (*pl.* **Mitnagdim**)—Opponent of Hasidism
Mitzvah (*pl.* **Mitzvot**)—Religious commandment; good deed
Musaf—Service recited on Sabbaths and festivals after the reading of the Torah
Neilah—Prayer of Yom Kippur concluded at nightfall
Neshamah Yeteirah—"Additional soul" which one receives on the Sabbath
Nigleh—Legal, or non-mystical literature; *Halakhah*
Niggun—Song without words
Nistar—Mystical literature
Parnas—President, or elder of the congregation or community
Purim—Feast of Lots
Rav—Communal rabbi; *Halakhic* authority
Rebbe—Hasidic rabbi
Responsa (*sing.* **Responsum**)—Answers to questions on Jewish law given by *Halakhic* scholars in reply to inquiries
Rosh Hashanah—The Jewish New Year
Rosh Hodesh—The beginning of the Hebrew month, also known as New Moon
Selihot—Penitential prayers especially before Rosh Hashanah
Seraph (*pl.* **Seraphim**)—An angel
Shaharit—Morning prayer
Shammash—Sexton
Shavuot—Feast of Revelation
Shekhinah—Divine Presence
Shema—"Hear, O Israel, the Lord our God, the Lord is One"; the Jewish credo
Shir ha-Yihud—Song of God's Unity
Shofar—Ram's horn, blown in the synagogue at services on Rosh Hashanah
Shohet—Ritual slaughterer of animals and poultry
Siddur—Prayer book
Simhah—Joy
Simhat Torah—"Rejoicing over the Torah," the last day of Sukkot, celebrating the completion of the yearly cycle of the reading of the Torah
Sukkah—Booth for the Festival of Sukkot, symbolically recalling the forty years' wandering in the desert

Sukkot—The Feast of Tabernacles, the fall harvest festival
Tablets of the Law—Received by Moses at Sinai and placed within the Ark of the Covenant
Tallit (*pl.* **Talleitim**)—Prayer shawl
Takkanah (*pl.* **Takkanot**)—Ordinance promulgated for public welfare, or for strengthening religious and moral life
Talmud—The post-Biblical Rabbinic compendium containing legal and moral teachings
Tefillah—Prayer; the *Amidah*
Tefillin—"Phylacteries," or leather cases containing quotations from the Pentateuch, worn on the forehead and on the left arm during morning prayers
Tehinot—Devotional literature for women, usually in Yiddish
Tekiah—A sound of the *Shofar*
Teshuvah—Repentance
Tishah b'Av—"The ninth day of the month of Av," a fast commemorating the destruction of the Temple
Torah—The Five Books of Moses; all Jewish religious literature
Tzaddik—Righteous one; saint; Hasidic rabbi
Tzedakah—Righteousness; charity
Viddui—Confession
Weekday—In contrast to Sabbath
Yeshivah—Talmudical college
Yidn—Jews
Yihus—Ancestry
Yom ha-Din—Day of Judgment
Yom Kippur—Day of Atonement
Zikhronot—Part of Rosh Hashanah liturgy

Bibliography

IN ENGLISH

Buber, Martin. *Tales of the Hasidim: The Early Masters,* Vol. 1. New York: Schocken Books, 1947.

Dresner, Samuel H. *The Zaddik.* New York: Schocken Books, 1974.

Encyclopaedia Judaica, Vol. 11, p. 102. "Levi Isaac ben Meir of Berdichev." Jerusalem: Keter, 1971.

Minkin, Jacob. *The Romance of Hasidism.* New York: The Macmillan Company, 1935.

Rabinowicz, Harry M. *The World of Hasidism.* New York and Bridgeport: Hartmore House, 1970.

Scholem, Gershom G. *Major Trends in Jewish Mysticism.* New York: Schocken Books, 1946.

Wiesel, Elie. *Souls on Fire.* New York: Random House, 1972.

IN HEBREW

Aaron of Zhitomir. *Toldot Aharon.* Lemberg, 1864.

Berger, I. *Eser Orot.* Pietrokov, 1907.

Citron, Mendel. *Shivhei Tzaddikim.* Warsaw, 1883.

Deutschesman, H. *Sh'muot Tovot.* Warsaw, 1896.

Dubnow, S. *Toldot ha-Hasidut.* Tel Aviv: Dvir, 1960.

Elazar ben Aharon. *Safran Shel Tzaddikim.* Lublin, 1919.

Erlich, Israel. *Rabbi Levi Yitzhak mi-Berditchev.* Tel Aviv: Bar Giora, 1947.

Gutman, Matityahu. *Migiborei ha-Hasidut.* Tel Aviv: Mosad Harav Kook, 1953.

Gutman, Shalom. *Tiferet Bet Levi.* Yasi, Rumania, 1909.

Horodetzky, S. *ha-Hasidut v'ha-Hasidim,* Vol. 2. Tel Aviv: Dvir, 1928.

Israel ben Levi Yitzhak. *Toldot Yitzhak ben Levi.* Berditchev, 1811.

Kleinbaum, Y. M. *Shema Shlomo.* Pietrokov, 1928.

Levi Yitzhak. *Kedushat Levi.* Jerusalem: Mosad l'Hotzaat Sifrei Musar v'Hasidut, 1958.

Meir ben Levi Yitzhak. *Keter Torah.* Part 1, Mezirov, 1803; Part 2, Zhitomir, 1806.

Steinman, Eliezer. *B'er ha-Hasidut: ha-Maggid v'Talmidav.* Tel Aviv, Keneset.

Wilensky, M. *Hasidim u-Mitnagdim.* Jerusalem: Mosad Bialik, 1970.

Yitzhak of Neshkhiz. *Toldot Yitzhak.* Pietrokov, 1928.

Yoetz Rakatz. *Siah Sarfei Kodesh.* Lodz, 1928-31.